MYTH OF THE SOCIAL VOLCANO

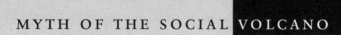

MYTH OF THE SOCIAL VOLCANO

Perceptions of Inequality and Distributive Injustice in Contemporary China

Martin King Whyte

STANFORD UNIVERSITY PRESS

STANFORD, CALIFORNIA

Stanford University Press
Stanford, California

Library of Congress Cataloging-in-Publication Data

Whyte, Martin King.
  Myth of the social volcano : perceptions of inequality and
distributive injustice in contemporary China / Martin King
Whyte.
      p. cm.
  Includes bibliographical references and index.
  ISBN 978-0-8047-6941-9 (cloth : alk. paper)—ISBN
978-0-8047-6942-6 (pbk. : alk. paper)
  1. Equality—China—Public opinion. 2. Distributive
justice—China—Public opinion. 3. China—Economic
conditions—Public opinion. 4. China—Social conditions—
Public opinion. 5. Public opinion—China. I. Title.
  HN740.Z9W58 2010
  305.0951'09045—dc22   2009035620

Typeset by Westchester Book Group in Sabon 10/13

Dedicated fondly to the memory of Leslie Kish,
who cared as much about social justice as he did about
sampling methods

CONTENTS

ILLUSTRATIONS

Figures

Tables

ACKNOWLEDGMENTS

The research project that formed the basis for this book began more than a decade ago and involved a large number of supporting researchers, students, and institutions. As a consequence, there are many people to thank for helping this book finally see the light of day. As with any complex enterprise of this type, none of those who helped this research along the way should be held responsible for any of the shortcomings in the resulting book.

My initial thanks go to Leslie Kish for suggesting—in a conversation in the living room of the home of his daughter Carla in Silver Spring, Maryland, in 1998—that I come up with a new research question and project suitable for survey research in China. Leslie had been a cherished colleague and neighbor from my days as a faculty member in sociology at the University of Michigan, and he had been supportive and helpful in my earlier forays into China survey work. As a result of his stimulus, I decided that I wanted to conduct research on how ordinary Chinese viewed the growing inequalities that had been unleashed by China's market reforms after 1978. Leslie died in 2000 and didn't see the results of his advice and enthusiasm. I gratefully dedicate this book to his memory.

I also owe considerable intellectual and other debts to the project research team that has worked with me to produce first a pilot survey on inequality and distributive justice attitudes in Beijing in 2000 and then the national survey with the same focus that forms the basis of the present book, which was carried out in the fall of 2004. The other members of the project research team include Jieming Chen, Chunping Han, Pierre Landry, Albert Park, and Wang Feng on the U.S. side, and Shen Mingming and Yang Ming and the staff of the Research Center for Contemporary China at Peking University (and particularly RCCC Associate Director, Yan Jie) on the China side.

I received financial support from the Beijing Office of the Ford Foundation for an initial planning meeting in Ann Arbor, Michigan, in 1999 to prepare for the Beijing pilot survey, and I am grateful to that office's director at the time (now my colleague at Harvard), Tony Saich. Attending the Ann Arbor planning workshop were Duane Alwin, Bao Shuming, David Featherman, Gail Henderson, Leslie Kish, David Mason, Albert Park, Ellen Pimentel, Carl Riskin, Jan Svejnar, Kathy Terrell, Steven Tuch, and Wang Feng on the U.S. side, and Shen Mingming, Yang Ming, Feng Xiaotian, Hao Hongsheng, Lu Hanlong, Pan Rongkang, and Qiu Haixiong on the People's Republic of China side, as well as Hong Yung-tai from Taiwan. I am particularly grateful to Duane Alwin and David Mason, leading figures in the International Social Justice Project (ISJP) surveys conducted in Eastern Europe and in other countries during the 1990s (see the comparative analysis of survey results presented in Chapter 4 of the present volume), for explaining at the planning workshop the logic of the ISJP attitude surveys on inequality and distributive injustice and providing a guide to the publicly archived data from those surveys. My thanks also to Bernd Wegener and Jean-Yves Gerlitz at Humboldt University in Germany, to Hynek Jerabek at Charles University in the Czech Republic, and to Antal Örkeny at Eőtvős Lorand University in Hungary for facilitating access to the new ISJP survey data collected in 2005 and 2006.

The final planning meeting for the 2000 Beijing pilot survey was conducted at the RCCC offices in May 2000, where we were hosted by Shen Mingming and Yang Ming. Participating from the U.S. side were Albert Park, David Featherman, Wang Feng, and myself. At that meeting a final module of questions about inequality attitudes, many of them translations of questions used in the earlier ISJP surveys, was finalized and incorporated into the Beijing Area Study (BAS) survey that RCCC carried out in China's capital later in the year.

The fact that we were able to carry out the Beijing pilot survey without incident emboldened our project team to seek funds for a national survey on views about rising inequality. At this stage Pierre Landry, who had not been involved in the Beijing pilot survey, joined the project team and took on major responsibility for designing the sampling plan for a national survey using an innovative sampling method he helped devise (for details, see Chapter 2). We received the major funding for the 2004 national survey from the Smith Richardson Foundation, and the author is very grateful to that foundation and to program officer Allan Song for their generosity and support during the extended period from initial grant to the completion of this book. Additional funding was provided by Harvard's Weatherhead Center for International Affairs, the Center for the Study of Democracy at the University of California at Irvine, and Peking University. Our colleagues at RCCC again hosted a final planning meeting on the Peking University campus in the spring of 2004, at which the national survey questionnaire and sampling plan were finalized, with Jieming Chen, Chunping Han, Pierre Landry, Albert Park, and the author participating from the U.S. side. My U.S.-based colleagues and I are very grateful to RCCC and to Shen Mingming, Yang Ming, and Yan Jie particularly for their skill and efficiency in conducting the survey fieldwork in the fall of 2004 and then preparing the survey data and documentation for distribution to all project members the following spring.

All of the funding for this project was expended carrying out the survey fieldwork and data preparation, and I did not have another grant to support the analysis of the data and preparation of research reports. Fortunately, I was able to draw on the supplemental financial support available to me as a Harvard faculty member and the assistance of multiple graduate students in Harvard's doctoral program in sociology in analyzing the rich and complex survey data our 2004 interviews produced. Tao Lin and Chunping Han assisted me in analyzing data from the Beijing pilot survey, and as a result of this experience, Chunping evolved from a research assistant into a full-fledged member of the research team for the 2004 survey. Subsequently, I was assisted by Jundai Liu, Patrick Hamm, and Min Zhou, while Alison Denton Jones carried out the "back-translation" from Chinese to English of the 2004 questionnaire. More recently Maocan Guo, Edward Weihua An, and Dong-Kyun Im helped me with statistical analyses keyed to the specific chapters of this book and contributed in vital ways to its completion. Without the dedicated assistance of a very large share of recent Harvard sociology doctoral students interested in China, I would not have been able to produce this final report on our survey findings.

While working on this book and earlier papers reporting our survey results, I also benefited by opportunities to present preliminary talks about popular attitudes toward inequality in China in a variety of settings, and from the comments and suggestions I received at those sessions. In that connection I would like to particularly thank M. Scot Tanner (then at the Washington office of the Rand Corporation), Deborah Davis and Ivan Szelenyi at Yale University, Kevin O'Brien at the University of California at Berkeley, Scott Rozelle at Stanford University, James Lee (then at the University of Michigan), Ralph Thaxton at Brandeis University, and here at Harvard, William Kirby, Marshall Goldman, and William Alford, who hosted different versions of my attempt to explain how ordinary Chinese feel about the inequalities within which they live.

Finally, I would like to thank the staff members at Harvard who have helped facilitate my work, and particularly Barbara Bontempo for grant management and my secretary, Mary Quigley, for general assistance at every step in the process. Last but not least, I am grateful to my wife, Alice

Hogan, and my daughter, Julia Hogan Whyte, for being understanding and supportive over all the years that it has taken to produce first the China inequality surveys and now this book.

Martin King Whyte
Cambridge, Massachusetts

Introduction: Is Rising Inequality Propelling China Toward a "Social Volcano"?

A house may be large or small; as long as the neighboring houses are likewise small, it satisfies all social requirement for a residence. But let there arise next to the little house a palace, and the little house shrinks to a hut.
—Karl Marx, 1847

Some people in rural areas and cities should be allowed to get rich before others.
—Deng Xiaoping, 1983

Because many people believe that wealth flows from access to power more than it does from talent or risk-taking, the wealth gap has incited outrage and is viewed as at least partly responsible for tens of thousands of mass protests around the country in recent years.
—Joseph Kahn, *New York Times*, 2006

China's post-1978 economic reforms have been remarkably successful in many respects, producing close to 10 percent economic growth rates for three decades, rising income levels, massive inflows of foreign investment, extraordinary success in exporting Chinese products overseas, and growing integration of the nation into the world economy. A society once known as the "sick man of Asia" and later as the site of the largest documented famine in human history[1] has now lifted hundreds of millions of its citizens out of poverty and displays mushrooming skyscrapers, limited access highways, shopping malls, private automobiles, and all the other trappings of an increasingly modern and wealthy society. During this period China's sustained economic growth has surpassed the record of previous East Asian "tigers," and this has been accomplished for a complex continental economy that currently counts more than 1.3 billion people. Even for those suspicious about the accuracy of Chinese economic statistics, there is no doubt that this is a record of stunning economic success.

However, there is at least one darker side to this story. During the reform period, China has gone from being a society that was relatively equal, at least in terms of the distribution of incomes, to being a society that is very unequal. As judged by the Gini coefficient that social scientists often use to measure overall inequality (with 0 equal to perfect equality and 1 equal to total inequality), China went from an estimated very modest Gini .29 in 1981 to .45 or even higher in 2002 (World Bank 1997; Khan and Riskin 2001, 2005; Gustafsson, Li, and Sicular 2008). By this measure China is still less unequal than such societies as Brazil and South Africa, but more unequal than the United States, Japan, and such populous Asian developing countries as India and Bangladesh.[2]

The changes the reforms have produced in regard to inequality go far beyond a more unequal distribution of the incomes of Chinese citizens. The entire system of distribution that had been constructed in the era of Chinese socialism (from 1955 to 1978) has been thoroughly dismantled, replaced by a market-oriented system that looks very much like capitalism, even if China's leaders still do not dare to call it by this name (and forbid their citizens from doing so as well).[3] As a result, forms of wealth and privilege that the revolution set out to destroy have returned with a vengeance—for example, millionaire business tycoons, the exploitation of Chinese workers by foreign capitalists, and gated and guarded private mansion compounds. The downsides of capitalism that socialism had eliminated have also returned with a vengeance—unemployment, inflation, loss of health insurance, company bankruptcy, and confiscation of housing and farmland in shady deals with property developers. Chinese who had learned to survive by playing by the rules of Mao-era socialism have had to adapt to a fundamentally changed distribution system in which there are plenty of losers alongside the many winners. Some who feel they should be honored for their contributions to socialist construction find themselves unexpectedly out of work and facing bleak prospects for the future, even as they see other Chinese becoming millionaires and even billionaires.

The present volume examines how ordinary Chinese citizens weigh the balance between a booming economy and rising inequality in evaluating the social order in which they live. Do most ordinary Chinese accept the new market-based and highly competitive society China has become and feel that it offers improved opportunities for them to get ahead and to make better lives for their children? Or is it more common to feel threatened by these changes and to feel that most of the benefits of China's prosperity are being monopolized by the well-connected and corrupt, while ordinary workers and farmers are being left behind? Which social order do Chinese today feel is more fair, the current go-go but very unequal society, or the less dynamic but perhaps more equal society of Mao-era socialism?

Such questions motivated the research whose results are reported in this book, and the answers are of more than academic interest. Given the fundamental changes from a socialist to a market economy and from modest income gaps to sizable ones, how Chinese citizens have adapted and view the transformed social order may well affect China's future political stability. The epigraphs at the beginning of this introduction convey a debate that has been going on around the world for centuries and that is very much alive in China today. In the mid-nineteenth century Karl Marx noted that the same basic facts of a person's living conditions feel very different and less satisfying if one's neighbor lives in a palace than if the neighbor has a house much like one's own. Early in the reform era the leader of China's market transition, Deng Xiaoping, took a different stance regarding inequality. For Deng and his fellow reformers, having some people get rich before others would be a positive development because it would show the rest of the population what was possible and stimulate people to try to get rich themselves. If Deng had been able to debate the question with Marx, he might have pointed out that the person living in what he now considers a hut might be stimulated to become rich enough to build or buy himself a castle.

The final epigraph, a quotation from a China correspondent of the *New York Times* in 2006, takes an even more negative view than did Marx. Joseph Kahn asserts that China's poor don't simply feel bad about their difficult living conditions; they also suspect that their newly prosperous neighbors do not deserve their wealth because it was obtained by unjust means rather than by talent and effort. In other words, Kahn asserts that there is a widespread popular feeling that China has become a very unjust society.

Even in a nondemocratic society such as China, the sentiments of the population on inequality issues cannot be ignored. To the extent that Chinese citizens feel that life is getting better, that differences between the rich and the poor are for the most part deserved rather than unfair, and that there are ample opportunities to get ahead for those willing to play by the rules of the market society in which they now live, they will tend to accept the contemporary social order and may even feel gratitude toward their leaders and support current policies and practices. However, if they come to feel that current inequalities are fundamentally unjust and that there is a corrupt alliance between the wealthy and the powerful at the expense of ordinary citizens, the implications are likely to be quite different. Feelings of injustice and resentment are likely to build up and lead Chinese citizens to resist and disobey authority, or even to be willing to join protest activity aimed at denouncing and correcting the injustices they see on a day-to-day basis. If sufficient resistance and protest activity occurs, China's political stability may be threatened.

So how do Chinese citizens feel about current inequality patterns and trends? Before the research reported in these pages, the answer would have been, "We don't really know." Questions of distributive injustice were considered too politically sensitive in China to permit systematic research on popular attitudes about inequality issues. However, the absence of systematic research did not prevent informed speculation and debate on how Chinese citizens feel about current inequalities. That debate, both within China and among China analysts outside, can be summarized in terms of two dramatically different scenarios.

In the first scenario, some analysts contend that China's robust economic growth, improved living standards, and ample new opportunities promote general optimism, acceptance of current inequality levels, and little nostalgia for the bygone socialist era. According to this view, although some individuals and groups experiencing unemployment, downward mobility, and abject poverty may be angry and feel that the current social order is unjust, for the bulk of the population the benefits produced by market reforms far outweigh the disadvantages and promote broad acceptance of the current system as at least relatively just. This broad acceptance of China's market system helps prevent local grievances and social protests from escalating into general challenges to the system. According to this view, China today might best be characterized as enjoying "rocky stability" (see Shambaugh 2000).

The contrary view is that rising income gaps and popular beliefs that current inequalities are unjust are threatening to turn China into a "social volcano," with China's social and political stability at risk. Perhaps stimulated by apparent sharp increases in local social protest incidents in recent years, the social volcano scenario has gained wide currency both in China and in the West.[4] For example, a poll of senior officials conducted by the Central Party School in 2004 concluded that the income gap was China's most serious social problem, far ahead of crime and corruption, which were ranked two and three (Xinhua 2004). On a similar note, a summary of the 2006 *Blue Book* published by the Chinese Academy of Social Sciences (an annual assessment of the state of Chinese society) stated, "The Gini coefficient, an indicator of income disparities, reached 0.53 last year, far higher than a dangerous level of 0.4" (Ma 2005).[5] Reports in the Western media echo these themes, particularly regarding rural protest activity. A recent edition of *The Economist* declares, "A spectre is haunting China—the spectre of rural unrest (Economist 2006)," while *Time* magazine's Asian edition tells us that "violent local protests . . . are convulsing the Chinese countryside with ever more frequency" and uses phrases such as "seeds of fury" and "the pitchfork anger of peasants" (Time Asia 2006).

In recent years this second view, that China's inequality trends are producing growing popular anger that may threaten to turn China into a social volcano (see He 2003), has gained general, even if not universal, acceptance.[6] For this reason I will refer to this second scenario as the "conventional wisdom" or "conventional view" in subsequent pages and chapters. There are additional themes in this conventional view that will be developed at greater length in later chapters. For present purposes, I summarize the components of the conventional wisdom this way:

1. Current inequality patterns are widely seen as unjust, and as a result the majority of Chinese citizens are angry about inequality trends and patterns.
2. The particular features of current inequalities that Chinese object to most are those associated with a return to a social order divided into social classes based on differential wealth and property ownership, rather than features that survive from the socialist period.
3. The Chinese who are most angry about inequality patterns and trends are the "losers" and disadvantaged groups in the wake of China's reforms, particularly those who remain at the bottom of the social hierarchy—especially China's farmers. However, those who have prospered as a result of the reforms or who have good prospects of doing so are more likely to accept current inequalities than to feel anger. In other words, objective advantage translates into acceptance of current inequalities, while disadvantage translates into anger.
4. If major efforts are not made to reverse growing inequalities and respond to popular anger about inequality trends, discontent is likely to accumulate further, eventually threatening China's social and political stability.

This conventional view, which implies fear of a looming social volcano due to rising inequality, is influential beyond researchers and policy analysts in China and abroad. China's leadership has accepted it as well, beginning in the closing years of Jiang Zemin's leadership,[7] and even more so since the succession to leadership of the Chinese Communist Party (hereafter CCP) and the government of Hu Jintao and Wen Jiabao in 2002–2003. Since taking the reins of leadership in China, Hu and Wen have introduced a number of important policy initiatives that will be described later in this book, all of them intended to improve the lives of China's poor citizens in general, and poor farmers in particular, and thus to steer China away from the looming social volcano and toward Hu's proclaimed goal of a "harmonious society."

However, we need to ask whether this conventional account of popular views about inequality patterns and trends is correct. The current study reports the results of the first systematic national survey of the attitudes of Chinese citizens on inequality and distributive injustice issues. The analyses are based on a survey of a representative sample of Chinese adults who were interviewed in the fall and winter of 2004. Our goal in conducting this survey was to answer several questions about which only speculation had been possible previously because of the perceived political sensitivity of the issues:

1. In general, how angry or how accepting are ordinary Chinese about current patterns of inequality in their society?
2. Which features of current inequality patterns are Chinese citizens most angry about, and which other features do they view in a positive light?
3. Compared to citizens in other societies, are Chinese more angry or less angry about current inequalities in general, and about particular features of current inequality patterns?
4. Within China, in which social groups and in which local areas is there the most anger about inequality and distributive injustice issues, and in which groups and localities is there the most acceptance of the status quo? In other words, what are the social contours of distributive injustice feelings within China?

We address these questions in a systematic way in the remaining chapters.

However, lurking beyond them is a fifth question that we cannot answer definitively based on our survey results:

5. Does the pattern of Chinese citizen responses to our questions about inequality and distributive injustice issues indicate that popular opinion in these realms is a potential source of future political instability?

We can at least explore the implications of the evidence from our survey for this final question. We assume that speculations based on systematic survey evidence are better than speculations based on hunches and untested assumptions.

The remainder of this study is organized as follows. The four chapters in Part I provide the necessary background and evidence to assess how much anger or acceptance Chinese feel toward current inequalities. Chapter 1 presents an overview of China's recent history focusing on the nature of inequality and social mobility patterns during that society's socialist era in order to provide a historical context for the post-1978 transformation of China from a socialist to a market society. An important part of the discussion in that chapter, as well as in later chapters addressing specific features of Chinese inequality patterns, is a consideration of whether socialist China before 1978 was an egalitarian social order that Chinese citizens might look back on with nostalgia or a rigid and unfairly stratified social order from which today's market society might be seen as a welcome escape (to state contrasting arguments in exaggerated form).

Chapter 2 describes the nature of the 2004 national survey and the sampling method and questionnaire we employed. Chapter 3 presents evidence to answer the first two research questions: In general how angry or accepting are Chinese citizens about current inequality patterns, and which features are they most and least angry about? In Chapter 4 we use comparative survey data from other countries, both post-socialist societies in Eastern Europe and advanced capitalist societies, in order to answer the third research question: Compared to citizens of other nations, are Chinese citizens more or less angry about current inequality patterns?

Part II examines variations in inequality attitudes across the social and geographical terrain of China. Chapter 5 introduces the distinct inequality attitude domains examined in subsequent chapters and describes the social, demographic, and geographic measures used to examine which respondents have critical attitudes and which have accepting views in each of these domains. Chapters 6 through 9 then address the fourth research question regarding the social contours of feelings of distributive injustice through parallel analyses of four different clusters of inequality issues: perceptions of the fairness or unfairness of current inequality patterns (Chapter 6), preferences for greater equality or appreciation of the benefits of inequality (Chapter 7), opposition to contemporary status transmission patterns and perceptions of inequality conflicts (Chapter 8), and pessimism about mobility opportunities and social justice (Chapter 9). Finally, the Conclusion summarizes the major findings from our survey, interprets the most surprising and unexpected survey results, and presents thoughts on the implications of current citizen attitudes for China's future political stability.

PART I HOW ANGRY ARE CHINESE CITIZENS ABOUT CURRENT INEQUALITIES?

CHAPTER ONE

China's Post-Socialist Transition and Rising Inequality

Since 1978 China has carried out fundamental reforms of its economic system, transforming itself from a centrally planned socialist economy largely isolated from the outside world to a primarily market-oriented system fully integrated into the global economy. As noted in the Introduction, in the process of market reforms China has become much more unequal in multiple ways, and many of the forms of status differentiation, elite privilege, and disadvantages of the poor that China's revolution had attacked and abolished have returned with a vengeance.

The study reported in these pages analyzes the results of a national survey conducted in 2004 devoted to determining how ordinary Chinese citizens view inequality trends and distributive injustice issues. Do most Chinese feel that the overall improvements in living standards and increased opportunities to become prosperous make the heightened inequalities of the reform era acceptable, or perhaps even necessary? Or is it more common to feel angry about the inequalities and unfair distribution of opportunities in Chinese society today, or perhaps even nostalgic for the now officially repudiated socialist patterns of distribution? In order to set the context for later discussion of these and related questions, the current chapter describes the nature and importance of the socialist transition in general and then provides a description of the complicated steps and stages through which China first created its socialist system and then, after 1978, proceeded to dismantle it.

THE IMPORTANCE OF THE POST-SOCIALIST TRANSITION

Arguably the most dramatic and important change in the global political economy in the last century is the rise and then collapse of the challenge to world capitalism posed by centrally planned socialist economies. After the Bolshevik revolution in 1917 and then the establishment of a centrally planned socialist economy in the USSR in the 1930s, the Soviet Union proclaimed that socialism provided a route to economic development that was both more rapid and more equitable than capitalism could provide. That challenge remained provocative but isolated until after World War II, when a combination of the advance of Soviet troops into Eastern Europe and the victory of the Chinese Communist revolution in 1949 (as well as the establishment of socialist systems in Yugoslavia, North Korea, North Vietnam, Laos, and, after 1959, Cuba) produced a situation in which close to one-third of the world's people were living under socialism.[1]

During the 1950s and 1960s, the challenge to world capitalism posed by this much enlarged group of socialist countries appeared formidable. Given the more rapid rates of economic growth of most socialist economies in that period, as well as such stunning accomplishments as the Soviet launch of the world's first artificial earth satellite in 1957, many observers found convincing the claim made by Soviet leader Nikita Khrushchev that the USSR was poised to overtake the United States and lead the way to dominance of the socialist camp over the capitalist world. We all know that this is not what happened. For a variety of complex reasons that we cannot go into in detail here, by the 1970s and 1980s the world situation had changed dramatically, with capitalism again ascendant and socialism in retreat. Economic difficulties and slower growth rates in Eastern Europe and political turmoil and economic troubles in China, when combined with the revival of Western Europe and the dramatic rise of East Asian capitalist economies, helped negate the triumphalism of the advocates of socialism and hastened the eventual dismantling of most socialist systems.

Efforts to enliven faltering socialist economies by introducing markets and private enterprises as supplementary devices began in Eastern Europe in the late 1960s and early 1970s, led by Hungary (see Szelenyi 1988). These limited reforms were not sufficient to cure the growing problems of socialist economies, and China's launching of gradual but eventually much more extensive market reforms after 1978 gets credit as the beginning step that led to the collapse of socialist economic systems generally.[2] Vietnam followed the Chinese example by launching its own program of market reforms (*Doi Moi*) in 1986, and 1989 saw the sudden collapse of Communist Party rule throughout Eastern Europe, followed in 1991 by the collapse of Communist Party rule in, and the breakup of, the Soviet Union, the latter two events leading to the dismantling of centrally planned socialism and a rapid and chaotic effort to create (or re-create) capitalism in the former Soviet bloc. As a result of these turbulent changes, within a decade and a half socialism as an economic system virtually vanished from the globe.[3] Today a system that once organized the daily lives of close to a third of the world's population survives only in two marginal places with a combined population of less than 35 million: North Korea and Cuba.[4] Even in these two countries, some timid experiments with market reforms have begun.

As already noted, China's path and experience in market transition have been substantially different from those of the countries of the former Soviet Union and Eastern Europe. Communist Party rule did not collapse, and in fact the Chinese Communist Party (CCP) has led and guided the process of market transition throughout.[5] Chinese leaders also rejected the advice (followed to some degree in Eastern Europe) that they needed to introduce market reforms and a full range of capitalist institutions quickly and more or less simultaneously (referred to as the "big-bang" approach to market reforms). China has instead introduced market reforms incrementally and gradually, as captured in the famous phrase of the leader of the reform effort, Deng Xiaoping, "crossing the river by stepping from stone to stone."[6]

Despite these and other distinctive features of China's reform experience that will be discussed in greater detail in subsequent pages and chapters, China shares with all the other formerly socialist states undergoing market reforms a common set of challenges: how to create and gain acceptance of institutions, attitudes, and indeed an entire way of life necessary for a market-oriented economy in a historical context of a population indoctrinated for decades to believe that socialism was good and capitalism was evil. If the market transitions in formerly socialist societies are the most important change in the political economy of the world in our lifetime, the future prosperity and stability of the world depend to a considerable degree on the extent to which this market transition is successfully completed. Success entails not only altered institutions and rising prosperity, but convincing the populations that capitalism (or at least "market competition") is good, and that socialism, if not exactly evil, is at least outmoded and unworkable and not to be mourned. The current study is a detailed examination of the attitudes of ordinary Chinese citizens to see how successfully this challenge is being met in China. The remainder of this chapter provides background that is necessary to place this examination in historical context.

THE FIRST OF CHINA'S TWO SOCIAL REVOLUTIONS: THE MAO ERA

If one considers the personal histories of the oldest Chinese in the People's Republic of China (PRC) today, what is striking is that they have been through at least two wrenching, near-total social revolutions, each involving more pervasive changes in the political and social order and patterns of daily life than anything experienced in the entire history of the United States or most other nations.[7] The first social revolution dates not from the political revolution of 1949, but from the launching of China's socialist transformation in 1955, and the second from the launching of China's market transition process in 1978. As already implied here, this second revolution could also be considered a counterrevolution, since it involved a gradual but eventually quite thorough repudiation of socialist institutions and practices and their replacement by the institutions prevalent in capitalist societies around the world.

The turning points in 1955 and 1978 involved changes in the economy first and foremost, but in reality almost everything about the way Chinese society was organized and people lived their daily lives was affected, including the institutions and values of distribution, stratification, and social mobility that are the central focus of the current study. Although the socialist transformation of the 1950s and the market reforms since 1978 represent the most comprehensive changes in the organization of Chinese society and in the accompanying official policies and ideology, they were not the only important disruptions of the status quo experienced by Chinese citizens in the last half of the twentieth century. It is important to briefly and in simplified form describe the major subperiods of recent Chinese history in order to comment on their potential implications for Chinese views about distributive justice and injustice.

Stratification in China Before the 1949 Revolution (Late Nineteenth Century to 1949)

The Chinese Communist Party came to national power in 1949 based in substantial measure on an influential critique of the inequities of the existing social order (both in the republican era from 1912 to 1949 and in the late imperial system that preceded it) and the pledge to create a more just society. Many different aspects of the prevailing social order were attacked by the CCP, including the huge gap between rich and poor, the pervasiveness of poverty, the privileges enjoyed by foreigners, and the exploitation of Chinese farmers and workers by rural landlords, urban capitalists, and foreign business owners. In many CCP treatments of the ills of the social order before 1949, that order was described as feudal or quasi-feudal, characterizations reflecting the Marxist conceptual scheme the CCP used to interpret the world.

While portions of this critique are unobjectionable, the use of the term *feudalism* is highly misleading. A striking fact about the nature of social order in late imperial China is that, with the exception of a small portion of the population at the very top (the imperial family and its relatives) and bottom (people engaged in a small number of "mean occupations" on a hereditary basis) of the social pyramid, there were few legal or other impediments to social and geographical mobility. The republican revolution in 1911 largely eliminated these minor inherited status barriers at the bottom and top of Chinese society. Given the huge size of the population and the small number of officials, wealthy merchants, and other elite positions, the odds against a poor rural or urban resident rising to the top were daunting. But it was not impossible, as one's station in life was not fixed at birth. On the other side of the equation, a wealthy rural landlord or merchant family enjoyed no legal claim or aristocratic pedigree that prevented the family, or perhaps its children or grandchildren, from falling back to the bottom of society. The greatest CCP animus was directed against rural landlords, but the latter were small potatoes in comparative perspective, definitely not feudal manor lords of the sort seen in medieval Europe or in Tokugawa-era Japan. Chinese rural landlords owed their ability to live privileged lives to their ownership of a disproportionate share of village land and to the resources that ownership allowed them to wield to protect their positions, but they had no special legal status granted by a monarch or any other authority, and any of their neighbors who managed to amass a similar amount of land could be transformed similarly from farmer into landlord.[8]

What do these characteristics mean for how ordinary Chinese viewed the structures of inequality in which they lived in the late nineteenth and early twentieth centuries? Obviously we do not have any national surveys comparable to the one whose results are discussed in this book. However, a variety of kinds of evidence indicate that most Chinese saw their society, both in late imperial times and in the republican period, as very unequal but at the same time very open. Chinese had their own versions of American Horatio Alger success stories—of poor but talented and ambitious individuals and families who by dint of extraordinary efforts and taking advantage of opportunities managed to rise to the top ranks of society in terms of status and wealth. The most cherished avenue for such mobility in dynastic times was via the imperial examination system. Through years of diligent study and by passing multiple, highly competitive bureaucratic examinations, an individual could attain a career as an official, with resulting high status and potential access to considerable wealth (see Ho 1962; Elman 2000).

However, many more Chinese of humble origins rose to wealth and high status through other routes, particularly through market competition and commercial success, leading to purchases of land and the establishment of successful businesses (see, for example, Chow 1966). Throughout the country, Chinese families were famously obsessed with trying to rear their children to succeed in schooling and excel in market competition in order to become prosperous and bring their families along with them. In this sense, China's historical traditions before 1949 emphasized the diligent pursuit of opportunities and upward social mobility, not the sort of resigned acceptance of one's fate that one might expect in a genuinely feudal society (see Rawski 2007). These same tendencies dominated popular consciousness in the republican

era between 1912 and 1949, although the much more chaotic and disorderly society of the time made figuring out what to do to be successful more
risky and difficult.

Initial Changes After the 1949 Revolution (1949–1954)

When the CCP leaders came to national power in 1949, they introduced a
large number of changes in institutions and policies that affected the
structures of inequality and opportunities, but they did not initially begin
to systematically eliminate private enterprises, private property ownership,
and market distribution and replace them with public property ownership and
central planning (socialism). However, considerable numbers of wealthy
capitalists and other elites fled to Hong Kong and Taiwan, and for the most
part their enterprises and other property were nationalized and run by the
state. Most foreign owners were similarly forced out, with their firms taken
over by the state. In the countryside the land reform campaign from 1950 to
1953 took much of the land away from those designated in the struggle as
landlords, with large numbers of the latter physically abused or even killed.
The land confiscated from landlords and rich peasants was given to, and
farmed by, other rural families as private family farms. In the cities most
enterprises and employment remained in the private and market-oriented
sector, although with government controls and restrictions on markets and
private enterprise steadily increasing.

During the period from 1949 to 1954 the most important changes
affecting inequality structures and opportunities were not a product of
the as yet limited encroachments of the state against the still predominantly
market-based economy. Rather, the new revolutionary government launched
major expansions of the government bureaucracy, used Soviet assistance to
build new heavy industrial enterprises and construction projects,[9] and promoted rapid expansion of schooling at all levels. The political stability that
was established by the CCP and its major initiatives and investments, when
combined with the strong economic growth of the period,[10] helped generate
a large number of new and desirable jobs and mobility opportunities, and
the latter contributed to a heightened sense of optimism and even gratitude
toward the new government (see Whyte 1991). Since for the most part individuals and families still operated within an environment of market competition and unrestricted migration, this period also witnessed a surge of
individual and family moves to take advantage of the new opportunities,
resulting as well in a rapid expansion of China's urban population. Many
older residents in Chinese cities today were born in villages and small towns
but joined the exodus into cities that was still possible during the 1950s,
fueled by the new opportunities generated by state actions. In other words, in
what could be seen as the obverse of the patterns used to describe the

changes in the economy early in the reform era (as described below), before 1955 economic expansion mainly involved the state sector's growing out(side) of the market (cf. Naughton 1995), rather than through wholesale conversion of private enterprises to state ownership.

The Socialist Transformation and the Great Leap Forward and Its Aftermath (1955–1965)

By 1955 Mao Zedong had become impatient that initial experiments with voluntary formation of socialist work organizations had made little headway, particularly in the countryside, and he launched the national socialist transformation drive. In agriculture this involved mobilizing pressure on farmers to yield their land to, and become members of, newly formed versions of collective farms, then called agricultural producers' cooperatives (APCs; see Shue 1980). By 1956 the socialist transformation in the countryside had been completed, although rural families retained the right to use a small portion of village land as private plots and to engage in modest private handicraft and marketing activities, as in Soviet collective farms.

In the cities socialist transformation involved two types of efforts, one targeted at large firms and the other at small-scale and family-run firms. The private owners of large firms and companies, already quite cowed by political campaigns and government restrictions and taxation before 1955, were convened for meetings in which they were pressured to turn over their enterprises to the state. They were promised that if they cooperated they could continue to receive salaries as well as interest payments based on the state's calculation of the value of the assets they had relinquished. Within weeks the owners of large firms had seen the writing on the wall and agreed to the deal. For small enterprises the effort took somewhat longer, since it involved pressuring them to agree to cease independent operations and join others in the same craft or trade in cooperatives (of barbers, jewelry carvers, and so on), where profits would be pooled collectively to fund more predictable wages and fringe benefits. These two types of socialist transformation gave birth to the two forms of socialist work organizations of the Mao era, state-owned enterprises (SOEs) that dominated the important sectors of the economy and smaller collective enterprises that in principle were not funded by the state budget but had to fund themselves.[11]

By early 1957 the socialist transformation of urban industry and commerce had also been completed, and from that point onward the entire economy was socialist in form and was managed by central planning, rather than primarily by market distribution. The advent of socialism and central planning in 1955–57 has a large number of implications relevant to our concern with inequality and social mobility. It became possible for the state to begin to bureaucratically control job assignments and labor mobility, with new employees assigned to a firm rather than hired through a process of market competition. One important aspect of this state control over labor is that systematic regulations were promulgated in 1958 to prevent virtually all voluntarily initiated rural-to-urban migration, and thus to insulate the cities from labor pressures from the countryside (see Cheng and Selden 1994). In addition, income derived from property or self-employment essentially disappeared, and wages became the primary source of income for virtually all Chinese.[12] Wage payments for urbanites were henceforth bureaucratically set, rather than being based on market competition and employer discretion. The result was a set of extremely complex wage and fringe benefit scales based on education, seniority, job responsibility, local costs of living, and other factors and provided in manuals used by state authorities to determine the wage and nonwage compensation of state employees (see Korzec and Whyte 1981). For those who worked in the state sectors of the economy (about 80 percent of the urban economy, with the remainder organized in collective firms with their somewhat lower wage levels and fringe benefit coverage), socialism provided what became known as an "iron rice bowl"—secure employment and wages combined with a wide range of fringe benefits that citizens of other developing societies could only envy (see Whyte and Parish 1984). China's collective farmers did not receive fixed wages but had their efforts recorded in variable work points, with the value of each work point depending on the harvest and state procurement prices, and they lacked the subsidies and benefits enjoyed by urbanites (see Parish and Whyte 1978). In most respects, the socialist economic institutions China developed were modeled on, and adapted from, those established earlier in the Soviet Union.

This newly consolidated centrally planned socialist economy was just beginning to find its footing when it was disrupted by the launching of the Great Leap Forward in 1958.[13] For our purposes it is sufficient to note a few key developments of that period. First, in the ambitious and utopian enthusiasm of the early Leap, severe labor shortages were predicted, and factories and other enterprises were allowed to recruit and employ extra laborers to enable them to cope with the predicted sharp increase in workers needed. So the newly proclaimed limits on rural-to-urban migration temporarily fell by the wayside, and about 20 million new rural-to-urban migrants swelled the populations of China's cities. The same utopian enthusiasm in the countryside led to the forced merger in 1958 of APCs into much large collective agricultural organizations, the rural people's communes, which eliminated private plots and marketing and established communal mess halls and child nurseries in order to deemphasize the interests of individual farm families and maximize participation in labor on the collective fields.

As is well known, the Great Leap Forward became an economic and demographic disaster, producing not record economic growth but a depression and famine in which, it is estimated, more than 30 million deaths beyond the number normally expected occurred—a period subsequently referred to as the "three bitter years" (from 1959 through 1961). In an effort to recover from this disaster, Mao and the other CCP leaders were forced to introduce retrenchment policies and reforms. Some methods of pursuing recovery, such as allowing rural families to contract plots of village land and cultivate them as family farms, were experimented with locally, but were denounced and prohibited once Mao gave a negative signal (see Yang 1996). However, the communes were subdivided into smaller units, the experimental mess halls and other innovations were abandoned, and by 1962 communes had essentially become the old APCs, but with one additional management level added on top.[14]

In cities the collapse of the Leap led to mass layoffs of newly hired personnel and to the mobilization to return to the countryside of those affected. The result was a huge reverse migration, again of about 20 million people, thus shrinking cities back to something close to their pre-Leap population sizes (see Murphey 1980). An additional important result was that, after 1960, the migration restriction regulations promulgated in 1958 began to be enforced very harshly and systematically, as they would continue to be for the next two decades.

The collapse of the Leap also largely negated the optimism spurred by the rising opportunities of the 1950s. During the three bitter years, even though urban areas did not experience the massive number of deaths that occurred in some parts of the countryside, there were sharp reductions in food and other rations and constant hunger. Even after the economy began to improve after 1962 and ration amounts increased, urban shortages of food items and consumer goods became endemic, trying the patience and testing the ingenuity of urban consumers. Urban youths faced more difficult prospects than had their older siblings and relatives, since most urban factories and organizations were taking on fewer new employees, while university enrollments had declined even as the number of youths completing high school and trying to get into college had increased sharply due to the school expansions of the 1950s. The result was rising tension and competition among urban youths about their future prospects, a development that some analysts feel contributed to the factional violence of Red Guard struggles that erupted after 1966 in the Cultural Revolution (see Shirk 1982; Unger 1982). Although urban parents generally had no such insecurity about employment, they were also affected by the retrenchment and more cautious policies that followed the post-Leap recovery. The regular wage increases and improvements in housing and other benefits they had been led to expect socialism to produce ended, and many urban employees were paid the same monthly wage for years or even for the next two decades, while the urban housing stock became more and more cramped and dilapidated.

For rural residents the first decade under socialism produced gains in realms such as access to rural schooling and improvements in health care, but more ominous outcomes in other realms. Even localities that did not suffer major losses of life during the Leap found themselves hard-pressed to meet basic food and other consumption needs because of declining state investment in the countryside. In addition, after 1960 the centuries-old escape route from rural poverty of out-migration was eliminated through migration restrictions (see Chan 1994). The resulting situation is one of the supreme ironies of China's socialist revolution: A new regime that proclaimed that it was going to eliminate feudalism and feudal vestiges and create a more equal and just society developed institutions and policies that bound to the soil the 80 percent or more of the population born in rural areas (who thereby inherited agricultural household registrations—see the discussion in Potter 1983; Wang Fei-ling 2005; Whyte 2010a).[15] Egalitarian revolutionaries, most of whom originally came from rural areas (as did Mao Zedong), ended up transforming a social order that was anything but feudal into a system of collectivized farming that was tantamount to "socialist serfdom."

The Cultural Revolution and Its Aftermath (1966–1976)

It would divert us too far from the main story to discuss why the Cultural Revolution was launched by Mao and his supporters in 1966 and to describe the chaotic and violent events that ensued during its mass movement phases, which lasted until 1969 in the cities and the early 1970s in some rural areas. Suffice it to say that one of Mao's major goals in launching the Cultural Revolution was to try to shift China to a different and purportedly superior form of socialism than existed in the Soviet Union.[16] Mao did not want to abandon most features of the Soviet model of economic development, including state-owned industrial firms and rural collective farms, primary emphasis on heavy industry and urban development, bureaucratic controls over labor, and most other features of the Stalinist command economy that emerged in the USSR in the 1930s. However, he and his radical supporters had come to believe that the Soviet Union was too unequal, hierarchical, and competitive, and that in many respects it operated in ways fairly similar to capitalist countries, despite the existence of socialist property relations and central planning rather than private property and markets.

In order to avoid following these "revisionist" tendencies of the USSR, the Cultural Revolution's struggles were in part designed to make China a more egalitarian social order. This meant, in particular, the effort to eliminate or sharply reduce the use of material incentives to motivate greater work efforts and improved individual performance. Production workers' bonuses were eliminated in favor of fixed monthly wages, and royalties for writers, monetary prizes for innovations and inventions, and even fancy uniforms and signs of ranks for military officers and other forms of status distinction were similarly denounced and abandoned.

The egalitarianism of the Cultural Revolution was not promoted by efforts to increase the incomes and living standards of the poor and disadvantaged—in other words, by what we would call affirmative action policies. Instead, the entire emphasis was on "leveling down" to prevent those with higher education, rank, professional qualifications, or other advantages from showing that they were different in any way from ordinary workers and peasants.[17] This period generated a large number of radical experiments designed to foster this sort of leveling down, including requiring youths who had completed high school to spend at least two years in manual labor or military service before they could be considered for college enrollment, sending bureaucrats and intellectuals for extended stints of agricultural labor in "May 7th cadre schools," and universalizing a drab and unisex style of dress that largely obscured the varying status of individuals (except for small signs, such as a fountain pen in the shirt pocket or a wristwatch; on these efforts, see Parish 1984; Whyte 1981). Perhaps the most dramatic status-reversal effort of the period was the campaign to send educated urban youth to the countryside to engage in farming, which rusticated more than 17 million city youths between 1968 and 1978 (Bernstein 1977).[18]

In the countryside the major manifestation of the leveling-down policy was a more determined effort than earlier to inhibit or eliminate entirely the ability of rural families to improve their incomes through work on their private plots, household handicrafts, and rural marketing activity, restrictions justified by the effort to make all members of the rural labor force totally dependent on what they could earn through labor in the collectivized fields. So not only was the response to rural poverty of migration to the cities now blocked, but the similarly age-old remedy of leaving farming to engage in family business activity was essentially banned as well.

The image of drab uniformity in clothing and other consumption behavior tends to shape our view of the egalitarianism of Mao-era socialism. However, it is important to note the ways in which this egalitarian image is misleading. First, it was mainly in the wake of the Cultural Revolution, in the period from 1966 to 1978, that the leveling-down program was zealously pursued. Before the Cultural Revolution, China exhibited the inequalities, incentives, and differentials, not to mention variations in styles of dress, that are fairly normal for a socialist society, and in this respect China was not so different from the Soviet Union or the Soviet satellites in Eastern Europe. (That, after all, was Mao's complaint when he launched the Cultural Revolution.)

Second, the egalitarianism of the Cultural Revolution was segmental and partial; this was also a period of dramatic and even rising inequalities. In income distribution and consumption patterns, the inequalities within any one work organization, urban locale, or rural community were relatively modest. However, across work organizations, locales, villages, and regions, there were often sharp differences in income, housing, schooling, and other resources, and neither socialism from the 1950s nor the Cultural Revolution's leveling down did anything to limit those gaps. (This pattern of sharper inequalities across, rather than within, organizational and geographic boundaries continues to shape income distribution in China today; see Wang 2008.)

The tendency for actual inequalities to increase despite the appearance and slogans of egalitarianism is most glaringly visible in the urban-rural gap in family incomes and in regard to virtually all other kinds of resources and opportunities. The combination of institutions of socialist serfdom and Mao's Stalinist priorities for urban and industrial development produced an unusually large and widening gap between urban and rural residents in the pre-1978 period in comparison to other societies (roughly three to one in income terms in the late Mao era, and even higher if one takes into account the monetary value of the subsidies and services received only by urban residents), a gap that continues to be the primary social cleavage in China today (see Whyte 2010a).

A final qualification to this image of China as an egalitarian society in the late Mao era is that minimal distinctions in clothing and even in household income don't tell the whole story. Since China was not a market society, many important goods and services were distributed bureaucratically and in a highly subsidized fashion according to one's work organization and rank and couldn't be purchased by ordinary citizens. As in any state socialist society, income was much less important in determining family consumption levels and access to resources than is the case in a capitalist society. Even as China denounced the revisionism of the Soviet Union, a very complicated system of special vacation resorts, official limousines, special hospital clinics, restricted bookstores, and many other highly differentiated special facilities continued to exist behind the scenes. To take the most extreme example, Mao Zedong's official salary was not very high (generally around 600 to 700 yuan a month, compared to about 60 yuan for an average industrial worker), but he didn't have to pay a *fen* (1/100 of a yuan) when he visited any one of the dozens of special villas that were maintained for his private use in different parts of the country.

The Cultural Revolution policy innovations in general, and the systematic leveling-down policies designed to inhibit elitism and conspicuous consumption in particular, had a number of very damaging consequences for China's economic development prospects. In a period when the rest of East Asia was beginning to grow at a very rapid pace, China's economy was growing slowly and fitfully, and China was falling behind rather than catching up. Even the more modest growth (compared to the 1950s) that did occur was highly inefficient, maintained by extraordinarily high levels of state investment that did not allow increases in popular consumption levels. Within work enterprises, motivations and incentives were problematic, with loafing and absenteeism common despite mobilization of "moral incentives" to try to increase productivity. Also, China's universities did not turn out any new graduates in the seven-year period between 1966 and 1973, and even when a flow of college graduates resumed after that, they were fewer in numbers than before the Cultural Revolution and of low quality academically.

In terms of popular morale, even when the chaos and factional struggles of the Cultural Revolution died down after 1969, the prospects for substantial improvements in living standards or anything else were bleak. For urban youths in particular, the Cultural Revolution had destroyed what had seemed like predictable paths to secure and rewarding lives. Before 1966 urban youths studied hard in primary and secondary school in order to either be assigned to a secure urban job or gain admission to a university and be on the path to an even more desirable urban job. In the wake of the Cultural Revolution, the direct path to university admission was closed, and most urban adolescents faced the daunting prospect of being forced to leave for the countryside and a life of agricultural labor, without any certainty about whether they could ever return to the cities.[19] Youths who came of age in urban areas during these years are often referred to as China's lost generation, and it is little wonder that many are bitter, since their prospects for advanced schooling, good jobs, and even marriage were harmed or at least delayed, resulting in less rewarding lives than were generally enjoyed by their counterparts who came of age before the Cultural Revolution and by those who came of age after the launching of market reforms.[20] In general, the sense of uncertainty and pessimism about economic and other conditions of the mid-1970s contrasts markedly with the optimism and enthusiasm that characterized popular attitudes during the 1950s.

The nature of the egalitarianism pursued during the Cultural Revolution provides a testimonial to a social science finding regarding popular preferences in societies around the world. It appears to be quite easy for most citizens in any society to support greater equality if it is pursued via raising the living standard of the poor and disadvantaged—in other words, through some variant of affirmative action policies. However, social equality pursued by the sort of leveling-down experiments that Mao promoted during the Cultural Revolution, designed to limit and penalize the advantaged rather than raise up the disadvantaged, is much less likely to be popularly accepted (see Hirschman and Rothschild 1973; Kluegel and Smith 1986). This same tendency is reflected in the 2004 Chinese survey responses presented in Chapter 3.

Summing up the nature of the structures of inequality and of Chinese socialist distribution in practice before 1978 is difficult because of the sharp changes in economic conditions and state policies over the subperiods after 1949. In general, the system after 1955 required individuals to submit to the will of the state and its subordinate bureaucratic officials. In exchange for diligent performance of the required work and other tasks in a person's bureaucratic niche, the system provided a fairly predictable level of remuneration and fringe benefits, with levels differing substantially across other niches in the bureaucratic system as well as being sharply affected by when individuals started their work careers. Many time-honored tendencies and behaviors that had served Chinese well in their pursuit of economic security and prosperity until 1955 were fairly thoroughly negated in this system— for example, families harnessing their labor and ingenuity in a family business, individuals leaving their home communities to seek their fortunes elsewhere, and entrepreneurs taking risks to start new businesses or finding low-cost goods in one locale they could sell at a higher price in another locale.

On the other hand, under socialism, even though people did not have opportunities to prosper through individual effort and market competition, they also didn't have to face the risks of going bankrupt, losing all their property, and becoming unemployed and destitute. Even a farmer in a very poor community was to some extent protected from destitution by the resources of the other families in his or her production team.[21] In urban areas, particularly among employees of state enterprises, the broad range of material resources and services to which urbanites were entitled provided security in life, even if not much opportunity to change their station or become more prosperous. In other words, even though socialism is often seen as providing more equality than markets and capitalism, in fact socialist systems are distinctive not so much in terms of equality, but more so in terms of the predictability and security that come from submitting to the bureaucratic management of the state and its administrative appendages.[22] However, even that predictability was often illusory in the case of Mao's China, since the state could and did change the rules, sometimes quite dramatically, and life plans and ambitions formed under one set of conditions proved a poor guide or even became counterproductive under changed conditions. Not only one's place in the geographical and bureaucratic system, but also one's age and when one started work heavily influenced whether individuals saw socialism as a secure and rewarding system or a limiting, unpredictable, and arbitrary controller of their fates.

CHINA'S SECOND SOCIAL REVOLUTION: POST-1978 MARKET REFORMS

It would take us too far afield to discuss in detail how and why Deng Xiaoping and other CCP leaders repudiated most of the socialist institutions that they themselves had help create in the 1950s and set China on a path toward a goal that Mao Zedong had dreaded—essentially the restoration of capitalism (see the accounts in Naughton 1995, 2007; Brandt and Rawski 2008).[23] The remainder of this chapter is devoted to a brief overview of changes in economic institutions and policies after 1978 and how they might be expected to affect popular attitudes regarding inequality trends and distributive injustice issues.

The Early Stages of Market Reforms, 1978–1994

As indicated earlier, China's reform leadership adopted and implemented specific market-oriented reforms gradually and sequentially, rather than in the sort of comprehensive (big-bang) fashion attempted later in the former Soviet Union and Eastern Europe. Despite this incremental approach, a large number of specific changes occurred in the initial years of the reforms. Some of them were related not to switching from socialist planning to market distribution, but more to political healing. For example, millions of victims of the Cultural Revolution and earlier political campaigns were rehabilitated; the class struggle policy that had stigmatized and blocked opportunities for millions of Chinese who came from "bad class backgrounds" was repudiated (with class background information deleted from personnel files and household registration records); and the mass campaign to send educated urban youths to the countryside was terminated, with millions still in the countryside allowed to return to the cities and resume urban lives and jobs.

In addition, the leveling-down policies of the Cultural Revolution decade were criticized as economically irrational and unfair and were rapidly reversed. In the educational sphere this entailed a return to pre–Cultural Revolution policies of strict academic standards, grades, and testing to determine progression up through what was once again a competitive and hierarchical educational pyramid, with direct entry to college resumed and largely determined by scores on the national college entrance exam, which was restored in 1977.[24] Cash bonuses, royalties, innovation prizes, and other forms of material incentives were restored, while promotions were increasingly based on educational credentials, technical competence, and other meritocratic criteria, rather than on the class origin purity, political loyalty, and class struggle enthusiasm criteria that had been dominant in the late Mao era (see Whyte 1981).[25] Wage increases, new apartment construction, and other measures were introduced in an attempt to relieve the consumer frustrations that angered the urban population. Such measures did not constitute a new social revolution, but more an effort to return to something like "normal socialism" after the excesses of the Cultural Revolution.

Other measures introduced in the first years of reforms went much further and constituted the beginning steps toward a transformation from socialist planning to market distribution. The open-door policy was launched in 1978, and special export zones that provided tax concessions and other inducements were established along the coast in 1979 in an effort to entice foreign manufacturers to invest there.[26] It was also acknowledged that the government could not provide employment for all of those coming of age and seeking jobs, and small-scale domestic private firms were allowed again for the first time since 1956.[27] The nature of the state financial system was also changed in ways that provided local governments and state enterprises with incentives to make extra money that would not have to be turned over to the state, as had been obligatory in the past. In particular, they were encouraged to produce goods and services to meet market demands as long as they could still meet their obligations to the state, and they were able to retain most of the profits from these market-oriented operations to spend on improving the living conditions of their workers and communities and expanding their market-oriented business operations (see the discussion in Whyte 2009).

Even though in a strict temporal sense the initial market reforms were not confined to the countryside, in terms of the actual dismantling of socialist economic institutions it is fair to say that the second social revolution began in rural areas. Several important rural transformations occurred in the 1978–84 period. In virtually all of rural China collectivized agriculture was dismantled, replaced by the contracting of village land to farm families (under the "household responsibility system"). Even though they didn't own the land contracted to them, rural families were once again in charge of farming, and insofar as they could meet their remaining agricultural tax and grain procurement obligations, they were free to engage in other agricultural and nonagricultural activities. The Cultural Revolution–era restrictions on private family business activity and marketing were eliminated, and within a short time entrepreneurial rural families were growing produce and making things that they transported to rural markets or into the cities to meet the needs of often distant consumers.[28] In addition, the combination of changed village finances and surplus rural labor freed from collectivized farming made possible a rapid growth in village factories, which became known as township and village enterprises (TVEs) and which by the early 1990s had more than 100 million employees.

The other major change that transformed the lives of China's rural population was the relaxation of the migration restrictions imposed at the end of the 1950s. Villagers began to leave not only farming but also their villages to seek employment elsewhere, as they had been able to do before the imposition of socialist serfdom. Usually migrants could not obtain urban household registrations if they moved to a city, but given the general shift to market distribution and the decline of urban rationing, if they could find a job in the city they could generally rent housing and purchase goods and services with their new earnings. In fact, the booming factories and cities in the special export zones would not have been possible without this loosening of migration restrictions. Estimates of the size of this floating population of migrants vary, but by the early 1990s they numbered at least 30 million, and their numbers grew further after that, eventually exceeding 100 million.[29] This combination of major changes in institutions fundamentally altered the lives and family calculations of China's rural population by the mid-1980s. No longer were people confined to their villages and collectivized farming for life, with little opportunity to augment the meager work point income that came from their production teams. Instead they had a variety of options, including continuing to concentrate mainly on farming, although perhaps growing more specialized and commercial crops;[30] engaging in household craft production or establishing a business to cater to the needs of others; seeking wage employment in a nearby TVE; joining rural-based construction companies that began to acquire contracts that enabled much of the new urban building boom; or migrating elsewhere, most often to a town or city, to seek wage employment in factories, hotels, and other branches of the newly flourishing urban economy.

During the earliest years of the reforms, until about 1985, China's rural population increased its average income more rapidly than the urban population did, resulting in a sharp reduction of the number of Chinese living in poverty and a reduction as well in the urban-rural income gap—from about 2.5 to 1 to 1.8 to 1 according to official statistics (see Naughton 2007, pp. 132–33).[31] However, the early immersion of China's rural population into a market environment had other consequences that were less favorable. As China's farmers now relied much more on their own family efforts to manage and succeed, and as collective finances in many areas withered, existing collective goods and services that had been supported by the commune system were weakened or eliminated. Almost all of the village cooperative medical insurance systems that had provided rudimentary protection disappeared, with rural families having to seek medical care on a fee-for-service basis (and with many avoiding seeking medical treatment due to cost concerns) in the 1980s and 1990s.[32] In addition, the financing, teaching staffs, and other bases of rural secondary schooling were negatively affected, leading to a sharp drop in secondary school enrolments in rural areas after 1978, with only gradual recovery since then. So China's rural population faced early the mixed blessings of the switch from socialism to markets, with much higher incomes possible, but with collective services and facilities undermined.

Starting in 1984 China's leadership proclaimed that market reforms in urban areas would take center stage. Initially this proclamation did not mean that urban residents would face as dramatic a change in their way of life as rural residents had experienced earlier. For the remainder of the period up through the early 1990s, more and more private and foreign firms began operating in the cities; fewer goods and services were distributed within the state system of distribution and rationing, with more and more distributed via market-set prices; and heavy state investments and increasing imports fueled improvements in urban housing stock, infrastructure, goods available in stores, and standards of living. Once again urban incomes and consumption levels grew more rapidly than their rural counterparts, raising the urban-rural income gap close to 3 to 1 by the early 1990s, according to official statistics.

During this period state authorities announced that the previous job and benefit security that had been enjoyed by most urban residents, particularly those employed by the state, would have to be reformed and phased out. For example, urbanites were told that the prevailing Chinese permanent employment system in state enterprises would be discontinued, and after 1986 all new hires would be on limited three- to five-year contracts. However, until the mid-1990s the iron rice bowl of employment, wage, housing, and fringe benefit security was not much affected for those already in the urban labor force. Through about 1994, at least, few urbanites actually took jobs in the private sector, and the great majority continued to live in subsidized, if shabby and cramped, rental housing distributed to them through their work organizations. State-owned enterprises were encouraged and pressured to orient themselves increasingly to producing goods and services for markets, rather than according to state planning targets, but many did so only grudgingly and not very successfully, producing severe problems of SOE bank loans that were not repaid.

The most dynamic growth in the economy and in employment was elsewhere, in foreign, TVE, and private-sector firms. In this period, the Chinese strategy was not so much to reform or privatize the state sector as to force state firms to compete with new entrants that provided most of China's growth, a strategy Barry Naughton (1995) has termed "growing out of the plan." Another important aspect of this strategy was the maintenance of a "dual-track economy," with a stagnating state sector persisting alongside booming private and foreign sectors, facilitating something close to "reform without losers" (Lau, Qian, and Roland 2000). In other words, major groupings of Chinese citizens enjoyed significant improvements in their living standards, while no significant group or sector was displaced and threatened with impoverishment. However, this relatively happy pattern did not continue.

The Reforms Advance: The Smashing of the Iron Rice Bowl and Other Laments (1994–)

China's reforms entered a new phase after Deng Xiaoping symbolized the reenergizing of the market transition when he toured China's southern special export zones in 1992, and even more so when Zhu Rongji took over primary responsibility for the national economy in 1993.[33] The latter half of the 1990s saw an ambitious and strict set of further reforms of state enterprises pushed through under Zhu's leadership. Before that time, China's SOEs had been pressured to reorient themselves increasingly to production for, and competition in, the marketplace, but employees of these firms still for the most part continued to enjoy the iron rice bowl of secure jobs, bureaucratically set wages, work unit–subsidized and allocated rental housing, and a substantial array of fringe benefits and subsidies.

Zhu's efforts were designed to smash the iron rice bowl, making individual employees as well as the firms in which they worked face the discipline of market competition. This change had a wide range of manifestations. Firm managers were given increased power and autonomy to make decisions on personnel and wages, and employees faced new hazards of being demoted, having their pay reduced, being fined, and being laid off entirely. Firm bankruptcy legislation had been on the books since the mid-1980s with little effect, but now some failing firms faced bankruptcy, threatening the jobs and livelihoods of their entire workforce. Benefit cuts also were widely enacted; for example, in the socialist period workers received full medical insurance for themselves and half-coverage for all family dependents, but now only the worker was covered (and only if the worker was a regular employee, not a migrant, and after paying increased copayments when seeking medical treatment). Firms and their managers also exercised increased authority in hiring new employees, rather than following the prior pattern of simply accepting everyone assigned to them by local labor bureaus.

These more extensive market reforms contained carrot incentives as well as sticks. The increased authority of firm managers enabled them to use expanded wage increases, bonuses, and other incentive payments to reward and promote their most valued and productive employees. Firm employees were no longer consigned to work at their posts indefinitely, without any other options. As a labor market began to emerge, those employed in SOEs could "go down into the sea" (*xiahai*) by leaving their jobs and going to work in the market sector in a variety of kinds of destinations ranging from self-employment and starting their own businesses to working for foreign corporations operating in China. Similarly, college graduates no longer had to accept state assignment to work posts, but could compete for jobs through job fairs, employer interviews, and a variety of other venues familiar in a market society.

Perhaps the most important economic gain of the urban population during the late 1990s, however, didn't come about through market competition, but via the long-established mechanism of bureaucratic allocation. A national drive to privatize urban housing was launched in the mid-1990s, and the dominant form this drive took was to have work units transfer to their employees ownership of the apartments they were already living in, with the transfer occurring by means of highly subsidized prices and loans from the work units.[34] By early in the new millennium the great majority of registered urbanites (not the migrants) had been transformed into homeowners, but with the size, quality, and amenities of their housing differing sharply depending on the resources of the work unit and the job title and rank of the employee within that unit (and without any market competition for the housing being privatized—see the discussion in Tomba 2004).

One important consequence of the accelerated market reforms of the 1990s is that it became increasingly possible for many Chinese citizens to at least supplement their family budgets with property income, and for some to begin to depend primarily on this source. This possibility is especially notable for individuals and families that developed successful private businesses, leading to a surge in new millionaires and the emergence of lists of the richest Chinese. (As of 2007, *Forbes* magazine reported that there were 66 billionaires in China in dollar terms, and that in comparative terms, Americans such as Donald Trump and David Rockefeller would not even rank within China's top ten; see Flannery 2007.) The opening of stock markets in Shanghai and Shenzhen in 1990 and the advent of public stock trading made it possible for many more Chinese to invest in stocks and try to augment their wages or other earnings with stock-based property income.[35] Urban housing reform provided another source of potential property income. Individuals and families can now rent their housing to others, purchase new housing for rental or resale, and if they are very successful leave wage employment entirely to manage their properties. Some of China's richest individuals and families—those that own and run real estate development companies—are at the apex of upward mobility through this strategy. The growth of such property-based income and the tendency of those most successful to be located in, or to relocate to, China's cities have contributed to rising urban incomes, increasing inequality within cities, and an enlarge-ment of the urban-rural income gap.[36]

CONCLUSIONS

As noted in the Introduction, China's transition from a socialist to a market economy has been successful in many ways, accelerating the pace of eco-nomic development, substantially increasing the average Chinese citizen's standard of living, and decreasing poverty. According to official figures, dur-ing the socialist era from 1952 to 1978 the gross domestic product in-creased at an average rate of 6 percent, or 4.1 percent per capita, but in the reform period from 1978 to 2005 these figures accelerated to 9.6 percent and 8.5 percent respectively (cited in Naughton 2007, p. 140). Whereas 71 percent of the labor force was still engaged in farming in 1978, by 2004 this figure had fallen to under 50 percent. Chinese official statistics indicate that rural poverty decreased from 250 million people in 1978 to 26 million in 2004 (cited in Naughton 2007, p. 212); even allowing for some exaggera-tion, there is no doubt that the record of Chinese poverty reduction has been impressive.[37] Unlike in the former Soviet Union, market reforms have not been accompanied by a deterioration in health conditions or reductions in life spans. In fact, life spans have continued to increase according to offi-cial statistics, from 67.8 years in 1980 to 68.5 years in 1990 and 70.9 in 2002 (cited in Naughton 2007, p. 222). Many other statistics also attest to the economic gains of the reform period, but the general point is clear: The average Chinese has made many more gains during the reform period than during the prior period of socialist planned development, and more than citi-zens of most other societies. Research indicates that in recent decades the income distribution of the population of the entire world has gotten a bit less unequal than in earlier decades, due largely to the major improvement in family incomes experienced in China primarily and, secondarily, in India (see Firebaugh 2003).

However, as noted at the outset of this study, the problem with such statements is that not all Chinese are average. Accompanying the impressive growth and improvement in average living standards has been an enlarging of most indicators of inequality. Visually, the days of drab uniformity of dress and lifestyles of the Mao era are gone, and many if not most Chinese seem to have taken to heart Deng Xiaoping's exhortation that "it is good for some people to get rich first."[38] Conspicuous consumption has gone from being politically hazardous to acceptable, and China's impoverished and unem-ployed citizens are regularly confronted with images of newly minted mil-lionaires living in gated and guarded mega-mansions, of foreign and Chinese business magnates hurrying to meetings in fancy imported limousines, and even of a growing Chinese middle class shopping in glittering shopping malls, spending lavish amounts on fancy weddings, traveling to foreign resorts, and in general living a life that is out of reach of even ordinary Chinese, not to mention the very poor.

Throughout the reform period there has been popular grumbling and suspicion that much of the newfound wealth that is being so garishly displayed was obtained not through hard work and talent, but via special connections and family ties to people with political power as well as through graft and corruption. Feelings of distributive injustice are now being openly expressed in China, despite the general improvements in living standards and other average indicators. As noted in the Introduction, it has become the conventional wisdom among analysts both inside China and in the West that China's social and political stability is increasingly threatened by popular resentment against the rising inequalities spawned by market reforms. China's leaders, wanting to head off the prospect of the country becoming a social volcano, have in recent years introduced a number of important policy initiatives designed to spread the benefits of economic growth more widely, particularly to western regions of the country and to the Chinese countryside. These initiatives, which are described in subsequent chapters, are intended to transform China from a breeding ground of protests over inequality and distributive injustice into what Hu Jintao, leader of the Chinese Communist Party since 2002, terms a "harmonious society." Yet in China today it is not certain how widely shared and deeply felt are sentiments of anger and perceived injustice over inequality trends. When we began research on this topic, abundant survey and other data were available on trends in objective inequalities in income, access to education, and other realms, but no systematic evidence at all about Chinese popular attitudes toward inequality trends and distributive injustice issues.

How Chinese assess the more unequal society in which they now live and whether sentiments of distributive injustice are widespread are questions that occupy our attention for the remainder of this book. As noted earlier, in order to systematically examine Chinese popular attitudes on these questions we designed and carried out a national survey in China in 2004. Chapter 2 presents an overview of the survey methods and goals and thus provides a necessary context for the presentation of our national survey results in the remaining chapters.

The China National Survey on Inequality and Distributive Justice

How can one determine how ordinary Chinese citizens feel about the structures of inequality and social mobility opportunities within which they live? Can one even investigate popular attitudes regarding whether current inequalities are unjust, given the fact that China is still ruled by the Communist Party and that the limitations on freedom of expression in a communist system may make asking about or responding to questions on distributive injustice issues difficult or even dangerous? Even if it is politically feasible to conduct survey research on these issues in China, how can one draw a representative sample in a society in which access to systematic local data on population required for survey sampling is restricted and many people are regularly on the move from place to place? These are some of the questions that colleagues and I wrestled with in launching the research project whose results are reported in these pages.

I began my career of research on China during the late 1960s, when Americans could not travel to China. My initial research was based mainly on interviewing refugees in Hong Kong (see Whyte 1974; Parish and Whyte 1978; Whyte and Parish 1984). Even during the 1970s, when it became possible to visit China (my first trip to the People's Republic was in 1973), it was still not possible for Americans to stay in China for extended periods and to conduct research on the ground there. After Mao Zedong's death in 1976 and the establishment of diplomatic relations between the United States and China in 1979, the situation improved, but initially survey research on any scale remained off limits. My first successful project in China was a survey focusing on changes in mate choice customs and marriage relations that I directed in Chengdu, the capital of Sichuan Province, in 1987 (see Whyte 1990; Xu and Whyte 1990). In subsequent years I directed or was involved in several additional collaborative survey projects in other cities, but well into the 1990s the prospects for a foreign researcher designing and directing a survey that was national instead of local in scope remained dim. Therefore, until the present project I always had to present my survey results from various cities with local caveats—"at least that's how it is in Chengdu" (or Beijing, or Baoding).

As noted in the Acknowledgments, the inspiration for the current project came from a conversation in 1998 with my former colleague from the University of Michigan, Leslie Kish, in the living room of his daughter's home in Silver Spring, Maryland, a city in which I also lived at the time.[1] Leslie had just returned from a trip to China very enthusiastic about recent improvements in the prospects for collaborative survey research, and he urged me to think of a topic or problem that would merit a multicity or even national survey project. After discussing various possibilities, it occurred to me that one of the most interesting and contentious issues in China at the time (and still today) was popular reactions to China's market reforms and the widening inequalities they had spawned.

THE 2000 BEIJING PILOT SURVEY

I began making inquiries about applying for a research grant to conduct a large-scale survey in China on popular attitudes toward inequality and distributive injustice issues, but these inquiries were met with skepticism about whether such a survey was feasible, given that it would involve a research team that included foreign researchers asking citizens in a communist country about injustices in the contemporary social order. I was told by program officers at one foundation that if I could successfully carry out a local pilot survey in China without incident to demonstrate the feasibility of survey research on this topic, they would be willing to consider a funding request for a national survey.

With this possibility in mind, I was able to secure modest funding from the Beijing Office of the Ford Foundation to hold a planning meeting in Ann Arbor, Michigan, in 1999 to discuss how to carry out a pilot survey on Chinese popular attitudes toward inequality trends and distributive injustice issues. Among those attending the planning workshop were Shen Mingming and Yang Ming, professors of political science at Peking University and the director and deputy director, respectively, of Beida's Research Center for Contemporary China (RCCC), an organization dedicated to mounting survey research projects to assess social trends and public opinion in China.[2] I had learned that the RCCC had begun to conduct annual Beijing Area Study (BAS) surveys in China's capital, modeled after the Detroit Area Study course run by the Department of Sociology at the University of Michigan. At the meeting in Ann Arbor, Shen Mingming and Yang Ming discussed the possibility of including a module of questions about inequality and distributive injustice issues within the BAS survey planned for 2000,[3] as well as the possibility that, if this pilot survey was successful, they could be our China collaborators for a multicity or even national survey on the same issues.

In trying to design questions for a survey of popular attitudes toward inequality and distributive injustice issues, it was not necessary to start from scratch. Survey research on these issues had been underway for some years in the United States and in other societies (see, for example, Hochschild 1981; Kluegel and Smith 1986). Even more relevant was the fact that national surveys had already been conducted in Russia and in multiple countries in Eastern Europe during the 1990s to investigate citizen reactions to the effects on inequality patterns of the post-socialist transitions in that part of the world (see particularly Kluegel, Mason, and Wegener 1995; Mason and Kluegel 2000). Two rounds of surveys had been carried out already, in 1991 and 1996, by the International Social Justice Project (hereafter ISJP), and two of the researchers involved in ISJP, David Mason and Duane Alwin, attended the 1999 planning meeting in Ann Arbor and offered advice. As a result of their advice and assistance, a substantial number of questions about inequality and distributive injustice issues included in the ISJP surveys in Eastern Europe were translated and replicated in China, initially in the 2000 Beijing pilot survey and subsequently in the 2004 national survey. (Comparisons of views of Chinese citizens with citizens in ISJP survey countries on selected inequality and distributive injustice issues form the basis of Chapter 4 of this book.)

Although I served as the principal investigator of the Beijing pilot survey and the subsequent national survey, it was very much a team effort. In addition to Shen Mingming and Yang Ming, other key researchers who were involved since the Ann Arbor planning meeting include Wang Feng (professor of sociology, University of California at Irvine) and Jieming Chen (professor of sociology, Texas A&M University–Kingsville). Carl Riskin attended the Ann Arbor meeting to provide advice as an economist; when he was unable to continue with the project, Albert Park (then in the Department of Economics at the University of Michigan, now at Oxford University) took his place. David Featherman, professor of sociology at the University of Michigan and at the time director of that institution's Institute for Social Research (ISR), provided partial funding for the Beijing pilot survey from ISR and traveled to Beijing with us in May 2000 for a final planning session for that survey.

A module of questions on inequality and distributive justice issues, some translated from the ISJP surveys and some newly designed to assess the peculiarities of stratification in contemporary China, was included in the Beijing Area Study survey that went into the field toward the end of 2000. That survey interviewed a representative sample of 757 Beijing residents who were identified from official household registration records. In addition, five of the neighborhoods included in the sample for the BAS survey, localities that were known to have migrants from rural areas in residence in substantial numbers, became the locus of an effort to find and interview migrants as well as registered Beijing citizens. That effort resulted in 132 migrants also being interviewed with the same BAS questionnaire. The 2000 BAS survey was carried out without incident, with the data shared with the U.S. project team shortly afterward, providing the evidence we were hoping for that a survey on attitudes regarding inequality trends and distributive injustice issues was not too politically sensitive to be feasible. The BAS results have been reported in some working papers and publications (see Whyte and Han 2003; Whyte 2006; Whyte and Han 2008), but they will only be mentioned in passing in the current study (mainly in Chapter 4), given the fact that the national survey data became available after 2004.

THE 2004 CHINA NATIONAL SURVEY

While the success of the 2000 BAS pilot survey was encouraging, we still confronted an important unresolved problem regarding plans for a national survey. Given the increasing geographic mobility of Chinese made possible by the loosening of the migration restrictions discussed in Chapter 1, the household registers that had formed the basis for previous sample surveys in China, including the 2000 Beijing survey, were increasingly out of date and inaccurate. A variety of studies reported that in the early years of the new millennium, perhaps as many as 30 percent or more of the de facto residents of large cities in China were migrants and thus would not be included in the neighborhood household registers. Migrants who stay for any length of time are supposed to go to local police stations and fill out temporary registration forms, but some studies indicated that perhaps 50 percent or more fail to do so, making the temporary registers an unsatisfactory mechanism for sampling urban migrants. If we were going to conduct a high-quality and representative sample survey of Chinese adults nationally, we had to devise a different sampling method that relied on where people actually resided and not on inaccurate household registration data.

Fortunately, at around this time Shen Mingming was in contact with another former University of Michigan graduate student, Pierre Landry (who had joined the faculty in the Department of Political Science at Yale University) regarding spatial probability sampling, a promising alternative sampling method that was not yet widely known in the social sciences. Essentially, spatial probability sampling uses local population estimates and detailed maps as a basis for drawing a sample of actual physical locations in China with probabilities proportional to population size. Then using the geographic information system coordinates of the selected locations and

GPS devices, samplers and interviewers travel to the selected sites and interview one adult per household in every household found within designated boundaries around that location, regardless of whether the individuals and families residing there are officially registered or not.

Landry and Shen conducted a test survey in 2001 in Beijing that compared this newly devised sampling method with household registration–based sampling, and the results indicated even more serious problems than previously realized with registration-based sampling. About 45 percent of the adults located by spatial probability sampling methods in that Beijing survey were not registered where they were residing, almost as many of them Beijing residents who had moved from one part of the city to another as migrants from outside of Beijing (see Landry and Shen 2005).

Given this demonstration of the drawbacks of traditional household registration-based sampling, survey project members decided collectively to switch to spatial probability sampling. Pierre Landry agreed to join the survey project team and to take special responsibility for designing our national sample using this technique in cooperation with Shen Mingming and the staff at the RCCC. We applied for and received primary funding for the national survey from the Smith Richardson Foundation, with supplementary funding provided by the Weatherhead Center for International Affairs at Harvard, the Center for the Study of Democracy at the University of California at Irvine, and Peking University. On the basis of these plans, we began to prepare to carry out a national China survey in 2004 focusing on popular attitudes toward inequality and distributive injustice issues. In 2003 Chunping Han, then a doctoral student in sociology at Harvard, joined the project team—initially as a research assistant, but eventually as an equal collaborator and participant in the planning and field preparations for the survey.[4]

Given the fact that we were preparing for a survey involving roughly hour-long face-to-face interviews, rather than simply a module of inequality attitude questions as in the 2000 BAS survey, we worked together to design a full questionnaire. Most of the attitude questions used in the BAS module were retained and incorporated into the new questionnaire, and we added new questions about inequality and distributive injustice issues. A major task in designing the national questionnaire was agreeing on a wide range of questions about the social backgrounds and life experiences of our eventual respondents and members of their families, information that would be needed if we wanted to try to explain why some interviewees were more angry about inequality issues than others—the core question that we address in Chapters 6 through 9 of this book. The draft questionnaire we worked out was translated into Chinese and used as the basis for pretest interviews in China conducted by our colleagues at RCCC.[5] All the U.S.-based project researchers traveled to Beijing in the early summer of 2004 to discuss the results of the pretest interviews, and together with our colleagues at RCCC we reached agreement on the final questionnaire to be used later that year for interviews across the face of China.

In designing the sample, we faced a number of strategic decisions beyond simply whether to use spatial probability sampling. Our budgetary resources indicated that we could aim for a target sample size of 3,000 respondents. Based on a ballpark estimate that we would have something like a 70 percent response rate (in other words, for every ten selected respondents contacted, interviews could be completed successfully with seven), that number indicated that we should draw a sample of about 4,300 cases. We also wanted to make sure that we would have enough urban respondents to be able to perform separate statistical analyses for cities and for the countryside. Since China in 2004 was still about two-thirds rural, in order to achieve that goal we decided to over-sample urban areas. What this means in practice is that we first drew our base sample with probability proportional to size of population in the normal fashion, and then we drew additional respondents adjacent to the urban sampling points in order to ensure we would have enough urban cases to approximate a fifty/fifty (rather than sixty-seven/thirty-three) division between rural and urban respondents in the final pool of interviewees. We eventually ended up with a target of 4,344 respondents, with 2,645 in the basic sample and an additional 1,699 in the urban supplementary sample.

We also stratified the sample by geographic regions in order to achieve a desirable spread of interview respondents in all regions of the country. Based on our budget and number of interviewing teams, we planned to use forty basic sampling points. For that reason, and since some regions have much larger populations than others, we developed a sampling plan based on a variable number of basic sampling points in each of China's seven major regions, varying from three to nine depending on region population.[6] Within each of the forty primary sampling units eventually selected, sub-selections, again based on population density, were carried out, finally producing the final sampling locations, with one adult between the ages of eighteen and seventy interviewed per household in all of the households located within a ninety-by-ninety-meter square centered on the selected location.[7]

Using this procedure, the sample was drawn, and project interviewers were sent to the designated locales seeking interviews in the selected households. The final number of interviews actually completed was 3,267, slightly higher than we had expected, primarily because our response rate was 75.2 percent rather than 70 percent. Within this final sample, 1,785 respondents resided in urban areas (54.6 percent), while 1,482 resided in rural areas.[8] The sample includes cases from twenty-three of China's thirty-one provinces—all except Jilin, Inner Mongolia, Tianjin, Sichuan, Chongqing, Tibet, Qinghai, and Gansu.[9]

The actual field interviews for the national survey were carried out in the fall and early winter of 2004. The interviewers were locally hired individuals (most of them students attending local colleges in each region, recruited with the assistance of faculty at each institution) supervised by RCCC field staff, using procedures agreed to in advance with the U.S. participants. As in the BAS survey in 2000, no particular problems or political obstruction of the survey was experienced. After our RCCC colleagues received the completed questionnaires, entered and checked the data, and prepared the necessary documentation (sampling report, interviewing report, and so on), the data files and documentation were shared with all project members on both sides of the Pacific in the summer of 2005, and analyses of survey results began.

THE 2004 SURVEY AS A BASIS FOR JUDGING CHINESE OPINIONS ABOUT INEQUALITY

A few final words need to be said about the quality of our survey data and what they do and do not allow us to say about how ordinary Chinese citizens feel about inequality and distributive injustice issues. This sort of large-scale national survey has strengths and advantages, but also limitations, in China or in any other society. If I wanted to know what a particular individual thinks about how fair or unfair the society is (in terms of the patterns of inequality), I would not use the sort of conventional questionnaire we used in the 2004 China survey. Instead I would want to spend hours talking to that individual in depth about his or her life experiences, perceptions of rich people and poor people, whether the person felt he or she had been blocked from getting ahead by discrimination, and multiple other topics. A one-hour interview with dozens of questions asked, almost all of them with preset response categories that can be easily converted into numerical scores (such as 1=strongly agree, 2=agree, 3=feel neutral, 4=disagree, 5=strongly disagree) is too blunt and superficial an instrument for understanding the rich textures of joys and disappointments of a particular individual's life story and present situation. However, such an in-depth and lengthy interview process obviously is not suitable if you want to generalize about how a population feels, particularly if that population has 1.3 billion people. This is not simply a matter of numbers and time. It would also be impossible to get a representative sample of any population to take the time and be as revealing about their views and experiences as the in-depth interview process demands, and those willing to submit to this process would therefore be atypical and would not provide a solid basis for generalizing about how the larger population feels.

To be able to generalize about the views of an entire population, social scientists conventionally employ the methodology of sample surveys, as we do in the present study. But we do so knowing full well that in order to achieve the number and representativeness of interviews that we require, we cannot do much more than scratch the surface of how the particular individuals we interview feel about the issues. Again this is the situation with fixed-response questionnaire surveys in general, not a feature of surveys conducted in China specifically.

Given these constraints, we are confident that we carried out a high-quality survey based on a very good sample of China's adult population. All the researchers involved, on both the China and the U.S. sides, were well trained in the strengths and limitations of survey methods, and we followed accepted procedures designed to minimize biases that might distort responses of our survey respondents. For example, our procedures for protecting human subjects in research such as ours were checked and approved by the human subjects institutional review board at Harvard University and included a whole series of standard precautionary procedures:[10]

- Interviewers read out an obligatory "doorstep introduction" statement to each selected respondent, saying that the survey was being conducted by Peking University and was a purely academic study designed to learn about popular attitudes toward recent social trends. Respondents were told that we were not sent by or connected to any Chinese government agency and that no such agency would be receiving the data that we collected.
- Respondents were assured that their participation was entirely voluntary and that they could refuse to answer any questions that made them uncomfortable, or they could even terminate the interview entirely.
- They were urged to speak honestly and tell us their true opinions, rather than what they thought our interviewers might like to hear.
- They were told that there were no right or wrong answers to the kinds of questions we were going to ask.
- They were also told that their responses would be kept confidential and transformed into numerical data, so that nobody would be able to identify them or know what they had told us.
- Finally, they were told that no identifying information would be written on the completed questionnaire, which would in any case be stored in a secure location at Peking University under lock and key.[11]

We adopted other procedures designed to ensure that the survey data we were collecting would be of high quality. For example, the questionnaire was carefully constructed and pretested to make sure that the questions were all relatively easy to understand and answer and would not be threatening to respondents or make them uncomfortable in other ways. The interviews were all carried out by locally hired and specially trained Chinese interviewers familiar with local dialects. That training included special emphasis on the need to ask questions in a neutral tone without leading the respondent to select one response rather than another. Insofar as possible, interviews were carried out face-to-face between the interviewer and the respondent, without family members or others being present and able to overhear and possibly influence what was being said. The foreign members of the research team did not conduct any of the interviews, and respondents were not informed that foreign researchers would be analyzing the survey data for fear this would worry some of them.[12] Also, the sample itself was carefully designed, as described earlier, to ensure that the resulting respondents would be representative of the target population (noninstitutionalized Chinese adults between the ages of eighteen and seventy), with comparisons made with figures from the 2000 Chinese census to verify this fact. Finally, since one part of the study involves comparison of Chinese attitudes with the attitudes of citizens in other countries (see Chapter 4), we again followed standard procedures and hired an independent individual not involved in the project who was fluent in both Chinese and English to carry out a back-translation of our Chinese questionnaire into English, to enable us to judge whether the meaning of questions and response categories we were trying to replicate from studies elsewhere (particularly the ISJP) was preserved.[13]

Since some of the findings of our survey contradict conventional views about the current mood of Chinese citizens, let me close this discussion of our research methods by addressing one common criticism of surveys in China in general. Some critics suspect that, since China is still ruled by the Chinese Communist Party, there must be an underlying fear about getting into trouble with the authorities that no amount of interviewer reassurances can dispel. Insofar as this is the case, this tendency would be expected to lead Chinese survey respondents to give biased responses to many questions, responses that are more pro-government and pro-party policy than the "true feelings" they are afraid to reveal. Given the focus of our survey, how can we be sure that Chinese respondents don't have much stronger feelings of distributive injustice than they revealed to us through their answers to our surveys?

My response to this suspicion is on two levels. First, I think this criticism distorts the nature of the political atmosphere in China today. While it is true that certain kinds of public and organized expression of views critical of China's government and its policies can produce fearful consequences—harassment, detention, arrest, exile—in private conversations there currently is little of the pervasive fear that characterized social life in the late Mao era. In private, and even with strangers, Chinese are willing to bluntly express a wide range of critical attitudes with little fear of informers or worries about getting into trouble. The other level of responding to this criticism is to point to the pattern of answers to our survey questions. As the reader will see in regard to some questions we asked (particularly in Chapter 3), large majorities of our respondents expressed quite critical views, attitudes that directly contradict current official policies. For example, most respondents think there is too much inequality in China today, that it is unfair to lay off workers in order to make factories more efficient, that current discrimination against urban migrants is unjust, and that it is unfair for people who hold power to receive special privileges. These kinds of responses don't suggest a population that continues to be intimidated politically and afraid to express critical attitudes.

Based on the care and scientific procedures we employed in this survey project, we feel the 2004 survey provides a sound basis for assessing Chinese popular attitudes toward various inequality and distributive injustice issues and how those attitudes compare with other societies and vary within China. Is China headed toward a social volcano fueled by seething discontent over the unfairness of current patterns of inequality and of unequal opportunities? Or is there instead broad acceptance or even substantial satisfaction with the status quo? In other words, are Chinese popular attitudes toward inequality issues a source of potential instability or of stability? In the chapters that follow we construct our answers to these questions piece by piece.

CHAPTER THREE

What Do Chinese Citizens See as Fair and Unfair About Current Inequalities?

In this chapter and the next, we use our national survey data to provide an overview of Chinese adults' feelings about what is fair and unfair about current patterns of inequality and mobility opportunities in their society. How much acceptance is there of the fundamental changes fostered by China's post-1978 reforms in the principles of remuneration and distribution and of the resulting altered, and generally increased, inequalities? How much sign is there that substantial portions of China's population resent and resist these changes or even harbor nostalgia for the now officially rejected and discarded distributional principles and patterns of planned socialism? In this chapter we examine the responses to a wide range of questions dealing with both competing principles of distribution and perceptions of actual current patterns of inequality and social mobility. Our goal is to determine which inequality principles and patterns are seen as basically fair and which are seen as particularly unfair. In Chapter 4 we use survey data from selected other countries, including other post-socialist countries in Eastern Europe, to determine whether Chinese citizens are more or less critical of market principles and current patterns of inequality than are their counterparts elsewhere.

TOO MUCH INCOME INEQUALITY?

In response to a question about whether current income differences nationally are too large, somewhat too large, about right, somewhat too small, or too small, a substantial majority of respondents (71.7 percent) indicated that the gaps are to some degree excessive (see Figure 3.1a).[1] However, when we asked respondents their opinions about income differences within their own work units and in the neighborhoods in which they live, the proportion who said that such local income differences were excessive was much smaller—only 39.6 percent and 31.8 percent, respectively. In fact, the most common response was that income differences within the work unit and the neighborhood were about right, although more said that local

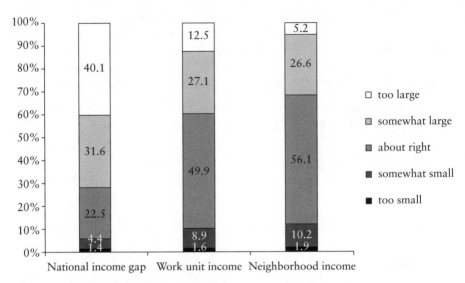

Figure 3.1a   Popular views on extent of inequality

income differences were too large than said they were too small. So these responses contain mixed messages. Clearly most Chinese feel that income differences in the entire nation are larger than they should be, but when you ask them about people in their local environment—those who more realistically would be used as their comparative reference groups—only about one respondent in three says that current income differences are excessive.

We asked a number of additional questions to gain more perspective on how Chinese citizens perceive current inequalities and inequality trends. Two questions concerned whether respondents thought the proportion of poor people and of rich people will increase, stay about the same, or decrease in the next five years.[2] As shown in Figure 3.1b, the most common responses were that the proportion of the poor will decrease (43.2 percent) and the portion of rich will increase (61.1 percent). In other words, the predominant tone in these responses is an optimistic expectation that the rising tide of economic development is lifting all boats, even if not at the same pace. (However, we should not ignore the 26.1 percent of respondents who expect the proportion of China's population that is poor to increase during the next five years.)

A somewhat different impression is generated by the pattern of responses to a question that asked respondents to register varying degrees of agreement or disagreement with the statement "In the last few years, the rich people in our society have gotten richer, while the poor people have gotten poorer." As shown in the left bar in Figure 3.1c, 60.1 percent of all respondents agreed or strongly agreed with this statement, which seems to be a

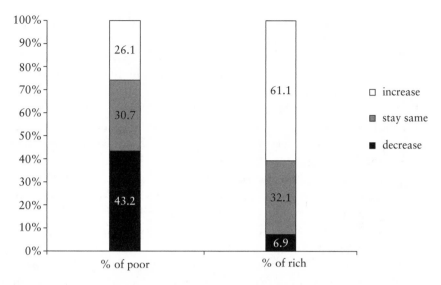

Figure 3.1b   Expected change in size of poor and rich

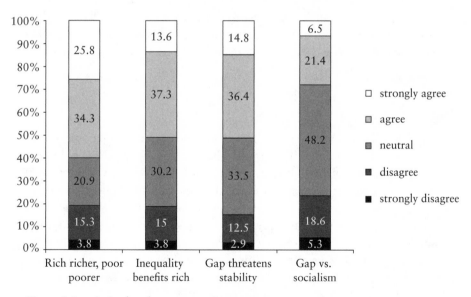

Figure 3.1c   Attitudes about current income gaps

puzzling contrast to the optimism about the proportion of China's poor declining in the future. The next bar in Figure 3.1c displays a similarly jaundiced
view: When presented with the statement "The reason why social inequalities
persist is because they benefit the rich and the powerful," 50.9 percent agree
and only 18.8 percent disagree. These responses suggest a popular suspicion

that in the country at large, those at the very top of the inequality pyramid are manipulating the system to their own selfish advantage.

Two other questions asked respondents to evaluate current income gaps in terms of whether they pose a threat to social stability and whether they violate the principles of socialism. As shown in the third bar in Figure 3.1c, 51.2 percent agree that the gaps threaten social stability, but as the fourth bar indicates, substantially fewer, only 27.9 percent, agree that the principles of socialism are being violated.[3] These responses raise the possibility that many respondents see current inequalities as excessive not so much because such large gaps are inherently unjust, but because the disparities threaten the desirable goal of an orderly and harmonious society.[4] As we examine the responses to other questions below, we will have further opportunities to probe the importance of social injustice sentiments compared to other types of negative reactions to current inequalities.

These initial questions about the size of inequality gaps yield mixed results. A large majority of Chinese citizens see the wide income differences in China nationally as unfair or undesirable, and they are particularly concerned about the prospect that such gaps could undermine social stability. Perhaps they also are suspicious of those at the very top of the social hierarchy. However, they are much less likely to see the income inequalities in their local communities and work organizations as excessive, and most do not expect the widened income gaps fostered by the reforms to translate into a growing problem of poverty in the immediate future.

THE ATTRIBUTION OF POVERTY AND WEALTH

In judging the fairness or unfairness of current inequalities in any society, more is involved than just deciding whether current gaps are too large, about right, or too small. It matters much more who is perceived to be at the bottom and at the top of the inequality hierarchy and how they are assumed to have ended up where they are. It makes a difference whether most rich people are perceived as enjoying ill-gotten gains or well-deserved fruits. Similarly, if people who are poor are perceived primarily as victims of discrimination and blocked opportunities, this will be seen as much more unfair than if the poor are seen as shiftless and incompetent. We thus enter the realm of the popular attribution of poverty and wealth.

Following the model of questions used in the International Social Justice Project, we asked each respondent to state whether various listed traits have a very large influence, a large influence, some influence, a small influence, or no influence at all on why people in China are poor, and we followed this up with similar questions about why people in China are rich. Attributions based on individual worthiness and merit and others based on external or structural causes are mixed together in each list.[5] The assumption underlying these questions is that if current inequalities are mainly attributed to variations in individual merit factors (such as talent, educational attainment, and hard work), they will tend to be seen as fair, but if inequalities are mainly attributed to external factors (such as unequal opportunities and discrimination), they will tend to be seen as unjust. The resulting weighted marginal distributions are displayed in Figures 3.2a and 3.2b.

In Figures 3.2a and 3.2b, one sees clearly that for most respondents, variations in individual merit factors much more than external and structural causes explain why some people in China today are poor and others are rich. In rank order, the top three attributions of poverty in China today are lack of ability or talent, low education, and lack of effort; for wealth the same three traits emerge as the most important, although in slightly different order, with ability and talent followed by hard work and then high educational level. However, one negative trait, variations in personal connections, is a close fourth in the ranking of attributions of why some people in China are rich.[6] Traits such as dishonesty, discrimination, and unfairness of the current economic system come out near the bottom in the rank ordering of reasons why some people are poor and others are rich.

These responses do not indicate that the dominant tendency in China today is for citizens to see the current patterning of wealth and poverty as attributable to social injustice. Rather, although perhaps a quarter of our respondents rank external or structural "unfair" sources as important or very important in explaining why some people are rich and others are poor, for the majority of respondents the primary explanations are found in variations in individual merit.[7] The dominant tendency is to see current inequalities as fair rather than unfair.[8]

How can these responses be squared with the fact that a large majority of respondents feel that there is too much income inequality in China today and that inequality exists because it benefits the rich and powerful? Two considerations may explain this apparent paradox. First, as suggested above, national inequality may be seen as excessive not so much because the gaps are inherently unjust but because they may threaten social stability. Second, it seems likely that when people respond to this series of questions about the explanations for why some people are poor and others are rich, they tend to focus on the rich and poor people in their immediate environment, rather than on invisible or dimly perceived rich and poor people in other parts of China. If that is the case, then as we saw in Figure 3.1a, most respondents do not see local inequalities as either particularly excessive or unjustly derived. If we can assume that, as in other societies, what matters most to individuals is how they see themselves compared to various local reference groups, rather than compared to the entire nation, it would appear that most respondents

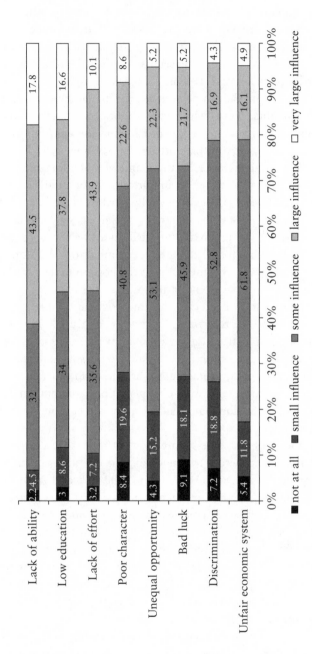

Figure 3.2a Attribution of why people in China are poor

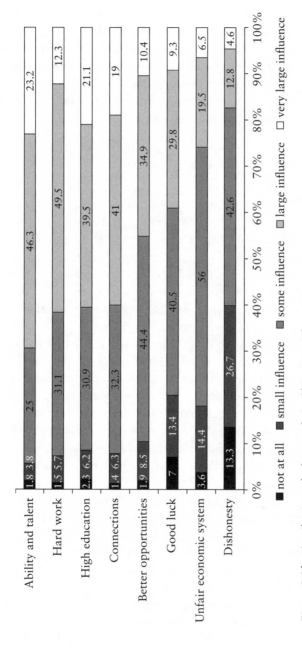

Figure 3.2b Attribution of why people in China are rich

see the inequalities around them as acceptable and even fair and do not harbor strong resentments and feelings that current inequalities are unjust, even if they worry about income disparities in the larger society.[9]

In short, the majority sentiment that current inequalities in China nationally are too large cannot be interpreted as indicating a general rejection of the current social order as unjust. Rather, there is a broad consensus that, at least in terms of the inequalities citizens see in their immediate environments, market reforms have produced new inequality patterns that are acceptable and viewed as primarily based on variations in individual merit rather than reflecting an unjust social order.

VIEWS ON EGALITARIAN DISTRIBUTION
AND REDISTRIBUTION

Since Chinese citizens have some objections to the size of current inequalities, it is worth considering how they would feel about a much more equal distribution of income and other resources and about government redistribution as a method of achieving such a result. Several questions relating to these issues are displayed in Figure 3.3. First are responses to the statement "Distributing wealth and income equally among people is the most fair method." As we can see from the first bar of Figure 3.3, opinions are divided on this issue, but with more respondents disagreeing than agreeing. Evidently, a strictly egalitarian distribution is not desired by most Chinese.[10] Nor is a need-based redistribution popular, as seen in the similar pattern of reactions to the statement shown in the second bar in Figure 3.3, "There should be redistribution from the rich to the poor in order to satisfy everyone's needs." However, judging from the third bar in the figure, there is much more popular approval of affirmative action efforts to help the poor, with 61.9 percent of respondents agreeing with the statement "It is fair to give people from lower social strata extra help so they can enjoy more equal opportunities."

The next four questions inquire about whether the government should take additional measures to reduce inequality. It is apparent that most Chinese do not favor limits on the maximum income individuals should be able to earn (see the fourth bar in Figure 3.3), with the pattern of responses very similar to those for the first two questions shown in the figure. However, there is much more support for the other three possible government actions, with 57.3 percent approving of government efforts to reduce the gap between high and low incomes, 75.7 percent favoring government guarantees of jobs to everyone willing to work, and 80.8 percent advocating the government's guaranteeing a minimum standard of living for everyone. Taken together, these responses suggest that the predominant view among Chinese

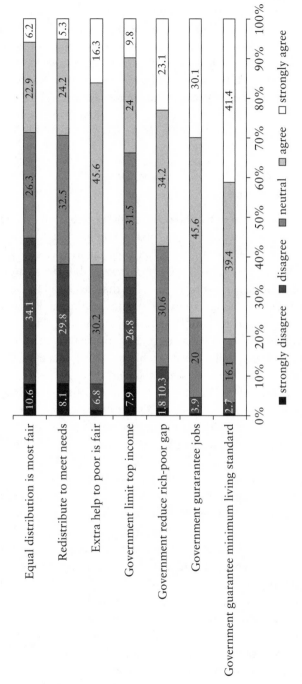

Figure 3.3 Attitudes toward egalitarian distribution and redistribution

citizens is that the ideal society would differ from the status quo mainly in having poverty eliminated by government-sponsored job and income guarantees, but without setting limits on the income and wealth of the rich or redistributing money from the rich to the poor. (Respondents were not asked to explain how the government could help the poor without extracting more from the rich.) This appears to be a formula for a market-oriented welfare state, not a socialist society,[11] and there is relatively little evidence here that most citizens harbor strong resentments against China's newly emerging class of entrepreneurs, millionaires, and, yes, capitalists.

THE BENEFICIAL EFFECTS OF INCENTIVES AND INCOME DIFFERENCES

Even if most Chinese are not in favor of equal distribution and egalitarian redistribution, are they willing to go further and say that the incentive effects of current inequalities are actually beneficial to society? When Deng Xiaoping contravened years of indoctrination in Maoist slogans extolling asceticism and egalitarianism by proclaiming that it is good for some people to get rich first, did he manage to persuade most Chinese? The abstract notion that inequalities are not simply tolerable, but may actually be desirable or even necessary because they benefit society (by increasing motivation, innovation, responsibility, and other desirable qualities), is central to the functionalist theory of stratification (see Davis and Moore 1945; Davis 1953), but it flies in the face of the Maoist condemnation of material incentives as the "sugar-coated bullets of the bourgeoisie." How successful have Chinese reformers been since 1978 in legitimating current inequalities by claiming that they are actually beneficial?[12] We can examine this issue by scanning the responses to questions in our survey that deal with the role of incentives and market competition, as displayed in Figure 3.4.

In the first bar of Figure 3.4, we see the pattern of responses to the statement "The good thing about market competition is that it inspires people to work hard and be creative." A solid majority of respondents (62.5 percent) expresses agreement with this statement, with less than 5 percent disagreeing. A more vague statement, "A free market economy is crucial to the economic development of our country," also is approved by a majority of respondents (53.8 percent) and disapproved by less than 5 percent. No other statement shown in the chart elicits such broad approval. A related statement meant to convey the central justification for markets by Adam Smith, "When every person can freely pursue his own interests, society as a whole will also benefit," elicits more approval (42.6 percent) than disapproval (13.8 percent), but the most common response to this claim is a neutral view (43.6 percent). There is a similar pattern of responses to another version of

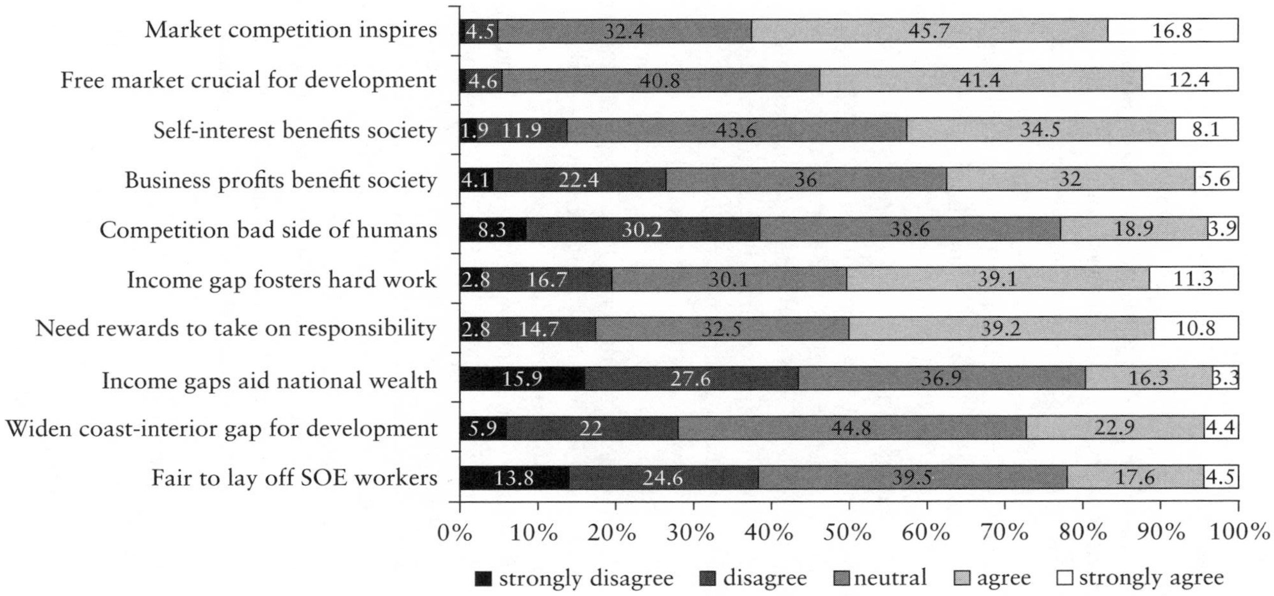

Market competition inspires
4.5
32.4
45.7
16.8
Free market crucial for development
4.6
40.8
41.4
12.4
Self-interest benefits society
1.9
11.9
43.6
34.5
8.1
Business profits benefit society
4.1
22.4
36
32
5.6
Competition bad side of humans
8.3
30.2
38.6
18.9
3.9
Income gap fosters hard work
2.8
16.7
30.1
39.1
11.3
Need rewards to take on responsibility
2.8
14.7
32.5
39.2
10.8
Income gaps aid national wealth
15.9
27.6
36.9
16.3
3.3
Widen coast-interior gap for development
5.9
22
44.8
22.9
4.4
Fair to lay off SOE workers
13.8
24.6
39.5
17.6
4.5
0%
10%
20%
30%
40%
50%
60%
70%
80%
90%
100%
strongly disagree
disagree
neutral
agree
strongly agree

Figure 3.4 Attitudes toward alleged benefits of markets, competition, and incentives

the same idea, but with a specific focus on the pursuit of profits by business-men: "It is acceptable for businessmen to make profits because in the end everyone benefits." Again there is more agreement that disagreement with this statement (by a smaller margin than was the case with the prior question: 37.6 percent compared to 26.5 percent), but the most common response is neutrality. A statement intended to express roughly the opposite attitude to those just discussed, "Competition is harmful because it brings out the bad side of human nature," not surprisingly finds more respondents disagreeing than agreeing, but again the most common response is neutrality. Clearly there is some support for market competition and incentives in the abstract among Chinese citizens, but also considerable uneasiness and uncertainty about claims that pursuit of self-interest and profit-seeking are generally beneficial for society.

The remaining statements in Figure 3.4 are designed to assess views on various versions of the claim that both carrots and sticks are needed to motivate individuals to behave in desirable ways so that society will bene-fit. These statements elicit even more divided reactions than was the case with the statements in the top two bars. Bare majorities agree with the statements "Only when income differences are large enough will individu-als have the incentive to work hard" (50.4 percent) and "Unless there are greater rewards, people will not be willing to take on greater responsibili-ties at work" (50 percent). When the same idea is expressed at the level of societal income gaps rather than individual incentives—in the statements "For the prosperity of the country, there must be large differentials in incomes" and "To develop our country's economy, it is necessary to increase the income gap between coastal and inland regions"—respondents express as much or more disagreement as agreement, and in both cases the most common response is a neutral position. Finally, the last bar of Figure 3.4 shows responses to the one statement directly dealing with the stick rather than the carrot side of incentives, "In order to reform state-owned enter-prises, it is fair to lay off large numbers of individuals." In this case as well, opinions are divided, and the most common response is neutral, but more respondents disagree with this statement (38.4 percent) than agree (22.1 percent).

Based on the questions considered in Figure 3.4, we conclude that China's reformers have been only partially successful in gaining popular accep-tance of the idea that market competition, material incentives, and income differentials are necessary and beneficial for Chinese society. To be sure, there is little sign in these responses that the notion Mao Zedong tried to instill in the population—that material incentives and the pursuit of profits and economic betterment are inherently evil—has many champions today. In general, however, uneasiness and uncertainty about claims that incentives and income differentials are beneficial and necessary are almost as common as approval of these ideas.

IS IT ALL RIGHT TO ENJOY THE FRUITS OF SUCCESS?

Attitudes about what forms of inequality are fair and unfair can be probed further by looking at a number of questions we asked about people who are successful and prosperous. These responses are displayed in Figure 3.5. Close to half of all respondents (48.8 percent) agree that it is fair for some occupations to receive more respect than others (see the first bar in Figure 3.5), and sizable majorities of our sample agree with statements that it is fair for the rich to pay for superior education for their children (64.2 percent) and to obtain superior housing (58 percent), although they are less certain that it is fair for the rich to obtain superior medical care (47.2 percent express approval and 27.6 percent disapproval). Also, a majority agree with the statement that rich people should be able to keep what they earn, even if this generates gaps between the rich and the poor (62.8 percent agree and only 6.3 percent disagree). Most respondents (61.2 percent) also say that inequality would be acceptable if China had equality of opportunity. However, the responses to a single question about elite status based on power rather than wealth generates a very different pattern (see the final bar in Figure 3.5). When presented with the statement "It is fair for people in power to enjoy a certain amount of special treatment," fully 55.8 percent disagree, while only 21.4 percent express agreement. Evidently, using acquired wealth to enjoy a better life than others is acceptable, but the translation of political power into a better life is not acceptable (even though the latter is every bit as common as the former, if not more so, in China today).[13]

DISCRIMINATION AGAINST PEOPLE OF RURAL ORIGINS

We have just seen that there is considerable acceptance of the rich and their families enjoying the fruits of their success. Now we shift our attention to look at popular attitudes toward a particularly important disadvantaged group—China's rural citizens. In one of the major ironies of China's socialist revolution after 1949, a leadership that had strong roots in the countryside and declared itself determined to eliminate feudalism and foster social equality produced something akin to socialist serfdom in actual practice, with those born into rural families effectively bound to the soil in all but rare circumstances, as discussed in Chapter 1. Even after this bondage ended in the reform era, with rural residents able to migrate and seek jobs in the cities, institutionalized discrimination against rural migrants (China's floating population, who possess agricultural household registrations—*hukou*—no matter

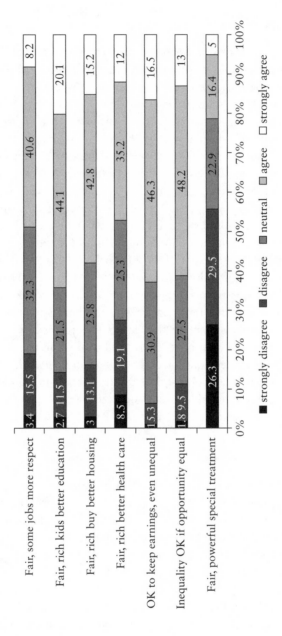

Figure 3.5 Attitudes toward the rich enjoying advantages

how long they may have lived in the city) has remained severe.[14] Our questionnaire included a range of questions to tap popular attitudes toward various aspects of this bias against people of rural origins. The distribution of responses is shown in Figure 3.6.

The figures in Figure 3.6 are quite different from those reviewed earlier. In every instance there is considerable sentiment that the various disadvantages suffered by rural people and migrants to the city are unjust. In the first bar of the figure we see that 45 percent of all respondents feel that the greater opportunities enjoyed by urban than by rural residents are unfair, while only 25.2 percent see them as fair. An even larger group, 59.2 percent of respondents, feels that denying urban household registrations to migrants from rural areas is unfair, while only 14.6 percent see this as fair. The sense of injustice is stronger still regarding rules preventing migrant children from attending urban public schools unless they pay special high fees, as well as the common practice of city regulations forbidding the hiring of migrants for a whole range of urban jobs. Here the consensus that these practices are unfair is 76.8 percent compared to 7.5 percent seeing them as fair for the school exclusion and 70.6 percent compared to 9 percent for the job exclusions. The figures in the next bar of Figure 3.6 confirm the pattern, with the jobs question asked the other way around: Overall 72.5 percent of respondents feel that rural and urban citizens should have equal rights to jobs, while only 7.8 percent disagree. The exclusion of urban migrants from welfare benefits enjoyed by China's urban residents is almost as unpopular, with 66.9 percent seeing this as unfair, and only 9.2 percent seeing it as fair.

The final two questions shown in the figure concern possible explanations for the higher income and other advantages that urban residents enjoy. Here the patterns are less lopsided, but they still show more rejection than acceptance of the idea that the advantages enjoyed by urbanites are deserved. When asked whether urban residents have enjoyed more of the benefits of the reforms than they deserve, 47.4 percent agreed compared with 21 percent who disagreed; when asked whether the advantages enjoyed by urbanites were due to the fact that they contribute more to the country and its development than do rural residents, only 21.7 percent agreed, while 45.4 percent disagreed. In sum, this set of questions shows the first clear-cut overall popular rejection of a current pattern of inequality.

Although we don't show the details here, these response patterns are not driven by the antipathy toward hukou-based discrimination of people of rural origin alone. Even urban respondents generally recognize the unfairness of current institutionalized discrimination against those with rural hukou, although their opposition is generally not expressed as strongly as that of migrants.[15] The institutionalized discrimination against people of rural origin in China in the reform era stands in contradiction to the pro-market

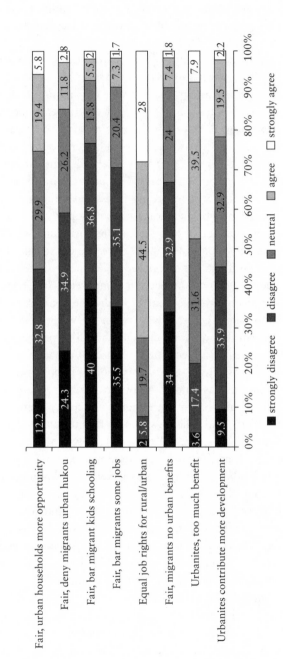

Figure 3.6 Attitudes toward urban bias

ideology that China's leaders are trying to persuade their citizens to accept. That ideology says that the ideal society has equality of opportunity, with the primary differences between the rich and successful and the poor and unsuccessful due to variations in talent, effort, and other nonascribed characteristics. The success of the leadership in gaining acceptance of these ideas, as we have seen earlier (particularly in Figure 3.2), almost necessarily means that the population will not agree that it is fair to maintain a large number of discriminatory practices against individuals simply because they were born into rural families.

PERCEPTIONS OF SEVERITY OF INEQUALITY-RELATED SOCIAL CONFLICTS

In any society with different social groups that have better or worse standards of living and access to opportunities, anger about inequality may be reflected not only in general sentiments that the situation is unfair, but also in feelings of resentment and antagonism directed toward other groups. Although members of disadvantaged groups are likely to feel such sentiments most keenly, advantaged groups may respond with hostility toward, and denigration of, the disadvantaged. As many inequalities have increased during China's reform era, one might expect the potential for social conflict between unequally situated groups to be on the increase. Still, whether Chinese citizens see their society as riven by sharp conflicts between different groups or instead as characterized by different groups that get along reasonably well is an empirical question.

Karl Marx recognized that exploited workers left to their own devices do not necessarily develop strong feelings of class consciousness and antagonism toward their exploiters. Mao Zedong formulated a complex theoretical framework around the question of whether particular intergroup relationships in Chinese society involved "non-antagonistic contradictions" or "antagonistic contradictions." Before the Cultural Revolution, the implication was that most inequalities in China fell into the former rather than the latter category.[16] As such there was no basis for strong feelings of resentment and antagonism between higher and lower status groups in Chinese socialism. The theme has returned to official Chinese policy in the new millennium with CCP leader Hu Jintao's emphasis on making sure that China remains a "harmonious society," even in the midst of rising inequalities.

Can the increasingly unequal and capitalistic society that China is today really be harmonious? To what extent do Chinese citizens see their society as characterized by sharp group conflicts related to inequality issues? Our questionnaire included a set of questions designed to assess perceptions of the degree of severity of a variety of inequality-related conflicts. Respondents

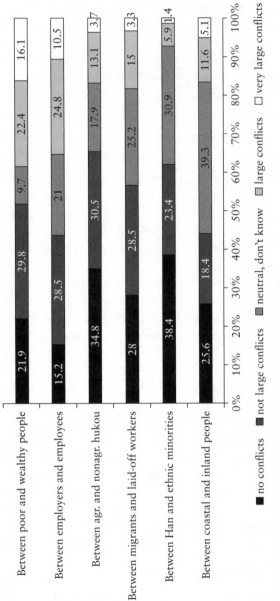

Figure 3.7 Perceptions of severity of inequality-related conflicts

were asked, "In our country, do you think the contradictions and conflicts between the groups listed below are very large, large, not large, or nonexistent?" The responses to six such potential group conflicts are displayed in Figure 3.7.[17]

It is hard to know what to make of the pattern of responses to these questions without comparable data from surveys in other societies.[18] On balance, however, we are struck by the preponderance of "no conflicts" and "not large conflicts" responses. Only in the first two bars, for conflicts between the rich and poor and between employers and employees, do we see something close to parity in the balance of "low conflict" and "high conflict" responses. In the remaining bars in the figure, less than 20 percent of respondents perceive social conflicts as large or very large, and the figure for relations between Han Chinese and ethnic minorities is only 7.3 percent. Most of the social cleavages dealt with in Figure 3.7 (with the exception of employers versus employees and perhaps rich versus poor) concern inequalities between advantaged and disadvantaged groups that tend to be geographically separated from one another and may not have much opportunity for contact, not to mention conflict. In any society groups with unequal status are most likely to come into sharp conflict if they are in the same social space and competing for the same resources.[19] Still, it is striking that most Chinese citizens appear to view these sorts of social cleavages as devoid of severe conflicts.

OPTIMISM AND PESSIMISM ABOUT
SOCIAL MOBILITY AND SOCIAL JUSTICE

The last set of attitude questions to be reviewed here concerns expressions of optimism and pessimism about the chances for individuals and families to get ahead and to live in a more just society. Statements relating to these questions are displayed in Figure 3.8. The first bar in the figure shows respondents' predictions about whether their families' economic situations will be much worse in five years than at the time of the survey, somewhat worse, about the same, somewhat better, or much better. The dominant mood is optimism, with 63.1 percent estimating that their families will be doing better in five years and only 7.5 percent predicting that their families will be doing worse. The dominant response to a more generic statement of optimism about upward mobility opportunities in China today—"Based upon the situation in the country today, the chances for someone like you to raise their living standard are still great"—is agreement (61.1 percent). However, the following attitude statements reveal that most Chinese recognize that equality of opportunity does not exist in China any more than it does in other societies. The statement "Currently, the opportunities to be successful are the same for all people" elicits nearly as much disagreement as agreement, and when the opposite view is stated, "People of different family backgrounds encounter different opportunities in society," almost 60 percent of respondents express agreement and only about 9 percent disagree. Despite this recognition of the inequality of mobility opportunities, when presented with the statement "In our country, hard work is always rewarded," most respondents strike an optimistic note, with 61.1 percent agreeing and only 15.4 percent disagreeing. Taken together, these responses indicate that most Chinese recognize that there is not a level playing field providing the same chances to all, but at the same time they do not think that the social order is so unfair that it is stacked against ordinary people, preventing them from getting ahead.

We see echoes here of the responses to questions about why some people are rich and others are poor (Figures 3.2a and 3.2b). There appears to be a strong belief that the diligent pursuit of social mobility through schooling, talent, and hard work will lead to social and economic improvement, with factors such as unequal opportunities and personal connections helping some undeserving individuals to succeed also, but not to the extent that deserving ordinary people are thereby blocked from getting ahead. This view of the world is substantiated when respondents were asked to indicate which of two statements they agreed with more: "Some people getting rich first will reduce the chances for others to get rich" and "Some people getting rich first will increase the opportunities for others to get rich" (not included in Figure 3.8). Many more respondents favored the second option (48.6 percent, compared to 11.1 percent who chose the first option), although a sizable 40.3 percent responded that it was hard to say or that they didn't know. Evidently most Chinese don't see the pursuit of wealth as a zero-sum game, and many accept Deng's view that it is good for some people to get rich first.

The final three bars in Figure 3.8 display responses to three statements designed to tap feelings of injustice and pessimism about achieving social justice: "Since we are unable to change the status quo, discussing social justice is meaningless"; "Looking at things as they are now, it is very difficult to distinguish what is just and what is unjust"; and "Government officials really don't care about what common people like me think." Opinions are very divided on all three statements. For the first two, disagreement is almost as likely as agreement, but the most common response is a neutral answer. A bare majority (50.1 percent) expresses agreement with the third statement, compared to 21 percent who disagree. (Chapter 4 includes discussion of how this level of negative feelings about government officials compares to other countries.) In general and taken together with the pattern of responses in Figure 3.8 as a whole, it does not appear that the dominant mood of Chinese

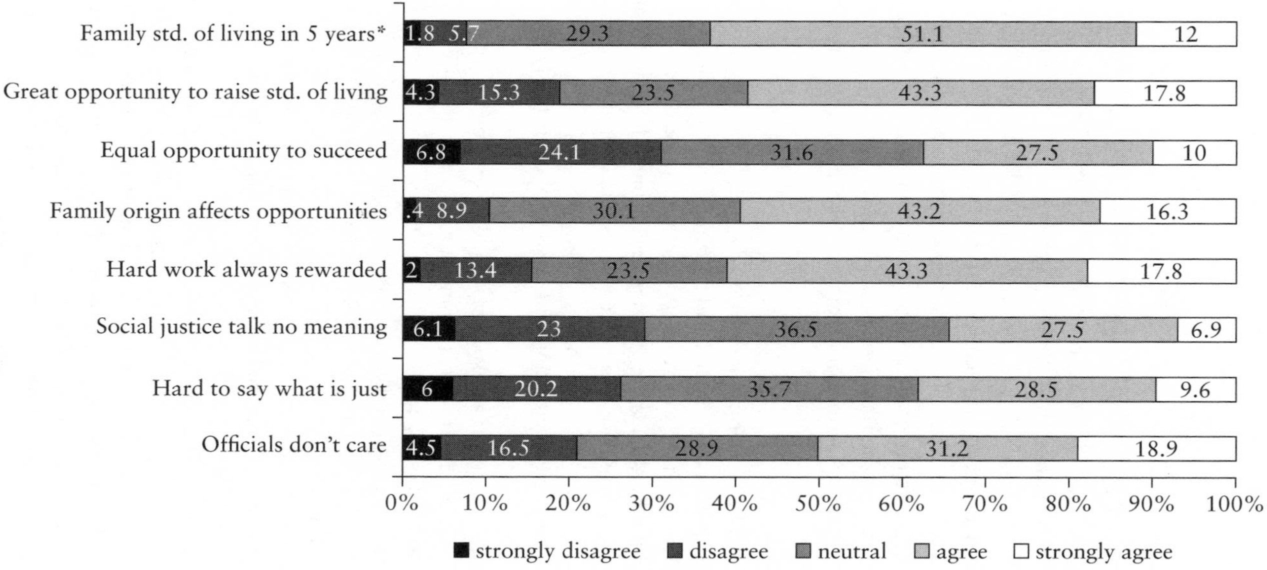
Family std. of living in 5 years*
Great opportunity to raise std. of living
Equal opportunity to succeed
Family origin affects opportunities
Hard work always rewarded
Social justice talk no meaning
Hard to say what is just
Officials don't care
1.8 5.7 29.3 51.1 12
4.3 15.3 23.5 43.3 17.8
6.8 24.1 31.6 27.5 10
.4 8.9 30.1 43.2 16.3
2 13.4 23.5 43.3 17.8
6.1 23 36.5 27.5 6.9
6 20.2 35.7 28.5 9.6
4.5 16.5 28.9 31.2 18.9
0% 10% 20% 30% 40% 50% 60% 70% 80% 90% 100%
strongly disagree
disagree
neutral
agree
strongly agree

Figure 3.8 Optimism and pessimism about social mobility and social justice
* Actual response categories: much worse, somewhat worse, no change, somewhat better, much better.

citizens, at least at the time of our survey in 2004, was anger at the fundamental injustice of current patterns of inequality or pessimism about the chances for ordinary citizens to benefit under the current system.

CONCLUSIONS

How can we summarize Chinese citizens' feelings about issues of inequality and distributive justice? Which aspects of current inequalities in China do they accept and view as fair, and which do they see as basically unjust? In general, our survey results indicate that the majority of respondents accept and view as fair most aspects of the unequal, market-based society in which they now live. There is little sign in our results of strong feelings of distributive injustice, of active rejection of the current system, or of nostalgia for the distributional policies of the planned socialist era.

The following principles for an ideal social order emerge from our survey results:

- There should be government-sponsored efforts to provide job and income guarantees to the poor and affirmative action policies to provide the disadvantaged with more opportunities to succeed.
- There should be abundant opportunities for individuals and families to improve their livelihoods and social status and to enjoy the fruits of their success.
- Insofar as possible, there should be equality of opportunity to succeed and prosper.
- Material advancement and success should be determined by merit factors, such as educational attainment, knowledge and skills, individual talent, and hard work, and not by non-merit factors (not only external unfairness, such as prejudice, unequal opportunities, and personal connections, but also age, gender, family size, household registration status, and so on).
- The pronounced social cleavage between China's rural and urban citizens and institutionalized discrimination against villagers and urban migrants are unfair.
- Since individuals and families vary in their talents, diligence, and cultivation and deployment of merit-based strategies for success, society will have a considerable amount of inequality of incomes and other resources. As long as society provides equal opportunity and merit-based pursuit of upward mobility, this inequality is acceptable.
- Upper limits should not be set on the incomes or other advantages that the upwardly mobile can enjoy, and there should not be a systematic government program to redistribute wealth from the rich to the poor (so long as wealth was obtained through equal opportunity and merit-based competition).

- It is acceptable for the rich to use their advantages to provide better lives for their families.
- People in positions of political power should not be entitled to special privileges or be able to use their positions to provide better lives for their families, and they ought to be concerned about the views of ordinary citizens on distributive justice issues.
- Despite acceptance of inequality of outcomes in general, it is desirable not to let inequality get too wide nationally so as not to increase the likelihood of social instability and political disorder.
- In general, the social groups in China that are divided by cleavages based on unequal rewards and opportunities should nonetheless have harmonious relations and mutual respect, rather than antagonism and conflict.

As noted earlier, this summary of the views of the majority of Chinese citizens about the ideal social order does not sound much like socialism and indeed is very different from the principles mandated during China's socialist era. Instead this seems like a generic formula for a market society supplemented by welfare state guarantees for the poor. An American or European citizen would likely agree with most of the same principles about the ideal distributive order (see Kluegel and Smith 1986).

Most respondents perceive that the society in which they live differs from these ideals in several important ways. In particular, there is no adequate safety net of government-provided subsistence guarantees for the poor,[20] and opportunities for social mobility are far from equal. Non-merit factors are seen as playing an important, even if secondary, role in access to opportunities; the politically powerful continue to enjoy privileges and special treatment; and no effective mechanism exists to prevent national income disparities from widening and provoking social turbulence.

This is the "glass half empty" side of the picture, and we also need to emphasize the ways in which the distributive glass is half full in the eyes of survey respondents: Upward mobility opportunities are perceived as plentiful. Individual merit factors are seen as playing the dominant role in enabling individuals and families to better themselves. No limits are perceived on upper incomes or on the ability of the rich to enjoy the rewards of their economic success. This mixed but generally upbeat picture provides the basis for our conclusion that most survey respondents see the gap between ideal and reality as acceptable rather than as huge and therefore that they view the current inequalities as more fair than unfair. As of 2004, at least, China's communist leaders seemed successful in gaining public acceptance of market-based inequalities.

Our conclusion that most respondents accept current patterns of inequality and don't harbor strong feelings of distributive injustice is tempered by three qualifications. First, the attempt by Chinese authorities to convince citizens that income gaps and competition for rewards are necessary and beneficial to society because they will stimulate economic productivity has not been all that successful. As seen in Figure 3.4, some questions along these lines elicit almost as much disagreement as agreement, with many respondents uncertain and settling for a neutral response. Although the authorities have been successful in counteracting the Maoist message that the pursuit of material success, upward mobility, and consumer goods is evil and socially harmful, they have not been nearly as successful in justifying and gaining popular acceptance of specific contemporary incentives and inequalities through the claim that these differentials make a positive contribution to productivity and economic growth. The skepticism surrounding claims that current incentives and disparities are generally necessary and beneficial may in some instances cause suspicion and anger, as in the case of the privileges enjoyed by political elites and mass layoffs of employees from state-owned enterprises.

The second qualification is that a majority of the population feels that some specific features of current inequality patterns are very unfair. In particular, most Chinese citizens feel that pervasive discrimination against rural residents and urban migrants is unfair (see Figure 3.6). Even though migrants are generally the most vocal in condemning discrimination based on China's hukou system, even urbanites do not defend these practices. The rural-urban cleavage, arguably the most important and extreme axis of inequality in Chinese society today, is widely seen as fundamentally unjust.[21]

The third qualification to the conclusion that current patterns of inequality are broadly accepted by Chinese citizens stems from the fact that throughout this chapter we have been focusing on modal tendencies and majority responses to survey questions. While the majority of survey respondents appear to accept the status quo and lack strong feelings abut the existence of distributive injustice, a sizable minority of respondents— generally 15 to 35 percent—responded otherwise to most of our attitude questions. For example, 26.1 percent of survey respondents predicted that the proportion of China's poor will increase in the coming five years; 27.9 percent said that current inequalities conflicted with socialist principles; 17.4 percent felt that dishonesty had a large or very large influence on who got rich in China; 26 percent said that the unfair economic structure had a large or very large influence on who was rich; 29.1 percent said that it would be most fair to distribute income and wealth equally; 33.8 percent thought that the government should place upper limits on how much people could earn; 27.6 percent felt it was unfair for the rich to obtain better health care for their families; 26.5 percent didn't think society benefits by allowing businessmen to pursue profits; 38.5 percent perceived large or very large conflicts between the rich and the poor; 19.6 percent disagreed with the statement that great opportunities to improve their standards of living currently existed for ordinary people; and 34.4 percent said that talking about social justice was meaningless because the current system could not be challenged or changed. To be sure, these figures do not tell us whether these critical responses to specific questions cohere. In other words, does the same roughly 25 percent of respondents see the current system as unjust across the board, or do these minority responses come from shifting groups of respondents who offer critical views on specific questions while agreeing with the majority's positive responses to many other questions? The answer to this question will be provided in the analyses presented in Chapters 6 through 9.

Regardless of the degree of coherence of such critical attitudes, these figures on minority response patterns give pause. If on most specific questions regarding distributive justice and injustice, a quarter or even more of China's citizens see the current system as unfair, the government will potentially have to contend with a sizable number of angry and alienated individuals. Social protest activity that is seen as threatening political stability does not require majority local sentiment, and there are clearly more than enough disgruntled people in China who feel that current patterns of inequality are unjust to pose a potential threat. Mao Zedong got pretty far in life by acting on his observation (in 1930) that "a single spark can start a prairie fire." While it appears that a majority of Chinese citizens accept most aspects of current inequalities and don't feel outraged by the gaps between current realities and an ideal social order, that is by no means sufficient to guarantee that China will remain politically stable in the years to come.

CHAPTER FOUR

Chinese Views on Inequality in Comparative Perspective

In general, as indicated in Chapter 3, the typical response of Chinese citizens to most aspects of current inequality patterns appears to be acceptance rather than rejection or anger. In other words, we do not see many signs in the 2004 national survey data that a large portion of Chinese adults feel that the social order in which they live is unjust (with some exceptions, particularly involving the injustice of pervasive discrimination against Chinese citizens with rural household registrations). Still, it is hard to know what to make of the figures presented in Chapter 3. Are the levels of support for contemporary inequalities stronger or weaker than in other societies? Do fewer Chinese express feelings that current patterns are unjust than do people in Eastern European societies that are making a similar transition from socialism to market-based capitalism? In general, how do views of Chinese citizens on inequality and distributive injustice issues compare with those of their counterparts in other post-socialist societies and in established capitalist societies? This chapter is designed to provide answers to questions such as these.

In designing the 2004 China national survey on attitudes toward inequality and distributive injustice issues, we took advantage of the fact that surveys on these issues had already been carried out in other countries, thus making it possible to place Chinese attitudes in comparative perspective. James Kluegel pioneered in this realm by directing a national survey on beliefs about social stratification in the United States in 1980 (see Kluegel and Smith 1986). Kluegel subsequently joined a collaborative research team, the International Social Justice Project (ISJP), that planned and carried out two waves of national surveys, in 1991 and 1996, designed to examine views about patterns of inequality of citizens in a variety of Eastern European societies making the transition from socialism to capitalism and in several advanced capitalist societies (see particularly Kluegel, Mason, and Wegener 1995; Mason and Kluegel 2000). The 1991 surveys were conducted in both advanced capitalist and formerly socialist societies: Bulgaria, the Czech Republic, Estonia, Germany (West and

East), Holland, Hungary, Japan, Poland, Russia, Slovenia, the United Kingdom, and the United States. The follow-up round of ISJP surveys in 1996 was confined to selected Eastern European transitional societies: East Germany, Hungary, Russia, Bulgaria, and the Czech Republic. A more recent round of ISJP surveys was even more selective—Hungary in 2005 and the Czech Republic and the former East and West Germany in 2006. We incorporated a range of questions from the ISJP project into our China survey work.

We are thus in a position to compare the pattern of responses to many but not all of the survey questions on inequality issues included in our 2004 China survey with responses from selected other post-socialist transition societies (Russia in 1996, Bulgaria in 1996, Hungary in 2005, the Czech Republic in 2006, the former East Germany in 2006, and Poland in 1991) and with selected capitalist countries (the United States, the United Kingdom, and Japan in 1991, and the former West Germany in 2006).[1] We can do this only for the questions we replicated from the ISJP surveys, not for the new questions summarized in Chapter 3 and discussed elsewhere in this study that were designed to assess distinctive aspects of inequality in China. So, for example, the very contentious issue of discrimination against individuals with rural household registrations (see Figure 3.6) is a distinctive feature of stratification in China, and we do not have comparative results about discrimination against rural residents and rural migrants in either advanced capitalist or Eastern European transitional societies.

COMPARING ATTITUDES TOWARD INEQUALITY AND DISTRIBUTIVE INJUSTICE

The remainder of this chapter roughly follows the order of presentation used in Chapter 3 to examine how the 2004 Chinese national survey results compare with results from other post-socialist as well as advanced capitalist countries. To simplify the presentation in the tables that follow, the figures for responses to statements with five response categories are the sum of the categories "agree" and "strongly agree." Where other response categories were used, the basis for computing the percentages shown in the cells of the table is indicated in the text. Although some detail is lost in reducing a question's results to a single percentage for each country, some simplification is necessary given the number of questions and countries involved in these comparisons.

Table 4.1a displays responses to a single question asked in each country: "Do you think that the current differences in income levels among people in this country are too large, somewhat large, about right, somewhat small, or too small?" The percentages shown in Table 4.1a are the total of those who said that the income gaps nationally are too large and somewhat too large. A substantial majority of Chinese respondents (71.7 percent) think that China's national income gaps are too large (see also Figure 3.1a). This percentage is actually on the low side in comparative perspective. In the ISJP surveys, citizens in every post-socialist transitional society other than Poland in 1991 agreed in substantially larger numbers that income gaps in their country were excessive, and about 95 percent of respondents in both Hungary and Bulgaria expressed this view in 1996. In fact, the tendency of Chinese citizens to see national income gaps as excessive is more on a par with the responses in the capitalist countries included in the 1991 ISJP surveys, with only citizens in the United States somewhat less likely to express this sentiment (65.2 percent).[2]

Table 4.1b displays the results of questions about whether the respondent thinks the percentage of poor people and of rich people will increase nationally over the next five years. The pattern of responses from Chinese citizens is strikingly different from all the other countries included in the table. In no other country surveyed do so few respondents predict that the percentage of poor people nationally will increase over the next five years (26.1 percent compared to between 37.2 percent and 79.6 percent), and in no other country does as high a proportion of respondents predict that the percentage of rich people nationally will increase (61.1 percent compared to between 29.1 percent and 57.9 percent). It is also striking that more than two times as many respondents in China predict an increase in rich people as predict an increase in poor people, whereas in all the other countries except West Germany, more respondents—often substantially more—see the percentage of poor people increasing than see the percentage of rich people increasing.

One could object that the timing of some of these surveys might affect the conclusions drawn. For example, respondents in both the United States and the United Kingdom would presumably have been more optimistic about increases in the proportion of the rich and decreases in the proportion of the poor at the end of the 1990s dot-com boom than they were in 1991. Even given such qualifications, the contrast of the Chinese patterns with so many other locales in different time periods is dramatic. In 2004, at a time when, as we saw in the Introduction to this book, many analysts claimed that the dominant mood in China was widespread anger caused by rising inequality, the most common pattern of responses was quite to the contrary and surprisingly optimistic. The mood is compatible with an upbeat "rising tide is lifting all boats" view that more and more people would become rich in the future while the numbers of poor in China would decline still further. Insofar as we can judge from Table 4.1 in general, Chinese citizens seem less angry and less concerned about income gaps and inequality trends than do citizens of other societies, whether capitalist or post-socialist.

TABLE 4.1a
Views on extent of inequality (percent)

	China 2004	Russia 1996	Bulgaria 1996	Hungary 1996	Czech Republic 2006	East Germany 2006	Poland 1991	United States 1991	United Kingdom 1991	West Germany 2006	Japan 1991
National income gaps too big	71.7	86.3	95.6	94.9	84.8	88.6	69.7	65.2	75.0	78.4	72.6

TABLE 4.1b
Expected changes (percent)

	China 2004	Russia 1996	Bulgaria 1996	Hungary 1996	Czech Republic 2006	East Germany 2006	Poland 1991	United States 1991	United Kingdom 1991	West Germany 2006	Japan 1991
Poor increase in five years	26.1	47.9	75.1	77.4	n.a.	79.6*	74.5	69.0	58.0	43.1*	37.2
Rich increase in five years	61.1	41.5	32.4	42.3	n.a.	45.1*	57.9	29.1	34.5	46.3*	36.7

n.a. = Data not available.
*Figures from 1996 ISJP survey.

This impression is strengthened by the responses of Chinese and citizens of other countries to questions about why some people in their society are poor while others are rich. The results of this comparison are shown in Table 4.2, with Table 4.2a displaying responses to a variety of possible reasons why some people are poor, and Table 4.2b showing the corresponding responses to a variety of possible explanations for why some people are rich. These questions about the attribution of poverty and wealth have five response categories: to a very large degree, to a large degree, to some degree, to a small degree, and not a factor at all. The percentages shown in all cells of Table 4.2 are a sum of those who gave "to a very large degree" and "to a large degree" responses. As noted in Chapter 3, we view this set of questions, translated from the ISJP surveys, as a key indicator of whether a respondent views current inequalities as fair or as unfair. Insofar as individuals perceive that such factors as ability and hard work are primary explanations of why some people are rich while others are poor, they are stressing meritocratic attributions of poverty and wealth and thus tend to see current inequalities as fair. Conversely, insofar as individuals perceive that such factors as dishonesty, discrimination, unequal opportunities, and an unfair economic structure are primary explanations of why some people are rich while others are poor, they are stressing structural or non-merit attributions of poverty and wealth and thus tend to see current inequalities as unfair.

The pattern of Chinese responses in Table 4.2 is very distinctive. Chinese respondents tend to stress individual merit rather than unfair external or structural explanations of why some people are rich and others are poor. The figures in Table 4.2 indicate that this tendency is stronger in China than in any of the other countries examined here, with the partial exception of Japan. In general, respondents in the other post-socialist countries included in the table are much more likely than their counterparts in China to explain being rich or poor in terms of structural rather than individual merit factors. Particularly striking is the fact that 61.3 percent of Chinese respondents see lack of ability as an important explanation of why some people are poor, while in other post-socialist countries the corresponding figures range from 26.6 percent to only 34.8 percent. Only 17.4 percent of Chinese respondents think that dishonesty is an important explanation of why some people are rich; in other post-socialist societies the comparable figures range from 43 percent to 82.4 percent. Sixty percent of Chinese respondents recognize the use of personal connections (*guanxi*) to become wealthy as important, compared to people in various Eastern European transitional societies, where anywhere from 72.7 percent to 89.3 percent stress manipulation of connections as an important explanation for why some people are rich.[3]

The distinctiveness of Chinese views on this issue also shows in a comparison of the responses from the three Western capitalist countries included

TABLE 4.2a
Why people in their country are poor (percent)

	China 2004	Russia 1996	Bulgaria 1996	Hungary 2005	Czech Republic 2006	East Germany 2006	Poland 1991	United States 1991	United Kingdom 1991	West Germany 2006	Japan 1991
Poverty—lack of ability	61.3	28.0	26.7	30.8	28.8	26.6	34.8	35.2	32.8	36.5	25.7
Poverty—bad luck	26.9	28.4	38.7	28.2	31.5	24.6	32.0	15.2	22.1	26.2	24.6
Poverty—loose morals	31.2	74.0	43.1	54.0	43.8	43.	75.	41.0	33.0	44.4	63.1
Poverty—low effort	54.0	39.1	35.6	28.5	45.3	32.0	42.8	47.8	34.9	44.0	62.0
Poverty—discrimination	21.2	40.8	23.0	27.0	22.3	40.4	11.1	36.4	31.5	31.4	22.8
Poverty—unequal opportunity	27.5	61.2	76.6	43.6	41.7	56.6	46.4	33.4	36.0	41.7	23.1
Poverty—economic structure	21.0	72.6	88.0	63.2	44.6	71.9	65.2	44.9	48.1	44.6	36.2

TABLE 4.2b
Why people in their country are rich (percent)

	China 2004	Russia 1996	Bulgaria 1996	Hungary 2005	Czech Republic 2006	East Germany 2006	Poland 1991	United States 1991	United Kingdom 1991	West Germany 2006	Japan 1991
Wealth—ability	69.5	48.3	34.1	42.0	54.5	51.8	46.0	59.7	53.9	59.5	65.1
Wealth—good luck	39.1	40.5	60.5	47.2	41.4	44.2	37.4	24.6	33.9	45.1	57.5
Wealth—dishonesty	17.4	74.1	82.4	48.1	64.9	43.0	62.4	42.9	35.5	33.3	27.8
Wealth—hard work	61.8	38.1	48.9	26.5	53.5	50.0	32.0	66.2	60.2	62.5	48.4
Wealth—connections	60.0	84.1	89.3	82.5	80.0	81.8	72.7	75.0	76.3	76.4	49.3
Wealth—more opportunity	45.3	55.3	82.3	80.1	58.2	75.6	55.8	62.5	64.7	71.1	54.4
Wealth—unfair economic structure	26.0	72.7	77.5	65.5	57.8	57.4	52.2	39.4	44.5	35.6	53.0

in the table, the United States, the United Kingdom, and West Germany. In these countries, there tends to be a bit more stress on merit factors, and somewhat less stress on external structural explanations, than in Eastern European transitional societies. But compared to China, the respondents in all three of these countries stress structural explanations more and merit explanations less. The country that comes closest to the Chinese pattern of responses is Japan, but even Japanese respondents are much less likely than their Chinese counterparts to stress lack of ability in explaining poverty (although they are slightly more likely to stress lack of effort) and much more likely to view an unfair economic structure as an important explanation of why some people are rich.

Looking at the results in Tables 4.1 and 4.2, we propose a rough ranking of countries and groups of countries in terms of people's perception of the degree of fairness or unfairness of inequalities within their societies:

Fair→China→Japan→Western capitalist countries→
Eastern Europe→Unfair

This ordering is striking. It conveys the idea that Chinese citizens view their country's inequalities, which have widened as a result of the post-1978 market reforms, in an even more favorable light than citizens in established and much more prosperous capitalist societies view inequalities in their countries. The residents of Eastern European societies undergoing their own market transitions are at the other end of the scale, with jaundiced or decidedly negative views that emphasize the unfairness of current inequalities. Of course, in China the market reforms took place twenty-six years before the survey was conducted, compared to Eastern Europe, where between two and seventeen years have elapsed, but the contrasts are nonetheless striking.[4] Furthermore, the length of experience with market-based inequalities cannot explain why Chinese citizens view current inequalities even more favorably than do their counterparts in the United States, the United Kingdom, and West Germany.

The contrasts of Chinese responses to these questions become even clearer when viewed visually in charts. Figure 4.1 displays the mean of the unfair inequality items for China compared to the same calculation for the ISJP countries.[5] From this chart it is clear that Chinese citizens (and their Japanese counterparts) are less likely than citizens in any of the other countries to explain the difference between who is rich and who is poor in terms of unfairness of the system. Figure 4.2 presents the same comparison for the merit-based inequality items. The education questions were not included in the ISJP surveys, so the calculations in Figure 4.2 are based only on the ability and effort attributions of poverty and wealth for all countries. In Figure 4.2 China is the country most likely to explain who is rich

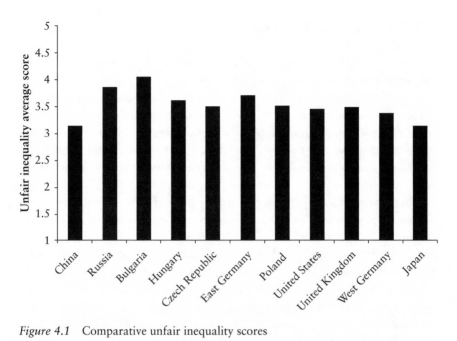

Figure 4.1 Comparative unfair inequality scores

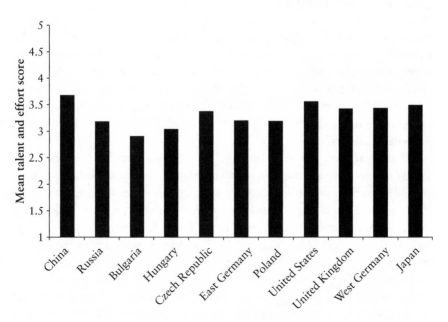

Figure 4.2 Comparative stress on talent and effort

and poor by differences in talent and effort (followed by the United States and then Japan).[6]

The next set of questions concerns preferences for more egalitarian distribution and for government efforts to promote greater equality. Did extreme promotion of egalitarianism in the Mao era, at least at the rhetorical level, leave an imprint on Chinese popular attitudes that is discernable today? The Chinese and comparative responses to six questions in this realm are displayed in Table 4.3. In this table the percentages are the sum of "agree" and "strongly agree" responses to the five statements read out to respondents.

In none of the countries covered here do more than a minority of respondents say it would be fairest to give everyone in society equal shares of resources, and China (where 29.1 percent agree with egalitarian distribution) is right in the middle of the pack. (Curiously, Japan stands out as the locale with the strongest support for egalitarian distribution, with 37.5 percent favoring this approach.) China is more distinctive in that fewer citizens favor redistribution from the rich to the poor in order to satisfy everyone's needs than do citizens in most of the other locales—only 29.5 percent favor this approach, compared to between 34.2 percent and 79.6 percent in Eastern Europe and between 45 percent and 69.3 percent in the three Western capitalist countries. (Japanese are about as unlikely as Chinese to favor this approach, at 30 percent, even though they are most likely to favor egalitarian distribution.) The third question concerns affirmative action. Respondents were asked whether it is fair to give extra help to the disadvantaged so they can enjoy more equal opportunities. Most respondents in all locales favored affirmative action, but only 61.9 percent of Chinese respondents agreed or strongly agreed with the desirability of giving extra help to the disadvantaged, a figure a little higher than in the Hungarian and Czech surveys, but much lower than the 75 percent to 88 percent who favored such measures in other Eastern European post-socialist societies and in advanced capitalist societies.

The final three rows in Table 4.3 are responses to statements about things the government might do to promote greater equality. Government-provided minimum income guarantees and the government as the last-resort provider of jobs to the poor are very popular in most of the included countries except the United States, and China's level of approval of these two approaches (80.8 percent and 75.7 percent) is not particularly low or high compared to the other countries. The final measure, government-imposed limits on the maximum income a person can make, tends to be favored more in the Eastern European transitional societies (with the exception of the Czech Republic) than in the capitalist countries, and the pattern of China's responses is closer to the latter than to the former. Specifically, only

TABLE 4.3

Attitudes toward egalitarian distribution and redistribution (percent)

	China 2004	Russia 1996	Bulgaria 1996	Hungary 2005	Czech Republic 2006	East Germany 2006	Poland 1991	United States 1991	Great Britain 1991	West Germany 2006	Japan 1991
Fairest—equal shares	29.1	28.6	32.4	22.5	13.0	30.9	19.1	19.2	28.9	22.3	37.5
Fair—redistribution to meet needs	29.5	44.9	36.8	67.2	34.2	79.6	50.9	45.0	46.7	69.3	30.0
Fair—extra help for disadvantaged	61.9	76.1	76.2	54.6*	61.3*	n.a.	88.0	82.1	79.5	n.a.	75.0
Government-provided minimum SOL guarantee	80.8	90.8	92.5	90.9	77.5	86.4	85.3	55.9	82.1	76.2	80.6
Government-provided welfare jobs	75.7	93.2	88.8	90.1	76.7	88.7	86.2	50.4	66.2	73.9	84.5
Government limit on top income	33.8	39.5	43.7	60.9	22.6	59.1	44.3	16.7	37.9	40.0	33.4

n.a. = Data not available.

*Figures from 1996 ISJP survey.

about a third of Chinese favor upper income limits, compared to about 39.5 percent to 60.9 percent in most Eastern European societies (but only 16.7 percent to 40 percent in the capitalist societies).

In the late Mao era Chinese citizens experienced more egalitarian rhetoric and policy than did their counterparts in Eastern Europe (see Parish 1984, Whyte 1981).[7] It would not have been unreasonable to expect this experience to produce broader support for social equality than exists in other state socialist societies. But perhaps unpleasant memories of the egalitarian experiments and rhetoric of the Mao era instead produced more ardent rejection of egalitarian distribution than in other societies. The data in Table 4.3 indicate that Chinese are less likely than citizens in most other societies to favor redistribution from the rich to the poor to meet popular needs or to favor affirmative action to help the poor, and they are also more similar to residents of established capitalist than of other transitional societies in being unenthusiastic about government-imposed maximum income limits. However, they respond similarly to respondents in Eastern European countries and Japan in being more likely to favor government provision of jobs to the poor than are their counterparts in Western capitalist societies. On balance, Chinese citizens today do not appear particularly egalitarian compared to citizens of other countries, and in some respects (regarding affirmative action and maximum income caps) they appear more skeptical of egalitarian policies. These data provide more support for the "reaction against," rather than the "legacy of," Maoist egalitarianism argument, but the distinctiveness of Chinese response patterns is more muted than elsewhere in these comparative data.

The questions in Table 4.4 are broadly concerned with whether current inequalities are not only acceptable, but actually desirable. They reflect the functionalist theory of stratification (see Davis and Moore 1945). According to that theory the differences between the rich and poor are not mainly the outcome of an unequal and perhaps unfair competition, but actually provide a necessary structure of incentives that encourage individuals to study and work hard, seek advanced training, take on extra responsibility, bear financial risks, innovate, and in general do all of the positive things that make an organization or even an entire society more productive and efficient and thus more prosperous. In this line of thinking, social equality can be harmful; without sufficient differentials and rewards, individuals will not be motivated to behave in optimal ways that will benefit society (see Okun 1975). China's reformers after 1978 contended that Mao-era socialism should be faulted on precisely those grounds and that for China to successfully compete in the world, more inequality had to be fostered (see Whyte 1993). However, as noted in Chapter 3, the official promotion of the idea that inequalities are necessary has not gained full acceptance. How do Chinese attitudes in this realm look in comparative perspective?

TABLE 4.4

Attitudes toward alleged benefits of markets, competition, and incentives (percent)

	China 2004	Russia 1996	Bulgaria 1996	Hungary 2005	Czech Republic 2006	East Germany 2006	Poland 1991	United States 1991	Great Britain 1991	West Germany 2006	Japan 1991
Free market vital to country	53.8	54.0	41.3	47.8*	72.8*	n.a.	n.a.	n.a.	n.a.	n.a.	n.a.
Business profits OK	37.6	39.2	13.1	17.7	34.5	32.3	49.5	51.1	42.0	38.9	51.3
Income gap fosters hard work	50.4	41.7	39.3	20.2	42.9	52.3	65.5	61.3	62.7	58.4	48.5
Reward responsibility	50.0	83.8	78.0	63.5*	74.3	71.5	82.0	69.7	82.8	73.1	39.6

n.a. = Data not available.
*Figures from 1996 ISJP survey.

The four questions in Table 4.4 allow us to examine this issue. The first row in the table shows the proportion of respondents in China and in other post-socialist countries surveyed who agree or strongly agree with the statement that the free market is vital to the country's development (the question was not asked in the 1991 ISJP surveys). Responses varied widely from locale to locale, and Chinese responses appear to occupy a middle ground. The same could be said of the responses to the next two statements: that it is all right for businessmen to make profits because all of society benefits, and that income gaps are necessary in order to foster hard work. In general Chinese respondents express less approval of these statements than do respondents in Western capitalist countries, but they are roughly in the middle of the pack in comparison with other post-socialist societies. The final row of the table presents levels of approval of a statement that unless people receive extra rewards, they won't be willing to take on greater responsibilities. Here Chinese respondents express less agreement than those surveyed in other post-socialist societies and in Western capitalist societies, often by a considerable margin (50 percent compared to between 63.5 percent and 83.8 percent). Japan is even more of an outlier, with just under 40 percent agreeing with the statement. On balance, based on this limited set of questions, Chinese citizens do not appear to be all that distinctive compared with citizens of other post-socialist societies, in which there is much variation but generally somewhat more skepticism about functionalist justifications of inequality than in Western capitalist societies. (Why Japanese citizens are even more skeptical about functionalist arguments in some respects is unclear.)

Table 4.5 includes questions about the acceptability of the rich keeping and enjoying their advantages and passing them on to their children. In this domain current policies and rhetoric in China ("it is good for some people to get rich first") constitute a sharp break with the Mao era, when pursuit of personal advantage and even slightly conspicuous consumption could be politically dangerous. The first question asks whether it is fair for some occupations to have more status in society than others, and here Chinese respondents express less agreement (48.8 percent) than do citizens in most of the other countries (about 55 percent to 77 percent), although more than do the Japanese surveyed in 1991 (36.4 percent). The next three questions ask whether it is fair for the rich to get better education for their children, better housing, and better medical care. Unfortunately we have responses to only the first of these three questions in several of the surveys. In general, though, the figures show as much or more approval of the rich enjoying the fruits of their success in China as in the other countries surveyed. The most distinctive contrast concerns the ability of the rich to obtain better medical care than others. Evidently respondents in the post-socialist societies of Russia,

TABLE 4.5
Attitudes toward the rich enjoying advantages (percent)

	China 2004	Russia 1996	Bulgaria 1996	Hungary 2005	Czech Republic 2006	East Germany 2006	Poland 1991	United States 1991	Great Britain 1991	West Germany 2006	Japan 1991
Fair—some jobs have more status	48.8	62.3	77.1	55.2*	59.7	67.0	55.8	68.0	66.0	63.6	36.4
Fair—rich kids get better education	64.2	60.0	60.1	30.3	35.1	37.4	67.9	65.2	56.3	42.8	50.9
Fair—rich have better housing	58.0	60.8	57.0	59.4*	n.a.	47.2*	n.a.	n.a.	n.a.	n.a.	n.a.
Fair—rich get better medical care	47.2	41.5	21.0	20.9	n.a.	6.4*	n.a.	n.a.	n.a.	n.a.	n.a.
Fair—people keep earnings	62.8	80.1	68.1	54.9	75.8	85.9	63.8	92.9	81.2	84.7	65.9
Fair—inequality with equal opportunities	61.2	74.2	73.4	68.8*	64.4	72.0	62.8	83.7	77.7	76.5	52.0

n.a. = Data not available.
*Figures from 1996 ISJP survey.

Bulgaria, Hungary, and the former East Germany see access to medical care more as a basic social right than as a market-distributed good, and they thus express strong disapproval of the statement. However, Chinese citizens are less likely to share this view, with close to a majority agreeing that the rich should be able to obtain better medical care than others.

The final two rows in Table 4.5 display responses to two abstract statements about the acceptability of inequality—that people should be able to keep what they have earned, even if this leads to inequality, and that inequality patterns are acceptable as long as there is equality of opportunity in society. Here Chinese respondents are on the low side in terms of their expressed approval of current inequalities. Only a little more than 60 percent of Chinese surveyed agreed with each statement, whereas in most other locales included in the table (except Japan) anywhere from 70 percent to more than 90 percent agreed with the statements (Americans were the most enthusiastic).

On balance there is no consistent pattern in the comparison of Chinese responses with citizens of other countries regarding the acceptability of inequalities and of the rich enjoying the fruits of their success; Chinese agree less with some of these statements and more with others compared to citizens elsewhere. Nor does there appear to be a distinction in responses in post-socialist societies and in established capitalist societies, as in some other tables. If anything, the Japanese respondents stand out as being the most uncomfortable with current inequalities and their reproduction over time. Most Chinese accept the specific aspects of current inequalities touched on in the questions in Table 4.5, but they are not unusually more or less likely to do so than citizens in the other societies surveyed.

Table 4.6 arrays responses to a variety of questions designed to assess general optimism and approval of current opportunities to get ahead in society in contrast to fatalism and pessimism about injustice. The first row in Table 4.6 shows a striking contrast, with 63.1 percent of Chinese respondents expecting their families to be doing better in five years than they are today, which is true of less than one-quarter of the respondents in the other post-socialist countries surveyed. (This question was not included in the 1991 and 2005–2006 ISJP surveys.) The next two rows in the table show the degree of approval (agree and strongly agree responses) of two favorable but empirically dubious statements about current opportunities. In regard to the first, a claim that equal opportunities to succeed exist currently, Chinese responses (at 37.5 percent) are in the middle, similar to responses from Japan, West Germany, the United Kingdom, and the Czech Republic (all with 30 percent to 40 percent agreeing), much lower than those surveyed in the United States (65.9 percent), but substantially higher than in the other post-socialist societies surveyed (between only 7 percent

TABLE 4.6

Optimism and pessimism about social mobility and social justice (percent)

	China	Russia	Bulgaria	Hungary	Czech Republic	East Germany	Poland	United States	Great Britain	West Germany	Japan
	2004	1996	1996	2005	2006	2006	1991	1991	1991	2006	1991
Higher family income in five years	63.1	22.0	20.5	21.1*	n.a.	22.3*	n.a.	n.a.	n.a.	n.a.	n.a.
Equal opportunities exist	37.5	22.8	7.1	11.9	31.2	20.3	25.5	65.9	41.8	31.8	38.1
Hard work is rewarded	61.2	10.7	2.8	25.9	22.7	34.7	8.5	37.4	18.7	47.0	16.6
Can't change injustice	34.4	45.5	50.1	43.3	41.2	52.7	49.2	27.6	34.4	46.1	28.6
Can't tell what justice is	38.1	54.4	62.7	64.8	59.9	65.2	64.1	58.8	61.9	52.3	62.9
Officials don't care	50.1	69.7	76.3	58.8*	70.0	76.6	72.3	64.0	66.5	65.9	74.7

n.a. = Data not available.

*Figures from 1996 ISJP survey.

and 26 percent). However, Chinese respondents express much higher agreement with the second statement, that hard work is always rewarded (by material success and social status improvement), than did respondents in any of the other surveys, and by a large margin compared to Eastern European countries, the United Kingdom, and Japan. Note the resonance of this Chinese attitude with the high proportion of respondents who saw hard work as an important explanation of why some people in China today are rich (Table 4.2b).

The final three rows of Table 4.6 explore more pessimistic or even fatalistic attitudes. Respondents were asked to express agreement or disagreement with statements that it doesn't make sense to talk about justice because nothing can be changed, that they don't know what justice means any more, and that officials don't care what ordinary people think. The pattern of Chinese responses is distinctive in regard to all three statements, particularly the last two. China is on the low side with the first statement, that there is no point discussing justice issues, thus indicating relatively high levels of disagreement, similar to the United Kingdom and slightly higher than the United States and Japan. In response to the latter two statements, fewer Chinese express agreement than in any of the other countries surveyed, post-socialist or capitalist. It is particularly striking that even though half of all Chinese respondents agree that officials don't care what ordinary people think, this is substantially fewer than in the post-socialist and newly democratic countries of Eastern Europe and established democratic countries in the West and Japan.

In general these figures reinforce the conclusions drawn in Chapter 3. Contemporary inequalities have not systematically fostered feelings of unusually strong anger and pessimism in China. Many, although not all, Chinese are decidedly optimistic about their own chances to improve their lot in society. It may not be all that surprising that Chinese feel more optimistic and less angry than citizens of Eastern European transitional societies surveyed in the 1990s and in 2005–2006, given the substantial economic depressions experienced at the beginning of the market transition in that part of the world. What is more surprising is that in some respects Chinese citizens have even more optimistic views and greater acceptance of current inequalities than do their counterparts in established capitalist (and democratic) societies.

CONCLUSIONS

This chapter has examined comparative data from China, six Eastern European transitional societies, and four advanced capitalist societies in an effort to determine what is distinctive about Chinese popular attitudes toward inequality and distributive justice issues. What can we conclude from this review of the available comparative evidence?

Broadly speaking, most of the questions examined here are designed to assess the degree of acceptance of current patterns of inequality or of ideas and principles associated with market distribution (as opposed to socialist planned distribution). The assumption lying behind surveying popular attitudes on these questions is that, for the post-socialist transition to be successfully consolidated in any country, the majority of the population must come to accept market-based inequalities as fair and as preferable to socialist distribution (sentiments that are presumed to be already widely held in established capitalist societies). If we adopt this general characterization, we can roughly categorize five response patterns in terms of what they tell us about whether Chinese attitudes are distinctive: On which questions do Chinese on average express (1) more critical opinions than all or virtually all of the other countries considered, (2) more critical opinions than many but not all of the other countries, (3) attitudes that are in the middle of the pack, (4) more favorable views than many but not all other countries, and (5) more favorable attitudes than all or virtually all the other countries? Table 4.7 presents the results of this rough sorting process.[8]

Table 4.7 reveals a clear overall pattern. Only for a small number of questions do Chinese citizens express somewhat more critical attitudes than do citizens in the other countries surveyed. In particular, with the exception of Japan, people in all the other countries agree more strongly than do Chinese that "it is fair for some occupations to have higher status than others" and that "unless there are greater rewards, people will not be willing to take on greater responsibilities." However, about 50 percent of Chinese respondents agree with both statements, so this is not an instance of a highly critical Chinese view, but only of a slightly less enthusiastic embrace of market-oriented maxims (Tables 4.4 and 4.5). In addition, a majority of Chinese agree that "it is all right for people to keep what they have earned, even if this leads to inequality" and that "inequality is acceptable as long as there is equality of opportunity," but in most other countries examined here (except Poland and Japan) people agree more strongly with both statements (Table 4.5). These are the only questions for which Chinese responses appear more critical than responses in most of the other countries, but in none of these cases do the majority of Chinese respondents express negative or anti-market attitudes.

For a large number of questions Chinese citizens are much more accepting of current patterns of inequality and much more optimistic about opportunities to get ahead than are citizens of any of the other countries. In particular, Chinese appear to see current differences between who is rich and who is poor in their society as much more due to merit, and less due to

TABLE 4.7
*How Chinese attitudes toward inequality compare
with attitudes in other countries*

1. *Chinese citizens are more critical than citizens in other countries*
   If you don't offer more rewards, people won't be willing to take on more responsibility (4.4)
   It is fair for some jobs to have higher status than others (4.5, except Japan)

2. *Chinese citizens are somewhat more critical than citizens in other countries*
   It is fair for people to keep what they have earned, even if this leads to inequality (4.5)
   Inequality is acceptable, as long as there is equal opportunity (4.5)

3. *Chinese citizens are in the middle, neither particularly critical nor uncritical*
   It would be fairest to give everyone equal shares (4.3)
   The government should provide minimum standard-of-living guarantees (4.3)
   The government should guarantee jobs to everyone willing to work (4.3)
   The government should place limits on maximum incomes (4.3)
   The free market is vital to the country's development (4.4)
   It is all right for businessmen to earn profits because in the end all benefit (4.4)
   Income gaps are necessary to foster hard work (4.4)
   It is fair for the rich to buy better housing (4.5)
   Equal opportunities exist in our society (4.6)

4. *Chinese citizens are somewhat more approving than citizens in other countries*
   View of national income gaps (4.1a)
   Poverty due to discrimination (4.2a)
   It would be fair to give extra help to the disadvantaged (4.3)
   It is fair for rich families to obtain better schooling for their children (4.5)
   There is no point talking about injustice as nothing can be changed (4.6)

5. *Chinese citizens are more approving than citizens in other countries*
   Proportion of poor in five years (4.1b)
   Proportion of rich in five years (4.1b)
   Poverty due to lack of ability (4.2a)
   Poverty due to low effort (4.2a, except for Japan)
   Poverty due to unequal opportunity (4.2a, except for Japan)
   Poverty due to unfair economic structure (4.2a)
   Wealth due to ability (4.2b)
   Wealth due to dishonesty (4.2b)
   Wealth due to hard work (4.2b, except for the United States)
   Wealth due to use of connections (4.2b, except for Japan)
   Wealth due to unequal opportunities (4.2b)
   Wealth due to unfair economic structure (4.2b, except for W. Germany)
   It would be fairest to redistribute to meet everyone's needs (4.3, except for Japan)
   It is fair for the rich to pay for better medical care for their families (4.5)
   Trend in family income in the next five years (4.6)
   Hard work is always rewarded (4.6)
   It is hard to say what is just and what is unjust anymore (4.6, except West Germany)
   Officials don't care what ordinary people like me think (4.6)

an unfair social structure, than do citizens of any other country (Table 4.2). They are much more optimistic that their families will be better off in the future and that hard work will be rewarded, and they are much less likely to feel that officials don't care about what ordinary people think (Table 4.6). On balance, these patterns reinforce the conclusions reached in Chapter 3. In general the average Chinese citizen has a relatively low level of feelings of distributive injustice not only absolutely, but also relative to citizens in other countries. Again, we see no evidence that China is heading toward a social volcano due to popular anger over rising inequality.

It might be argued that it is not surprising that Chinese citizens are more accepting and optimistic when confronting contemporary inequalities than is generally the case in Eastern European societies also undergoing post-socialist transitions. The Eastern European societies generally experienced severe economic problems in their economic transitions, in contrast with the fairly steady and even robust economic growth that has characterized the transition in China. Furthermore, some of the ISJP surveys were carried out fairly early in that transition (in Poland in 1991, in Russia and Bulgaria in 1996), before the substantial economic recovery that some of the countries have experienced since, and perhaps before market-oriented ideas and distribution principles could gain broader popular acceptance. Our China survey, in contrast, was conducted in 2004, twenty-six years after the launching of a successful market transition.

However, the distinctiveness of Chinese popular attitudes regarding current inequalities seems striking and unexpected in several respects. First, there is the common view that despite the overall success of China's reforms, the pattern of changes over time has to some extent been the reverse of Eastern Europe's path. Instead of serious economic problems followed by recovery and rising affluence, in China there was an initial dramatic improvement in the economy and living standards and sharp reductions in poverty, followed since the mid-1990s by continued robust growth but rising problems—increased inequality, rising urban unemployment and poverty, rising popular protests, and so on. Insofar as this shift from reform with no losers to reform with losers as well as winners captures the Chinese transition experience over time, one might have expected the greater passage of time since market reforms were launched to foster more critical opinions about contemporary inequalities, rather than more favorable opinions. But our comparisons show the opposite tendency—for Chinese citizens to be less critical of current inequalities.

Further confirmation of the relatively more positive attitudes of Chinese citizens toward current inequalities comes from a separate analysis I conducted with Chunping Han. That study, involving more nearly comparable survey timing but only two capital cities, Beijing in 2000 and Warsaw in 2001, yielded similar results and conclusions (Whyte and Han 2008). The Warsaw survey was conducted a decade later than the Polish survey used in the tables of this chapter, well after the economic recovery that began in Poland in 1992, but it didn't produce markedly more favorable attitudes toward current inequalities and market principles, while the Beijing survey four years earlier than the 2004 national survey didn't produce markedly more critical (or for that matter, markedly more favorable) attitudes toward current inequalities and market principles. Even when controlling for differences in sample composition between the Beijing and Warsaw samples (for example, the greater education of Warsaw respondents, the higher percentage of Beijing respondents who reported improvements in their families' standards of living), there were still significant differences in the attitudes expressed in Beijing and Warsaw on inequality issues, with Warsaw respondents generally markedly more critical.

Further confirmation that the quirks of survey timing cannot explain the relatively positive and optimistic views of Chinese citizens regarding current inequalities can be derived from the ISJP surveys conducted in Hungary (1996 and 2005), the Czech Republic (1996 and 2006), and the former East Germany (1996 and 2006). The initial draft of this chapter used the 1996 ISJP data for these three countries; the current text incorporates the 2005–2006 survey results kindly made available by the principal investigators, Bernd Wegener (East Germany and West Germany), Antal Örkeny (Hungary), and Hynek Jerabek (the Czech Republic). When I substituted the 2005–2006 figures for the 1996 survey results in the tables for this chapter, there were minor changes in percentages, but no change at all in the contrasts with the Chinese survey results. There was no detectable tendency for survey respondents in these countries to have more positive views about current inequalities in 2005 and 2006 than their compatriots had a decade earlier. Another ways of putting this conclusion is that citizens in Eastern Europe have maintained fairly critical views about market-based inequalities even as their experiences with the socialist alternative have receded further into the past. So the assumption that approval of market-based inequalities increases over time in post-socialist societies is wrong. In this context it might be noted that another study using different survey data from Eastern Europe (Kelley and Zagorski 2004) makes the opposite argument— that citizens in Eastern Europe were quite approving of large income gaps between high- and low-status occupations early in the post-socialist transition and became less approving in later years.[9]

A final consideration in support of seeing Chinese favorable views about current inequalities as genuine and surprising is that the views of Chinese respondents in regard to a substantial number of questions were more favorable than were the views of citizens in the United States, the United Kingdom, West Germany, and Japan. The conventional wisdom is that in established and wealthy capitalist societies, current inequality patterns are broadly seen as just rather than unjust, whereas in post-socialist transitional societies' doubts and criticisms of emerging and increased inequalities and of the rationales presented by advocates of market-based distribution will exist for a considerable period of time. On these grounds we might expect Chinese citizens to have more favorable views about current inequalities than their counterparts in Eastern Europe, but not in comparison with Americans, British, (West) Germans, and Japanese. How can we explain what now seems an unusually favorable view about current inequalities and the fairness of the distributive system in China, even in comparison with established and much more prosperous capitalist countries?

In pondering this question we leap from the relative firm grounding of survey statistics into the realm of speculation and conjecture. Several possible influences might help explain these favorable Chinese views. First and most obvious is the fact that China's economy has experienced a dramatic and sustained record of robust growth for three decades, despite the strains and problems mentioned above. This growth might reasonably be expected to produce widely shared optimism and acceptance of the possibilities for ordinary people to get ahead through merit despite the advantages enjoyed by the wealthy and powerful, and this optimism may generally sway popular responses to most questions about current inequalities in a favorable direction, even among Chinese citizens who have not (yet) become prosperous. Second, personal experience of the lack of opportunity for improvement in living standards and for upward mobility in the Mao era, in contrast with modest gains and new opportunities available in China now, may incline a large share or even a majority of the population to view current inequalities positively. Later chapters present considerable evidence that farmers—the largest single group of Chinese citizens—generally have experienced such improvements in their lives, and they seem particularly likely to have positive views about many inequality issues (despite their continued low social status).

Another consideration is the impact of the expectations that existed before the launching of market reforms. For the most part political isolation and tight controls over information from the outside world kept Chinese citizens in the dark about living standards in other countries. Official propaganda in the Mao era claimed that socialism was a superior system, and the population had no grounds for developing high or unrealistic expectations about how people would benefit from market reforms. When such benefits came, they may have been seen as a welcome and unexpected confirmation of the new post-1978 official propaganda message—that markets worked better than socialist allocation. Citizens in Eastern Europe in the 1980s, in contrast, were not so isolated and were aware of how much worse off they were than citizens in Western European societies.[10] As a consequence, many Eastern Europeans developed unrealistic expectations about how quickly and smoothly the end of socialism would result in the general prosperity enjoyed by, say, Austrians and West Germans (see, for example, Reykowski 2004). Even after the recovery from the "shock therapy" dismantling of socialism, the realities of life in the struggling new capitalist systems of Eastern Europe could not compare with the extraordinarily high hopes that had been built up before the transition. The realities of life in a market society were generally better than Chinese citizens had been led to expect, while to Eastern Europeans they were worse.[11]

A final consideration that may help explain the positive views of Chinese citizens is the fact that the Chinese Communist Party (CCP) still exercises considerable control over communication and information, whereas the mass media and public debate on issues of inequality and distributive injustice are more lively and critical in the other countries examined here, even in Eastern Europe. In Eastern Europe the post-socialist transition involved not only a shift from bureaucratic allocation and distribution to markets, but also the collapse of Communist Party rule. That dual transition makes the political atmosphere in Eastern Europe generally quite different from that in China. To be sure, in China the CCP's controls on the media, information, and ideas are much less strict than in the Mao era, and lively debate in the mass media and in the public square about issues related to inequality is now possible. However, there are limits on views that can be voiced publicly that do not exist in such societies as Poland and Hungary.[12] Views that there is too much inequality and that unequal opportunities are causing popular resentment can be expressed publicly in China. However, to suggest publicly that the current structure of inequality is a product of official favoritism toward the rich and powerful and of rampant corruption, or that most of the newly wealthy owe their success to being the children or other relatives of high officials, is to risk serious consequences.[13] There are still no fully independent media outlets in China, and there are frequent closures and suspensions of publication of magazines and other media that offend the authorities by spreading ideas that are deemed excessively critical.

Perhaps more important than the ability of Communist Party media controls and police surveillance (with the Internet being a particular focus) to limit the spread of critical views about inequality issues is the considerable power and resources of state-controlled media to regularly disseminate positive views and stories related to these issues—for example, to publicize rags-to-riches stories of newly emerging millionaires, to laud the increased efficiency that market competition produces, and to showcase China's top leaders expressing concern about China's poor and disadvantaged and taking steps to correct injustices. In promoting a favorable view of markets and contemporary opportunities to achieve prosperity, the Chinese Communist Party can be said to employ a public relations juggernaut that a Chamber of Commerce in the United States or any other capitalist society can only envy (see Brady 2008). So even though critical opinions about inequality and distributive injustice can more freely be expressed in China today than in the

Mao era, the critics still may be lonely voices buried under an avalanche of favorable stories conveyed by the official media.

These speculative comments lead to a paradoxical conclusion. We normally think that free markets and free politics go hand in hand (for example, see Centeno 1994), and many analysts have argued that China will eventually have to democratize. Whether this prediction comes true or not, for the moment the lifelong Communist Party bureaucrats in China are doing a better job of promoting support for, and gaining popular acceptance of, the fairness of their increasingly capitalistic and unequal society than are their counterparts in the newly democratized societies of Eastern Europe and even in the established and wealthy democratic and capitalist societies. At the end of this study we examine the paradoxical situation of lifelong communists presiding over the creation and widespread acceptance of a booming capitalist system.

PART II   THE SOCIAL CONTOURS
OF FEELINGS OF DISTRIBUTIVE
INJUSTICE

CHAPTER FIVE

Chinese Attitudes Toward
Current Inequalities

Chapters 3 and 4 use data from the 2004 China inequality and distributive justice survey to address three primary research questions: How angry in general are Chinese citizens about current inequalities (Chapter 3)? Which aspects of current inequalities do Chinese citizens accept, and which aspects do they criticize (Chapter 3)? How do Chinese popular attitudes toward inequality and distributive injustice issues compare to attitudes in other societies (Chapter 4)?

Regarding most aspects of current inequalities, the average Chinese citizen regards the status quo as more fair than unfair. Most respondents feel that opportunities to get ahead within the current structure of inequality are abundant, even if not equal. For the most part, the average Chinese citizen either has views similar to citizens in other societies or views that are more positive and optimistic, sometimes decidedly so. In particular, Chinese citizens have markedly more positive views than do their counterparts in post-socialist societies in Eastern Europe. The weight of evidence from the 2004 survey, then, leads us to question the conventional wisdom. The average Chinese citizen is less angry and feels more optimistic than is conventionally assumed, and certainly less than is implied by the scenario of a looming social volcano.

Despite this overall relatively positive picture of Chinese popular attitudes, a significant minority of survey respondents expressed negative and critical views about various aspects of current inequalities. For example, as indicated in Chapter 3, 26.1 percent of survey respondents expect the proportion of Chinese who are poor to increase during the next five years, 45.3 percent perceive that unequal opportunities helped some people get rich, 29.1 percent think rewards should be distributed equally among citizens, and 27.6 percent think it is inappropriate for rich people to be more able than less affluent people to purchase better medical care for their families.

Who is most angry about these issues and most pessimistic about the opportunities for ordinary people to improve their standards of living? In pursuit of an answer to this question, Chapters 6 through 9 are concerned with the fourth basic research question that motivated our project: How do inequality attitudes vary within China, and in which social groups, categories, and geographic locations do we find the most criticism of current inequalities and the strongest feelings of distributive injustice? These chapters map the social contours of critical opinions about inequality and distributive injustice issues.

To prepare the ground for this mapping process, the current chapter is devoted to a discussion of two important issues. First, what are the important dimensions or domains of popular attitudes about current inequalities that we should try to measure with our survey data so that we can map how they vary across the Chinese social landscape? Second, what social status, demographic, and locational characteristics of our respondents should we use to systematically examine who is more likely to approve of or disapprove of current inequalities, and how can we measure these background characteristics with our survey data?

DOMAINS OF ATTITUDES TOWARD INEQUALITY AND DISTRIBUTIVE INJUSTICE ISSUES

Some prior survey research on popular reactions to the post-socialist transition used a single question or type of question as a measure of feelings of distributive injustice (see, for example, Kelley and Zagorski 2004). In this study, in contrast, we follow the lead of other earlier research, particularly the International Social Justice Project (ISJP) discussed in Chapter 4, and conceive of attitudes toward current inequalities and distributive injustice issues as a complex, multidimensional terrain. However, it doesn't make sense to examine variations across China in the responses to each of the approximately seventy survey questions discussed in Chapter 3. The only reasonable way to proceed is to develop a conceptual scheme based on analytically distinct domains of attitudes and to construct a small number of survey-based measures for each distinct domain.[1] That said, it is not immediately obvious what the primary domains of inequality attitudes are.

There is no consensus on how to organize the complex conceptual terrain of inequality and distributive injustice attitudes into their basic underlying dimensions (see, however, Hochschild 1981; Kluegel and Smith 1986). The dimensions that researchers end up focusing on depend to a large degree on the specific questions included in their surveys and are affected as well by questions they did not think to ask. We included a large range of questions in the 2004 China survey, but we cannot claim to have fully covered every inequality and distributive injustice domain imaginable. Still, we collected evidence on how Chinese citizens feel about a broad array of issues, and the task here is to divide this terrain into distinct domains of inequality attitudes in order to make statistical analysis manageable and comprehensible.

The first domain of inequality attitudes involves perceptions that Chinese citizens have of the shape and nature of current inequalities. How do they view the actual inequalities they see around them, and to what extent do they think that current inequalities are excessive, unfairly derived, and harmful to society (compared to acceptable, fairly derived, and having benign implications for society)? Chapter 6 focuses on the social contours of variations in Chinese perceptions of current inequalities in an effort to determine which respondents view current gaps as relatively fair and which see them as unfair. The chapter draws on responses to the questions covered in Figures 3.1 and 3.2 and reduces those responses to four separate inequality perception measures.

The second inequality attitude domain concerns preferences for a different kind of social order. In other words, here we are dealing with respondent ideals about inequality patterns rather than perceptions of the status quo. In this second domain we want to know whether respondents would prefer China to be a more equal society than it is currently and whether they would like the government to promote greater equality through such measures as redistribution from the rich to the poor and affirmative action to aid the disadvantaged. We also want to know how acceptable or unacceptable respondents feel it would be to maintain or even increase current inequalities in order to provide some people with greater incentives and rewards for contributions to society. The domain of preferences for greater equality and of preferences for differentials and incentives is the focus of Chapter 7. That chapter draws on responses to the questions covered in Figures 3.3 and 3.4 and again reduces the available items to four separate measures of preferences for greater equality or acceptance of differentials.

The third domain of inequality attitudes concerns views regarding the perpetuation of inequalities over time and even over generations. In the language of sociology, this involves a shift away from an emphasis on current inequalities toward an emphasis on status transmission patterns or social stratification (see Duncan 1968). Because several kinds of status transmission are at play in China, including transmission based on wealth, on power, and on household registration status, Chapter 8 focuses on survey respondents' views about the acceptability or unacceptability of the various forms of social stratification. Because social stratification fosters status groups and social cleavages that can lead to conflict between haves and have-nots, Chapter 8 also focuses on respondent views on how much conflict exists across the status cleavage fault lines of contemporary China. Again four summary measures are used in the analyses, all derived from the survey questions summarized in Figures 3.5 through 3.7.

The fourth and final major domain of inequality attitudes concerns whether opportunities for ordinary citizens to improve their livelihoods and obtain social justice are abundant or scarce. Which types of respondents are relatively optimistic about the availability of such opportunities, and which are relatively pessimistic or even fatalistic? The issues regarding opportunities for social mobility and social justice are the focus of Chapter 9, using three summary measures derived from the questions covered in Figure 3.8.

Taken together, we employ fifteen separate measures or scales to capture a variety of specific aspects of the four domains of inequality attitudes. Because our measures of inequality attitudes are conceptually derived (even though they are shaped and constrained by the survey questions), there is no presumption that each of the four main inequality attitude domains or each of the fifteen specific measures is independent of the others empirically and thus statistically. Our starting assumption, based on conventional wisdom, is closer to the reverse. The initial expectation is that respondents who perceive current inequalities as excessive and unfair will also favor greater equality and government redistribution, be critical of current patterns of status transmission, and have a pessimistic view about the opportunities for ordinary citizens to improve their lot. Conversely, respondents who perceive current inequalities as reasonable and fair are expected to lack strong preferences for greater equality and government redistribution, to accept current patterns of status transmission, and to have fairly optimistic views about the chances for ordinary citizens to get ahead. If these kinds of tendencies are an accurate representation of how respondent attitudes are structured, there should be fairly consistent patterns of statistical associations among most or all of the measures we use in the next four chapters.[2] If it turns out that the various domains and specific measures of inequality attitudes are closely connected in popular thinking about inequality issues, and if we discover that some respondents tend to have critical attitudes pretty much across the board, even as others accept most aspects of inequality, such a pattern would give new life to the social volcano scenario, despite the generally accepting attitudes of the average survey respondent summarized in Chapters 3 and 4. Political instability is not usually a product of general dissatisfaction of the populace, but rather of angry and mobilized minorities. So even if the average Chinese citizen has fairly positive attitudes toward current inequalities, it is still important to determine whether there are clear and consistent pockets of critical views about inequalities in the Chinese social landscape.

However, we may discover that the variety of domains and specific measures of Chinese citizen attitudes are only loosely related to one another or even unrelated. On a given inequality attitude measure, for example, it is possible that farmers are angry while urban white-collar workers are satisfied, whereas on another measure farmers are relatively satisfied while urban blue-collar workers are most angry. To state the matter a different way, perhaps the 29.1 percent of respondents who favor equal distribution overlap very little with the 27.6 percent who oppose better medical care for people who can afford it. If this sort of pattern is more the rule than the exception, it would be additional evidence against the social volcano scenario. In other words, if the average Chinese citizen has a fairly accepting or even positive view about current inequalities, but a particular group is angry about some inequality issues and satisfied about others, it will be difficult to identify a particular group or social category with an across-the-board strong sense of distributive injustice. A pattern in which each social group feels a mixture of grievances and positive feelings is a recipe for social and political stability, not for instability.

The analyses presented in Chapters 6 through 9 will help us determine which of these opposing possibilities is closer to the truth—coherent acceptance of current inequalities by some social groups and critical attitudes by other groups, or much more selective and even inconsistent attitudes toward inequality issues among all groups. To proceed with this analysis, however, it makes sense to assume that some Chinese citizens are consistently more angry than others (to follow the first of these contending assumptions) and to use background characteristics of our survey respondents to try to look for the patterning, or social contours, of varying attitudes toward inequality issues.

BACKGROUND CHARACTERISTICS OF RESPONDENTS AS PREDICTORS OF INEQUALITY ATTITUDES

As noted in Chapter 1, China's reform process since 1978 has required a wrenching reorientation in how Chinese citizens plan and lead their lives and fundamental shifts in the rules governing access to resources and opportunities. This transformation has produced a dismantling of the distributive rules and procedures of a centrally planned socialist economic system and the substitution, gradually and increasingly rather than all at once, of a rival set of rules and procedures based on those operating in competitive, market-oriented capitalist societies. As a result of these fundamental changes as well as of China's robust economic growth over the last three decades, large numbers of individuals and families have improved their educational, income, and consumption levels. As noted earlier, initially these improvements were so widely shared that some analysts spoke of "reform without losers" (Lau, Qian, and Roland 2000). However, since the mid-1990s at least, with the deepening of the reforms through the dismantling of the iron rice bowl of security and subsidies previously enjoyed by those affiliated with urban state-owned enterprises, the existence and problems of the losers in China's reform process have become more apparent. China has also witnessed the emergence of growing numbers of millionaires and even billionaires, making the diverging fortunes of Chinese citizens a potentially contentious issue.

The conventional wisdom assumes that there is a fairly direct and strong connection between the variable fates of Chinese families since reforms were launched and citizens' attitudes regarding inequality and distributive injustice issues. The groups and locales that have been objective winners as a result of the reforms, according to this logic, should favor the market-oriented distribution principles from which they have benefited and should view the resulting patterns of inequality as acceptable or even desirable. There is an understandable tendency in any society for the advantaged and successful to feel that they are enjoying the fruits of their own meritorious efforts, rather than benefiting from ill-gotten gains and societal unfairness. This is not simply the conventional wisdom of the moment among China analysts, but reflects the findings of a substantial body of social science research in the United States and in other societies (see, for example, Hochschild 1981 and Kluegel and Smith 1986 on the United States; Ravallion and Lokshin 2000 on Russia; Alesina and Fuchs-Schündeln 2007 on Germany). Generally speaking, past research confirms that individuals with high incomes and other advantages are less eager about redistribution and other equalizing measures than their disadvantaged counterparts, which is not very surprising.

A list of Chinese winners might include those with high incomes, the well-educated, white-collar workers (particularly intellectuals, managers, and professionals), members of the Chinese Communist Party, private entrepreneurs, urban residents in general, residents of booming coastal provinces, and perhaps to some extent youths and men in general. People with low status, those who experience systematic discrimination, or those who have experienced downward social mobility are assumed by the same conventional wisdom to be angry about inequality and distributive injustice. In any society this is another understandable tendency; those who are doing poorly do not blame themselves, but feel that their poor circumstances are attributable to unfairness in the current social order. A listing of such losers in China's reform process would include rural residents in general, particularly those still mainly dependent on farming for their livelihood; rural migrants living in cities; people with low incomes and little schooling; the unemployed; factory workers; employees of financially troubled state-owned enterprises; non–Communist Party members; residents of China's interior (particularly in western provinces); and perhaps women and the middle-aged and older in general.

In the four chapters that follow, we use a variety of measures of winner and loser status as well as other background traits to try to explain variations in measures of inequality and distributive injustice attitudes. We want to determine whether the assumption that winners tend to approve of current inequalities while losers are angry is a useful guide to Chinese popular attitudes about current inequalities. The remainder of the current chapter is devoted to describing the range of the social background predictors we rely on to explain variations in inequality attitudes. These background traits, like our attitude measures, are derived from responses to our questionnaire.[3]

Objective Characteristics: Occupations and Residential Status Categories

Social scientists commonly view occupations in modern societies as fundamental markers of high and low social status and therefore use occupational categories to examine variations in popular attitudes—in our case, to see if people in low-status occupations are more critical of current inequalities than those in high-status occupations. In China occupational categories are entangled with an even more important status cleavage between those with urban household registration and those with rural household registration (hukou) status. For example, virtually all farmers have agricultural household registrations, but workers may have either nonagricultural or agricultural household registration status (the latter in the case of migrants from rural areas), and these two types of workers have quite different social statuses and entitlements. For this reason we use a composite occupation and residential status category measure with a total of twelve categories, four involving current agricultural household registrations—farmers, rural nonagricultural workers, migrants, and rural others (such as rural residents not in the labor force)—and eight categories involving nonagricultural registrations—unskilled and semiskilled workers, skilled workers, the self-employed (including private business owners), routine nonmanual workers, professionals, managers and administrative cadres, the urban unemployed, and urban others (mainly those not in the labor force).[4] According to the conventional wisdom, we expect to find the most critical views on current inequalities in the lowest status groups—particularly among farmers, migrants, the urban unemployed, and urban unskilled and semiskilled workers.

Objective Characteristics: Demographic and Socioeconomic Traits

In the analyses in Chapters 6 through 9 we employ a range of other measures of objective characteristics of respondents that might have some association with attitudes toward inequality and distributive injustice issues: gender (female=1, male=0), age of respondent, age of respondent squared (divided by 100),[5] number of years of education, marital status (married=1, all others=0), ethnicity (Han Chinese=1, all others=0), the logarithm of the respondent's household income in 2003[6] (self-reported in response to our survey questions), Chinese Communist Party (CCP) membership (yes=1, no=0), whether the respondent was currently or before retirement had been employed in a state-owned enterprise (yes=1, no=0), and a summary measure of the respondent's exposure to unofficial communications.[7] If the conventional wisdom is correct, individuals with advantageous social statuses (high education, high family income, CCP membership, and so on) will have views that are more approving and less critical of current inequality patterns, while those who are or were employed in troubled state-owned enterprises or who have access to a range of unofficial sources of information will be more critical.[8]

Objective Characteristics: Geographic Location Measures

We assume that an individual's attitudes toward various aspects of inequality and distributive injustice will be affected not only by personal and family background characteristics, but also by where the person lives and works. It has often been suggested, for example, that people located in booming regions, such as in Shanghai or in the Pearl River Delta in the southeast, will feel optimistic and accepting about the shape of current inequalities, while those located in distant interior locales or in areas that are more troubled economically, such as the "rustbelt" cities of China's northeast, will be more critical. Furthermore, as G. William Skinner (2005) often stressed, measuring location simply in terms of provinces is a very poor guide to almost any social variation because of the large gap between those located in the urban core and those in the distant rural periphery within each province or region.

We utilize three different measures to try to tap the complexity of geographic location factors that may influence attitudes toward inequality issues. First, we classify where respondents live in terms of the conventional division of Chinese provinces into east, central, and west regions as defined by China's National Statistics Bureau.[9] Second, reflecting our attempt to respond to Skinner's critique, we classify each respondent in terms of distance from a prefectural or higher-level city, using a scheme of eight categories ranging from 0 (resides in a prefectural or higher level city) to 7 (resides two hundred or more kilometers from the nearest prefectural or larger city).[10] Finally, to try to capture the fact that some provinces have been much more affected than others by market reforms and the economic activity they have spawned, we utilize research conducted by scholars in China (see Fan and Wang 2004) to categorize the relative degree of market transformation of all the provincial units in which our respondents live, with the values ranging from 3.61 for Ningxia to 9.74 for Guangdong (out of a maximum of 10).[11] In the conventional account, we expect to find more anger about inequality in central and western provinces, in locales far from any city, and in provinces that are backward in terms of the impact of market reforms.[12]

Subjective Indicators

Research in other societies has indicated that subjective perceptions of personal and family status and of status improvement or deterioration sometimes have as much or more influence on inequality and distributive injustice attitudes as do the objective socioeconomic characteristics of respondents (see, for example, Kluegel 1988; Kreidl 2000). With this consideration in mind, we also use a variety of measures of subjective status and experiences as predictors.[13] Three such subjective measures are employed in subsequent analyses: (1) a comparison of the respondent's family's living standard at the time of the interview with that of five years earlier (in 1999), ranging from 1=much worse to 5=much better; (2) a summary measure of relative social status compared to local reference groups (again using a five-point scale);[14] and (3) a summary scale of inequality-related bad personal or family experiences during the past three years, which we call simply "bad experiences."[15] In the conventional view respondents who reported that their families were doing better than five years earlier and better than local people with whom they compared themselves will tend to accept current inequality patterns, while those who had bad personal or family experiences in the highly competitive environment of China are likely to be more critical.[16]

This chapter has presented the conceptual framework that lies behind our examination of a wide range of inequality attitude measures, and it has also described the social background characteristics used to systematically test whether critical attitudes toward current inequalities are associated with low-status groups and social disadvantage in Chinese society. Together these discussions serve as preparation for systematic examination of social contours of the Chinese inequality attitudes in the next four chapters.

CHAPTER SIX

Perceptions of Current Inequalities

As discussed earlier, there is a strong consensus among observers both inside and outside China, and even among China's leaders, that rising inequality spawned by reform-era changes is generating widespread anger among ordinary Chinese citizens. The claim is that many or most Chinese perceive current inequalities as excessive, harmful, and unfair. There are at least two variants of this view. In one variant the size of the gaps in income, wealth, and consumption standards—between rich and poor, between rural and urban, and between residents of coastal areas and those of interior regions—is seen as too large and therefore unacceptable. For example, many press reports in China have claimed that when a society's Gini coefficient of income distribution rises above .40, that country enters a danger zone for social and political turbulence (see Ma 2005). Because the estimated Gini income distribution coefficient for China increased from .29 in 1981 to .45 or even higher by 1995 (World Bank 1997; Gustafsson, Li, and Sicular 2008), China has supposedly been in the danger zone for well over a decade. However, societies with Gini coefficients higher than China's, such as Brazil and South Africa (above .55), have avoided collapsing for many decades, so it is unclear how and why so many people in China believe in this Gini danger-zone formula. Nevertheless, this variant involves the claim that many Chinese perceive income and other status gaps as too large to be tolerated.

The second variant of the concern about perceptions of inequalities involves the claim that it is not the size of income and other gaps per se that is intolerable, but rather which kinds of people are rich, which are poor, and how they ended up where they are. The belief is that many Chinese perceive that a large proportion of today's high-status and rich individuals owe their advantages to special treatment, corruption, and the unfairness of the current system (see, for example, Kahn 2006), and that many who are poor and disadvantaged deserve better. In this variant unfair mobility opportunities that determine who is rich and who is poor, rather than too-wide income gaps, are particularly resented by ordinary Chinese citizens.

We saw in Chapters 3 and 4 that, in general, both variants of this consensus are wrong. Fewer Chinese than citizens of the other countries with whom we have compared them think that national inequalities are excessive, and the average Chinese citizen perceives the differences between who is currently rich and who is poor more in terms of variations in merit than in terms of societal unfairness. Nevertheless, a considerable number of our respondents disagree. The tasks in this chapter are to determine what sorts of respondents are particularly likely to perceive current inequalities negatively and to take the first step toward determining whether respondents who perceive current inequalities as unacceptable also have critical views in the inequality domains that will be examined in Chapters 7 through 9.

MEASURES OF NEGATIVE AND POSITIVE PERCEPTIONS
OF CURRENT INEQUALITIES

The focus in this chapter is on understanding the social sources of variations in popular perceptions of current patterns of inequality in China. Who views current income gaps as too wide? Who sees current inequalities as the product of unfair manipulation and as harmful to society? Who feels that current patterns of who is rich and who is poor are mainly a product of unfair institutions and practices instead of a reflection of meritocratic and fair competition? We are concerned here with the questions whose survey response patterns were displayed in Figures 3.1 and 3.2 in Chapter 3. To answer such questions, we need to first reduce these survey responses into a smaller and more manageable number of summary measures of views on the shape and fairness of current inequalities. Based on preliminary statistical analyses, we end up with four distinct measures of inequality perceptions.

The pattern of responses to the three questions in Figure 3.1a (whether income differences in the nation, in the respondent's work unit, and in the respondent's neighborhood are too large, somewhat too large, about right, somewhat too small, or too small) do not cohere well enough to be combined into a single scale. Thus we use in this chapter only the single question about national income gaps as our first focal measure of perceptions of current inequalities.[1] In subsequent pages, we refer to this first measure as our "excessive inequality" measure.[2]

Our second measure is a scale constructed to reflect the common content of the four questions summarized earlier in Figure 3.1c, all of which concern harmful origins and/or consequences of current inequalities—views that the rich are getting richer while the poor are getting poorer, that inequality persists because it benefits the rich and the powerful, that the disparity between rich and poor threatens social stability, and that the same disparity violates the principles of socialism.[3] In subsequent pages we refer to this as our "harmful inequality" measure.

In a parallel fashion we constructed two separate summary scales from selected items whose overall response patterns were summarized in Figures 3.2a and 3.2b. This set of questions, adapted from the International Social Justice Project,[4] includes both explanations based on individual merit (variations in talent and ability, effort, and education) and variations in external structural factors (such as discrimination, unequal opportunities, and unfairness in the economic system). We used the pattern of responses to this set of questions, regarding explanations of both poverty and of wealth, to construct two summary scales. The third summary scale we call "unfair inequality," and it was constructed from items emphasizing discrimination, lack of equal opportunity, and problems with the economic structure as explanations for poverty, and the items for dishonesty, having special connections, having extra opportunities, and unfairness of the economic structure as explanations for wealth.[5] The fourth summary measure we call "merit-based inequality," and it is based on emphasis on lack of ability, lack of effort, and low education as explanations for poverty, and ability, hard work, and high education as explanations for wealth.[6]

Given the nature of these four measures, our simple-minded prediction is that Chinese citizens who are particularly angry about the size and unfairness of current inequalities will tend to score high on the first three scales and low on the fourth. Citizens who are quite satisfied and accepting of the shape and fairness of current inequalities should score low on the first three measures and high on merit-based inequality. However, an examination of the pattern of statistical intercorrelations among these four scales defies these simple-minded expectations (see Table 6.1). Although as expected there are positive and statistically significant correlations among the first three scales indicating negative assessments of current inequalities (excessive inequality, harmful inequality, and unfair inequality), there are also positive and statistically significant correlations between each of these scales and the merit-based inequality scale, which we consider an indication of accepting and even favorable views about current inequalities.[7] These patterns indicate that a respondent who scores high on the first three measures will not tend to score low on merit-base inequality as we originally expected, and in fact will tend to score high. We return later to the question of how to explain the positive correlations in the bottom row of Table 6.1.

TABLE 6.1
Correlations among inequality perception measures

	Excessive inequality	Harmful inequality	Unfair inequality	Merit-based inequality
Excessive inequality	1.00			
Harmful inequality	.25***	1.00		
Unfair inequality	.14***	.39***	1.00	
Merit-based inequality	.10***	.08**	.20***	1.00

**$p \le .01$ ***$p \le .001$

RESPONDENT CHARACTERISTICS AND PERCEPTIONS OF CURRENT INEQUALITY PATTERNS

The remainder of this chapter examines how these four measures of perceptions of current inequalities vary within our national sample of Chinese citizens to determine what sorts of respondents are angriest about distributive injustice. In pursuing an answer to this question, we employ the strategy conventionally used by social scientists when analyzing sample survey data. In addition to asking a lot of questions about respondent attitudes toward a wide range of aspects of current inequalities, our questionnaire also inquired about a range of objective traits and subjective experiences that we thought might help us explain the patterning of inequality attitudes. For example, other things being equal, are China's farmers more or less angry about current inequalities than other Chinese citizens? How do the attitudes of Chinese Communist Party members differ from those of nonmembers? How do the attitudes of people residing in western provinces differ from the attitudes of those who live in eastern provinces? How do the attitudes of those who report that their family income has improved over the last five years differ from the attitudes of those who report stability or a decline in family income? As discussed in Chapter 5, many but not all of the background predictors we use in this analysis are designed to test the idea that those who currently have advantages or have been winners as a result of market reforms have more positive views about current inequalities than do those with low status or who have been losers in the reforms.

The three chapters that follow examine different inequality attitude domains but present analyses that parallel those in the current chapter. The first step is to examine the pattern of statistical association between a particular inequality attitude scale (here we examine four: excessive inequality, harmful inequality, unfair inequality, and merit-based inequality) and the full range of respondent background characteristics described in Chapter 5. In the jargon of social science we do this by computing and examining the bivariate correlation statistics between each dependent variable (our inequality attitude scales) and each independent or predictor variable (the available background traits of respondents).

Because our predictor variables are themselves associated in complex ways (for example, farmers tend to have less education and lower family incomes than urbanites), these correlations do not tell us the full story. If we observe a statistically significant negative correlation between being a farmer and viewing current inequalities as excessive, suggesting that farmers are less angry than other citizens, is this association due to being a farmer or mainly due to low education or low family income or some other trait that is confounded with the farmer/nonfarmer difference? To try to disentangle these complexities, the second stage of statistical analysis involves employing regression procedures to examine these same associations.[8] Regression analysis statistically controls for a range of other predictor variables simultaneously in order to see what the net association with a particular predictor is. In the example used here, the regression coefficient can tell us the net effect of being a farmer, while holding educational attainment, family income, and other confounding factors constant. By examining correlations first and then examining regression coefficients, we obtain as complete an understanding as possible of the variable impact of a range of respondent background characteristics on our inequality attitude summary measures. At the bottom of each column of regression coefficients in the tables in this and the next three chapters we show a summary R-squared statistic, which is an estimate of the proportion of variation in that inequality attitude measure that we can explain by taking into account all of the background predictors simultaneously.

Using the complex array of respondent background predictors of inequality attitudes described in Chapter 5, we are now in a position to examine whether and how each such predictor is associated with our four measures of perceptions of current inequality patterns. The results of this examination are reported in Table 6.2. In a manner we will follow in Chapters 7 through 9, this table displays two columns of associations with each measure of inequality attitudes—first the bivariate correlations that show the pattern of associations before we control for any of the other predictors listed along the left side of the table, and then the standardized regression coefficients that show each specific association once all the other predictors included have been controlled for statistically.[9] Given the size and complexity of the table, it is not useful to try to focus on and explain each coefficient individually. Rather, our approach is to scan across the rows and columns of the table, looking for general patterns. For example, do farmers, Communist Party members, people residing in western provinces, or people who report that their family incomes have deteriorated in the last five years have different perceptions of the fairness or unfairness of current inequality patterns than do other Chinese citizens?

TABLE 6.2

Correlations and regressions of perceptions of current inequality patterns

	Excessive inequality		Harmful inequality		Unfair inequality		Merit-based inequality	
	R	Beta	R	Beta	R	Beta	R	Beta
Objective: Occupation and residence								
Farmer	-.12***	-.11**	-.19***	-.17***	-.18***	-.11**	-.06***	-.04
Rural nonfarm	-.04*	-.07***	-.03	-.07**	-.02	-.04	-.01	-.03
Migrant	.08***	.06*	.01	-.05	.01	-.01	-.01	-.02
Rural others	-.12***	-.12***	-.06**	-.08**	-.01	-.01	-.05**	-.03
Urban others	.05**	-.01	.09***	-.02	.07***	-.03	.06**	.01
Urban unemployed	.07***	.04	.11***	.01	.04*	-.03	.02	-.00
Unskilled and semiskilled workers	.05**	omitted	.09***	omitted	.07***	omitted	.03	omitted
Skilled workers	.04*	-.01	.08***	.00	.09***	.04	.04*	.00
Self-employed	.01	-.01	.03	-.02	.03	-.02	.01	-.05*
Routine nonmanual	.07***	.02	.07***	-.00	.09***	.03	.01	-.04
Professionals	.07***	.03	.03	-.04	.06***	.01	.03	-.01
Managers and cadres	.02	-.00	-.00	-.04	.01	-.03	.01	-.04
Objective: Demographic and socioeconomic								
Female	-.04*	-.02	-.01	.01	.01	.03	-.01	.02
Age	-.00	-.06	.02	.14	-.01	.24	-.03	.20
Age-squared/100	-.00	.07	.02	-.07	-.01	-.18	-.03	-.20
Years of education	.14***	.15***	.15***	.15***	.16***	.09***	.11***	.06*
Married	-.00	.00	-.00	.01	-.05**	-.04	-.01	-.00

(continued)

TABLE 6.2 (continued)

	Excessive inequality		Harmful inequality		Unfair inequality		Merit-based inequality	
	R	Beta	R	Beta	R	Beta	R	Beta
Han ethnicity	.10***	.11***	.06***	.02	.06**	.00	.06**	.02
Log of household income	.08***	.03	.08***	-.02	.10***	.03	.09***	-.02
CCP member	.07***	.03	-.02	-.07***	-.00	-.03	.03	.01
SOE employed	.12***	.06**	.10***	-.00	.12***	.03	.01	-.04
Access to unofficial information	-.00	-.09***	.07***	-.03	.11***	.03	.14***	.10***
Objective: Geographic								
East region	-.07***	omitted	.01	omitted	.03	omitted	.01	omitted
Central region	.13***	.13ns	.07***	.11ns	.05**	.02	.06***	.03
West region	-.08***	.01	-.11***	.09ns	-.11***	-.04	-.10***	-.08ns
Distance to city	-.10***	.05^^^	-.23***	-.15***	-.19***	-.09ns	-.10***	-.04
Province marketization	-.02	.01	.07***	.09ns	.04*	-.02	-.01	-.06ns
Subjective								
Five-year standard of living trend	-.02	.01	-.13***	-.07***	-.10***	-.07***	.09***	.07***
Relative social status	-.06**	-.09***	-.05*	-.03	-.04*	-.05*	.11***	.05*
Bad experiences scale	.01	.04*	.03	.05*	.05**	.10***	-.04*	.02
R-squared		0.10		0.11		.08		.04

ns Coefficient no longer significant after correction for case clustering.

^^^ Coefficient significant beyond $p = .001$ level after correction for case clustering.

r=Bivariate correlation coefficients; beta is standardized regression coefficient from ordinary least squares regressions.

$* .01 < p \leq .05$ $** .001 < p \leq .01$ $*** p \leq .001$

The first pattern to note in Table 6.2 is that we are less successful in explaining variations in the merit-based inequality scale than in the other three measures. There is an expected tendency for the well educated and people who feel their family living standards have improved, and also people who feel they are doing better than their local reference groups, to stress the influence of hard work, talent, and education in explaining who is rich and who is poor in China today (see the last column in the subjective predictor section of Table 6.2). Less expected are tendencies for those with access to unofficial information to also stress the role of merit and for those who are self-employed to be less likely to explain poverty and wealth in terms of variations in merit. Overall, however, few background variables show much association with the merit-based inequality scale once we control for other predictors, and we are able to explain only a paltry 4 percent of the variation in this scale with the wide range of variables we use in our regression model (see the R-squared figure at the bottom of the last column in the table).

The failure to explain much of the variation in respondent views about the role of hard work, talent, and education in differentiating the rich from the poor is, in fact, one of the important substantive findings of our survey. This pattern indicates that there is relatively little variation in perceptions of the role of merit in explaining material success across the social contours and cleavages of Chinese society. We already know from Chapter 3 that there is very broad agreement on the importance of merit factors in explaining who is rich and who is poor (see Figure 3.2), and we also know from Chapter 4 that Chinese citizens generally stress the role of talent and hard work in explaining who is rich and who is poor more than do their counterparts in many other societies. In other words, there is a high level of agreement within Chinese society on the importance of factors like talent and hard work in getting ahead, and as a result there is not that much variation in responses to this set of questions. Furthermore, the variation that does exist in responses is not closely related to the social background characteristics of the respondents.

The hegemony of beliefs in merit-based inequality fits a pattern seen in prior research on inequality attitudes in other societies (see Kluegel and Smith 1986 for the United States). Within any society, certain core or dominant beliefs are widely shared and accepted, and social scientists cannot have much luck in explaining variations in such core beliefs. At the same time other secondary or more specific inequality beliefs are not so widely shared, and social background factors are much more likely to be associated with and help explain variations in them. It is not uncommon to find core beliefs and secondary attitudes about inequality that are apparently contradictory, as is the case in the puzzling pattern of intercorrelations of merit-based inequality and the other three inequality measures seen in Table 6.1. In other words, in societies other than China it would not be surprising to find individuals who say that hard work is a key to material success and who also feel that dishonesty and unequal opportunities have a big influence on who is rich and who is poor. For the remainder of this chapter, we will concentrate our attention on the other three measures of perceptions of current inequalities: excessive inequality, harmful inequality, and unfair inequality.[10]

Returning to Table 6.2, there is a general tendency for urbanites to express more-critical attitudes about current patterns of inequality than rural respondents (with the exception of migrants), as demonstrated by the correlations in columns 1, 3, and 5 in Table 6.2. Once we control for other background characteristics (in columns 2, 4, and 6) and use unskilled and semiskilled urban workers as our comparison group, it is apparent that the views on current inequalities of other urban occupational groups are not very different. However, the net effect of being a farmer, a rural nonagricultural worker, or in the rural other category is generally negative, although not all the coefficients are statistically significant. Farmers in particular, though, are significantly less likely to be critical on all three measures of perceptions of current inequalities than are urban unskilled and semiskilled workers, and thus by implication they are less likely to be critical than urban people in general. Rural migrants—see row 3 in Table 6.2—do not follow this rural pattern of being less critical. On two of these measures they do not differ much from the comparison group of urban workers and thus are more likely to be critical than are farmers. However, they are more likely than any other occupational group, rural or urban, to feel that current national inequalities are excessive.[11]

The distinctiveness of these attitudes of rural respondents, and of farmers in particular, is another important substantive finding from our survey, one that is echoed in many but not all of the survey findings presented in Chapters 7 through 9. According to the conventional wisdom, in general disadvantaged groups should be angry about current patterns of inequality, and advantaged or high-status groups should be more accepting or even approving. There are groups that are disadvantaged within both rural areas (farmers, migrants) and urban areas (unskilled and semiskilled workers and the unemployed). However, given the overarching importance of the rural-urban cleavage in structuring inequality and access to opportunities in China today, by any reasonable ranking farmers and rural migrants rank below disadvantaged urban groups, who are at least entitled to some urban public benefits that migrants (and farmers) are not eligible for. Following this line of thinking, we would expect to find more critical attitudes about current inequalities generally among rural people, particularly among those still relying on farming. However, what we find in this analysis is just the opposite.

Rural residents, especially farmers, are significantly less likely than their urban counterparts to see national income gaps as excessive, to feel that current inequalities are getting worse and harming society, or to feel that unfair external factors play a major role in explaining why some people are rich and others are poor. China's farmers' relatively favorable views about current inequalities despite being pretty much at the bottom of the contemporary Chinese social status hierarchy presents an intriguing puzzle, and we will suggest possible explanations at the conclusion of this study.[12]

The second section in Table 6.2 displays the correlations and regressions of these three perception measures with the demographic and socioeconomic background characteristics. The most striking pattern is again contrary to the conventional wisdom: Individuals with the most education are more likely to express critical attitudes than are others on all three measures of perceptions of current inequalities, even when other background variables are controlled for statistically. In the context of prior research in the United States and other societies, however, this pattern is not as unexpected. In such studies (see Kluegel and Smith 1986) material advantages tend to be correlated with acceptance of the status quo, but advanced education is associated with more-critical or even leftist attitudes. Another way of viewing this association is to say that advanced education is likely to lead to a more sophisticated awareness of patterns of bias and discrimination in society than is held by the less educated.

At first glance, two other measures of advantaged status (family income and membership in the Han ethnic group) also appear to be associated with critical views on all three inequality measures, but once we control for other background characteristics, only the tendency for the Han to be more likely than non-Han to view current national income gaps as excessive remains statistically significant. The latter pattern is also puzzling; research in other societies (e.g., Kluegel and Smith 1986) generally finds more anger about inequality within minority populations than within the majority ethnic group.

More in line with conventional expectations, affiliation with a state-owned enterprise (presumed to be a disadvantage) initially appears to be associated with critical responses on all three inequality measures, but once we control for other background characteristics, only the tendency for SOE employees to view current national income gaps as excessive remains statistically significant. An additional pattern that deserves comment involves the associations of our inequality scales with age and age-squared (divided by 100). From the regression coefficients it appears that curvilinear associations exist for all three inequality measures, with the middle-aged more likely than younger or older Chinese to view current inequalities as both harmful and unfair, but less likely to view current national income gaps as too large. However, none of these curvilinear patterns is statistically significant beyond the p=.05 level. What this finding means is that the patterns of regression coefficients are intriguing, but we cannot confidently rule out the possibility that they occurred by chance.[13] Overall, these patterns provide little support for the claim that individuals with advantaged statuses will consistently express accepting views about current inequalities and that disadvantaged individuals will express more critical views.

The associations of our inequality attitude scales and geographic location measures are displayed in the third section of Table 6.2. The correlation coefficients make it appear that inequality perceptions are affected by geographic factors, although in complex ways that are not easy to interpret. Once we control for the influence of other background factors in regression models and compensate for the clustering tendency in our geographic measures,[14] the regression coefficients for only the first two inequality perception measures and distance to the city remain statistically significant. These associations by themselves are also somewhat puzzling, since they indicate that, other things being equal, there is a net tendency for people located far from any city to view current national inequalities as excessive, but at the same time to be less likely to view current inequalities as harmful.

Finally, the fourth section in Table 6.2 displays the associations of our inequality attitude measures and several subjective scales. We find patterns here that are much more congruent with the conventional wisdom, with individuals who report that their family living standard has improved compared to five years earlier and those who report high status relative to local reference groups being less critical of current inequalities than others, and those who have had a high number of bad experiences in the last three years being more critical, although not all the regression coefficients are statistically significant. It appears from these results that, insofar as the conventional wisdom holds that critical attitudes about inequality issues are the product of low status and personal disadvantage, in our data only subjective measures of disadvantage display this effect, not the range of objective status indicators we examined and discussed earlier.

CONCLUSIONS

In Chapters 3 and 4 we saw that Chinese citizens are not as upset about the size and unfairness of current inequalities as many analysts and Chinese government officials have assumed. The current chapter casts further doubt on the conventional wisdom. In general China's most disadvantaged citizens are not the most likely to be angry about current patterns of inequality.

China's farmers, particularly those living away from the coastal region and far from any city, are at the bottom of the social status hierarchy. They are seen by many as left behind and.even victimized by the kinds of market activity and property acquisitions unleashed by China's post-socialist reforms. As noted in the Introduction, one recent Western press account uses such phrases as "seeds of fury" and "the pitchfork anger of peasants" to describe the mood among China's farmers (Time Asia 2006). China's top political leadership has shared the perception that groups left behind by the reforms, farmers in particular, need to be aided by state policy interventions in order to lessen the looming danger of rural unrest and political instability. These sentiments and fears have led to a series of ameliorating policies since 2002, including eliminating the state grain tax, waiving school fees in rural areas, and resurrecting village collective medical insurance systems.[15]

Our survey results indicate that, in terms of perceptions of the size, social danger, and unfairness of current patterns of inequality, the prevailing assumptions about who is particularly angry are for the most part wrong. In general urban residents, particularly well-educated urbanites, are most angry about these issues. In contrast rural residents, particularly those continuing to rely on farming for their livelihood, tend to have more accepting or positive attitudes about the shape and fairness of current inequalities. On these issues, at least, we see little sign of the claimed "pitchfork anger of peasants."

To be sure, one pattern does seem to confirm the conventional wisdom: In general respondents who feel that their living standards have improved in recent years and that they are doing better than other people tend to have accepting views about current inequalities, and those who have experienced economic difficulty, personal loss, and official mistreatment tend to have critical attitudes. However, these subjective ratings and experiences are not confined to any one social group or geographic location, and presumably there will be individuals who rank from high to low on these factors within any community or work organization. How people feel they are doing compared to the past and to their peers has an influence on whether they feel current inequalities are fair or unfair, but those feelings cannot be predicted simply by knowing that they are farmers, urban skilled workers, Communist Party members, or residents of a western province. As far as those objective social background characteristics are concerned, low status or disadvantage does not generally translate into anger about the shape of current inequalities.

Stressing that the conventional wisdom is wrong and that the most disadvantaged groups in China are not the most angry about current patterns of inequality should not imply the opposite. Even though some kinds of advantage (particularly more years in school) are associated with more-critical attitudes, those who are benefiting the most from the reforms are not consistently more critical of current inequalities. For example, the net influence of having a high family income, being a Communist Party member, working as a professional or a manager, or being self-employed is close to zero (as seen in the regression coefficients in Table 6.2). So we do not see a totally paradoxical situation in which the beneficiaries of China's reforms are very angry while those left behind and victimized are quite satisfied. Instead the social contours of feelings about current patterns of inequality are complicated, and some specific groups (particularly farmers) display more positive attitudes about inequalities than we would have anticipated.

In the next three chapters we examine patterns of variation in attitudes regarding other domains of current inequalities, and we are particularly concerned with whether the unexpected patterns analyzed in the current chapter are confined to the domain of perceptions of current inequalities, or whether they are only one piece of a much broader pattern affecting distributive injustice attitudes across the board. Only after we have examined the patterns of variation of other inequality and distributive injustice attitudes in the three chapters that follow will we be in a position, in the concluding chapter, to try to more comprehensively answer our fourth major research question: In which social groups, and in which locations, is there the most anger about current patterns of inequality.

CHAPTER SEVEN

Preferences for Equality and Inequality

Chapter 6 was concerned with one important domain of Chinese citizen attitudes toward current income and other gaps, how citizens perceive those inequalities, including whether they are seen as just or unjust. If ordinary Chinese are not happy with the shape of current inequalities, it is logical to ask what their preferred alternative would be. What kind of balance between equality and inequality would make for the best society? Do people want China to be a much more egalitarian society, perhaps with many resources and benefits distributed totally equally? Do they think the government should be more active in limiting or even reducing inequalities? Or do Chinese citizens object more to the way people become rich or poor (the unfair inequality syndrome analyzed in Chapter 6) than to the size of the disparities involved? Do Chinese citizens recognize the desirability or even necessity of certain kinds of differential rewards and reject the idea that a more egalitarian social order would be better? Do they find plausible the government's claim that differentials and inequalities help promote economic growth? In general, which social groups in China prefer a more equal society, and which groups are comfortable with the status quo and accept the government's claims that too dogmatic a promotion of social equality in the Mao era harmed China?

In exploring the social contours of variation in these attitudes, we focus on the questions whose overall distributions were reported in Figures 3.3 and 3.4 in Chapter 3. There we saw that only a minority of respondents in the 2004 survey agreed that equal distribution would be the most fair principle or that there should be systematic redistribution from the rich to the poor. However, this is not a small minority—about 30 percent either agreed or strongly agreed with each proposition (see the first two bars in Figure 3.3). At the same time there was less than enthusiastic endorsement of most statements reflecting the government's current pro-market arguments in favor of differentials and incentives, with half or more of all respondents uncertain about or disagreeing with a variety of statements of this type (see

Figure 3.4). So the most common response to these questions is for Chinese citizens to have reservations about both equal distribution and highly differentiated rewards and opportunities. In this chapter we examine which social groups and categories, and which locales, show the greatest support for these contrasting distributional principles.

DEBATES OVER SOCIAL EQUALITY
AND DIFFERENTIAL REWARDS

In popular writings it is sometimes assumed that socialist societies systematically favor and foster equal distribution, while capitalist societies systematically promote inequality. The reality, in terms of both policies and actual distribution, is a good deal more complicated. Much of the Western research conducted when socialist societies were in their heyday questioned whether there were any differences beyond minor details in the actual contours of inequality and differential social mobility patterns in socialist and capitalist societies (see, for example, Connor 1979).[1] As noted in Chapter 1, Mao Zedong shared this skepticism, at least regarding the Soviet Union, feeling that it had become a revisionist society that was more or less as unequal and as unjust as the leading capitalist society, the United States.

Karl Marx and his later followers rejected outright the idea that future socialist societies should practice equal distribution. Marx denounced "utopian socialists" for advocating "universal asceticism and social leveling in its crudest form," and in his *Critique of the Gotha Program* (1875) he specified that the ideal under socialism would be distribution according to the labor supplied by "producers" (workers and employees), which would inevitably be variable and unequal. On the eve of seizing national power in Russia, Lenin in *State and Revolution* (1917) struck a similar note, arguing that the entire national workforce in the socialist society he wanted to create, from workers to technicians, managers, and officials, could be compensated with "workingmen's wages," implying modest but nonetheless important differentials between lower and higher wage grades. Mao Zedong is also on record denouncing equal distribution. For example, his 1929 article "On Correcting Mistaken Ideas in the Party" includes a section about the mistaken idea of absolute equalitarianism (reprinted in Mao 1967, pp. 110–11). There Mao criticized, among other things, the demand that officers in the Red Army not ride on horseback because the soldiers they commanded were on foot.

Eventually the Soviet Union developed a standard verbal formula for the distribution system of a socialist society: "From each according to his abilities, to each according to his contributions." Even in the hoped for, but never achieved, future communist society, the preferred distribution principle would not be equality. Instead distribution under communism would be based on the variable needs of individuals and families, as in the standard formulation, "From each according to his abilities, to each according to his needs."[2] (Needs are inherently unequal, although presumably less so than contributions.) In other words, orthodox Marxists have consistently rejected egalitarianism as the general distribution principle for a socialist society.

The two main reasons for this rejection are not distinct to socialist theory, but rather share common ground with arguments widely accepted by promoters of capitalism and market distribution (particularly in the functionalist arguments for inequality summarized in Chapter 3). First, it would be unjust to give the same rewards to an individual who takes on major responsibilities, works very hard, provides special expertise, or devises useful innovations as to someone who does none of these things, or even fails to show up for work, fights with coworkers, damages equipment, or produces shoddy output. Given normal and expected variations in performance (the contributions in the socialist formula), instituting equal distribution would make those who contribute more than the average person feel dissatisfied and unappreciated.

Second, at a societal level, the resulting morale problems that would flow from equal distribution would be harmful to social cohesion and economic growth. Without sufficient rewards for acquiring special expertise, taking on extra responsibility, working harder, or innovating, individuals would be less likely to do any of these things, and the overall level of individual and organizational performance would be harmed. With equal distribution and no carrots and sticks to reward and punish variable performance, everyone would be a "free rider" (see Olson 1965), and societal efficiency and productivity would suffer (see Okun 1975). What a socialist society needs, then, is not equality but equity, and equity implies differentials and inequalities the population regards as fair because they reflect varying contributions to society.[3] These were the kinds of arguments China's reformers used to try to persuade citizens that the purported egalitarianism of the Cultural Revolution era was, in fact, manifestly unjust.

If orthodox Marxists share with advocates of market capitalism an aversion to egalitarian distribution and thus favor the use of differentials in income and opportunities as incentives, what makes the distribution system in a centrally planned socialist society distinctive? In principle, several features of a socialist society may produce at least relatively less inequality than in a capitalist society. First and most important, property ownership and inherited wealth can be used to produce income and special opportunities under capitalism—sometimes at levels beyond the imaginations of ordinary citizens—that are unrelated to the contributions to work or organizational success of those who possess such wealth. In a socialist system there is no private ownership of important property (Marx's "means of production"), so societal inequalities will not be enlarged by this factor.[4] (In the wake of market reforms and the rehabilitation of private enterprise and property after 1978, the role of property ownership and inherited wealth has once again become important in shaping China's income distribution.)

A second potential difference between socialist and capitalist societies concerns the extent of public goods. Even in a capitalist society, not all benefits and opportunities are distributed via market distribution and consumer purchase; some are distributed as public goods on the basis of the principles of equality or need—for example, mail delivery, police and fire services, public school enrollment, and, in almost all advanced capitalist societies except the United States, medical care. Socialist societies, given their proclaimed commitment to social equality and their desire to differentiate themselves from their capitalist rivals, tend to have a larger portion of desirable resources and opportunities distributed as public goods, and a relatively smaller portion distributed in the forms of goods and services for purchase. Insofar as they do so, this difference should lead to greater equality under socialism, since income differences won't affect access to the goods and services thus distributed.[5]

One important example of this difference concerns access to higher education. In socialist societies generally (including China until about a decade ago), students admitted to college (generally through competitive examination systems) not only didn't have to pay tuition, but received modest monthly living stipends from the state. Thus a family's ability to pay for college was not a barrier to college attendance in the way it can be in a capitalist society. As a consequence, this important source of future high status and income was not directly affected by family income.[6] (In this realm as well, policy changes in China in the last decade or so have altered the situation in basic ways, with tuition now charged for higher education, thus reviving a barrier facing a poor family that is seeking a better life for a son or daughter.)

A third potential difference between socialist and capitalist societies is that the primacy of central planning and the lesser role of market distribution in the former means that such factors as supply and demand play a lesser role in determining prices and the distribution of wages and benefits, which are primarily determined by bureaucratic decisions without much reference to market conditions. One might expect this difference to produce more inequality in capitalist societies than in socialist ones, and this is sometimes the case—as in the absence in socialist societies of the astronomical incomes received by star athletes, entertainers, and even doctors and lawyers in capitalist societies. Lenin's injunction in 1917 that all work in a socialist society could be performed "for workingmen's wages" implies very modest gaps between the lowest- and highest-paid personnel. The dominance of central planning and the minimal role of market competition also help make mass unemployment less of a factor in socialist societies than in capitalist ones, where lack of work is a major source of inequality.

However, the reality turns out to be complex. In a capitalist society most people's incomes and other benefits are not determined by some sort of pure market competition, but rather by a complex mix of bureaucratic decisions made by managers in organizations that operate within a larger market-oriented environment. So, for example, the pay a mechanic receives for work in an automobile repair shop depends not only on the market factor of how much auto repair business the shop is able to attract and how much it is able to charge for services, but also on how much the owner or manager of the shop decides to pay the mechanic and what range of fringe benefits to provide. Those decisions are in turn the product of a complex set of factors, including negotiations and demands from the mechanic, the manager's perception of what is fair, how long they have worked together, and what the mechanic could potentially earn by quitting and getting a job elsewhere.

For those of us in the academic profession the situation is similar, with salary increases and changes in fringe benefits for the most part determined bureaucratically by departmental committees, deans, higher administrators, and in some universities also by state legislators. The only exception is when an academic is being courted by another university and is using an outside offer to bargain for more than the typical increase. The differentials between the lowest- and highest-paid professors are a product of an accumulation of bureaucratic and market influences over many years, rather than a reflection of current market forces and supply and demand. To put it in the language of professional athletics, in capitalist societies most people in most jobs most of the time are not testing the free agent market, and the normal situation is governed as much or more by the bureaucratic hierarchy they are in as by the market. (For the classic work on these competing principles of distribution in a capitalist context, see Williamson 1975.)

In a socialist society as well as in a capitalist one, it is useful to think of overall inequality as composed of two aspects: inequality within organizations and inequality across organizations and locales. Within organizations, Lenin's injunction suggests that bureaucrats who determine wages and benefits in socialist societies should consistently try to keep the gaps between the lowest and highest paid within narrow bounds. However, in the years after Lenin's 1917 statement, the initial Soviet experiment with "war communism," with its preference for rationing and egalitarianism (1918–20), was repudiated in favor of the New Economic Policy (NEP) of 1921–27, under which private property and market distribution were rehabilitated and continued to be dominant in the Soviet economy. By 1921 and 1922 Lenin was sounding very different themes than he had voiced in 1917: "Every branch of the national economy must be built up on the principle of personal incentive" (quoted in Moore 1950, p. 184), and "No matter what happens we must assure that specialists, as a special social layer which will remain a special social layer right up to the achievement of the highest stage of development of communist society, live better under socialism than under capitalism" (1922, in Lenin 1949, p. 169).

Lenin died in 1924. Starting in 1928, socialist transformation was carried out under Stalin's command, and socialism was declared established in 1936. The completion of socialist transformation and the resulting triumph of central planning over market distribution did not mean a return to the spirit of workingmen's wages. Instead Stalin regularly and forcefully condemned "wage egalitarianism" as a deviation promoted by Trotskyites and other "enemies of the people." The Stalin era was characterized by enthusiastic use of material rewards and cash prizes, a preference for piece rates (even "progressive piece rates") instead of time wages for workers, and a wide range of signs of rank and status used as carrots to stimulate and reward the favored (while very large coercive sticks, including arrest, exile, and execution, awaited those who fell out of favor).[7]

In other words, the bureaucratic authorities in socialist societies who make decisions about wages and benefits do not necessarily always do so to minimize inequalities. In actual practice their actions have often enlarged the gaps in the remuneration and benefits of lower- and higher-ranked personnel. One study of experiments in Hungary to supplement central planning by allowing some market competition argued that market activity actually helped reduce gaps in incomes and in housing space and quality and thus undercut the highly unequal distributive principles followed by socialist bureaucrats in that society (Szelenyi 1983).

As noted above, we also have to consider how wage and benefit gaps are determined across organizations and locales. In a centrally planned socialist society, these horizontal inequalities are also amenable to policy intervention and bureaucratic reallocation. However, whether socialist planners and bureaucrats use their control over resources to minimize gaps and redistribute wages and benefits to disadvantaged organizations and locales is an empirical question, and usually they do not. Rather, socialist bureaucrats generally develop complicated systems of ranking of locales and organizations in terms of perceived importance to the state, and for the most part a disproportionate share of budgetary and other resources is directed toward the high-priority firms and locales, with those at the bottom of the system neglected and expected to fend for themselves. This tendency is particularly visible in the systematic preference for large, heavy industrial, and military-related firms in socialist societies, as well as in the neglect and exploitation of agriculture and rural areas to serve the needs of rapid industrialization and urban consumers.

There are also powerful tendencies within capitalist societies for large and important companies to seek special favors from the government to protect their interests, and for unsuccessful companies and poor locales to have difficulty promoting their interests. However, important differences between socialist and capitalist societies tend to foster more equality under capitalism. Socialist societies, given their penchant for central planning and predictable control over resources, tend to place obstacles in the way of firms closing down, people moving, and individuals and organizations changing their fates. So in many instances it is more difficult for organizations or individuals to take advantage of new opportunities than might be the case in a capitalist society. Perhaps the most extreme example is the policy noted in Chapter 1 that essentially bound Chinese rural residents to the soil for more than two decades after 1960 and even now makes Chinese born into rural families second-class citizens, unable to compete equally with their urban counterparts for new opportunities. The fact that under socialism favored organizations and locales don't have to contend with market pressures and with an influx of labor competing for jobs helps sustain greater inequalities, as disadvantaged individuals and locales cannot readily seek better fortunes.[8]

The historical context in China includes other influences beyond Marxist debates and the evolution of socialist institutions in the USSR. In particular, it is important to take into account the altered ideas and practices regarding inequality and distribution that Mao Zedong and his radical colleagues promoted during the Cultural Revolution era (1966–76), the period that immediately preceded the launching of China's market reforms. In that decade, in an effort to create a more pure or proletarian form of socialism for China, Mao and his followers repudiated both much that they themselves had created after 1949 and the form of socialism they saw in the Soviet Union. The distinctiveness of the Cultural Revolution innovations needs to be emphasized. It was Mao Zedong who was the revisionist of Marxist principles and practices, not the Soviet leadership.

First, there was a general denunciation of the use of material rewards and incentives as a way to motivate workers and employees to perform better. This change involved not only abolishing piece rates and material bonuses for workers in favor of fixed monthly wages, but also abolishing royalties for writers, prizes for inventors, and other similar payments, as noted in Chapter 1 (see Whyte 1981). The change did not mean that everyone was paid equally, but instead that members of the urban work force received set monthly wages regardless of performance, with movement up in wage ranks mainly determined by seniority in theory, but frozen for long periods of time in fact.[9] The use of material incentives to motivate workers was condemned as the "sugar-coated bullets of the bourgeoisie," as noted earlier. All Chinese in the workforce were expected to work to their fullest capabilities in response to moral incentives (such as love of Mao and devotion to socialism) and social pressure, rather than because doing so would increase their remuneration. During the Cultural Revolution decade, the socialist formula of distribution according to contributions was effectively abolished.

In general the Cultural Revolution ethos included a condemnation of any individual or family orientation to compete with other people in order to earn higher income or to rise into a higher rank or social status.[10] Rather, Chinese were expected to be willing to serve where they were assigned, even if this meant leaving a comfortable life in the city and toiling in a distant rural or border work post. In consumption and lifestyle, as well, any attempt to distinguish oneself from one's neighbors and colleagues became politically dangerous after the launching of the Cultural Revolution.[11] In addition, all progress was seen as mainly produced by the mobilized labor and creativity of ordinary workers, peasants, and soldiers, and the contributions of experts and intellectuals were denigrated. In general during the last decade of Mao's life there was a systematic attempt to implement leveling down to short-circuit the competitive and acquisitive tendencies of the population, and this effort involved the systematic elimination of virtually all the material incentive practices that had been employed since the 1950s.

The immediate context before the launching of China's reforms was thus a complex one in terms of principles of distribution. Mao and his Cultural Revolution colleagues did not, in fact, advocate equality as a general principle of distribution, and the Cultural Revolution did not do anything systematic to bridge the very substantial income and other gaps between organizations and locales. One recent study contends that China still has a distinctive profile of income distribution as a result, in which the boundaries and categories of horizontal inequality across firms and localities, relative to the vertical inequality across jobs and ranks within work organizations, remain much more important than is the case in other societies (Wang 2008). However, the Cultural Revolution did involve a repudiation of basic ideas associated with both orthodox Marxism and functionalist theory in sociology—that it is necessary to use a broad and appropriate range of material incentives and differentiated benefits (and penalties) in order to motivate individuals to gain skills and perform in desirable ways, and that it is normal and even desirable for individuals to orient their behavior in ways that will enable them to compete for and acquire greater material rewards and benefits.

Since the reforms were launched in 1978, China's leaders and propagandists have worked hard to repudiate the Cultural Revolution revisions in distributive ideology and practice. In particular, the use of material incentives and rewards of other kinds was revived and has been heavily emphasized, and Mao's denigration of the same was condemned for having harmed China's economic development. The launching of market reforms, the rehabilitation of private property and businesses, the demise of central planning, and the much reduced role of bureaucratic allocation have fundamentally altered the rules of the game by which both individuals and firms organize their lives. As noted in the Introduction, Deng Xiaoping famously declared in 1983 that "Some people in rural areas and cities should be allowed to get rich before others," and conspicuous consumption has now returned to Chinese society with a vengeance. The incentive sticks have returned along with the carrots, and the security provided to urbanites by the iron rice bowl of state employment has been replaced by the possibility of fines, demotions, layoffs, and unemployment.[12]

Since 2002 the new Chinese Communist Party (CCP) leadership has voiced concern about rising inequality and has instituted some measures to counter this trend, but on balance the major message of China's post-1978 leadership is in direct contrast to the Cultural Revolution policies. It is now regarded as normal and even desirable for individuals and families to compete with their neighbors to become more prosperous, and the competitive energies thus unleashed are a major source of China's post-1978 economic dynamism. In this sense China's leaders have presided over a return to the distribution principles and ideology that were favored both in orthodox Marxist regimes (in Eastern Europe before 1989) and in market societies (including China before 1955).[13] In general Deng Xiaoping and his successors have argued that the Cultural Revolution distribution patterns constituted distributive injustice and that incentives and widened differentials are more equitable and therefore just.

MEASURES OF PREFERENCES FOR EQUALITY OR FOR INEQUALITY

In which groups and in which locales is there the greatest resistance to the arguments in favor of material incentives, and what kinds of individuals think that more should be done to promote equality and to attack and reduce the increased inequalities that the reforms have generated? Our questionnaire included a range of questions related to preferences for greater equality and designed to measure the extent of agreement with the government's current market-oriented philosophy and its emphasis on the necessity of competition, differentials, and incentives. The overall response patterns to questions of both types were presented in Figures 3.3 and 3.4.

As in Chapter 6, it is necessary to combine and winnow the available questions in order to have a manageable number of measures of attitudes about egalitarian distribution and unequal rewards. After preliminary analysis, we settled on four measures of attitudes that will be examined for the remainder of this chapter. They include one single question and one scale intended to reflect a preference for more equality, and one question and one scale designed to capture a preference for differential rewards and market competition.

We discovered that the three questions we asked about preferences for equality (favoring egalitarian distribution, advocating redistribution to aid the poor, and approving of affirmative action measures to help the disadvantaged—the first three bars in Figure 3.3) could not be combined into a reliable composite scale. As a result, we examine here only the social contours of agreement and disagreement with the first of these statements: "Distributing wealth and income equally among people is the most just method."[14] We refer to this measure as "prefer equality."

From three of the four questions we asked about the role of the government in promoting increased equality, we constructed a composite scale we refer to as a preference for "government leveling." The three included items asked respondents to state agreement or disagreement with the following statements: "The government should assure that every person is able to maintain a minimum standard of living"; "The government should provide an opportunity to work for every person willing to work"; and "The government has the responsibility to shrink the gap between high and low incomes."[15] The tenor of these statements involves the view that the government should promote a more equal distribution mainly by affirmative action policies, or leveling up—by providing jobs and minimum incomes to the poor—rather than by the leveling down that was stressed during China's Cultural Revolution. The one question included in Figure 3.3 that was not included in the "government leveling" scale concerned approval of the government's placing a maximum income limit on the population—a leveling-down measure.[16] That item did not have high enough statistical associations with the other three items to make a reliable expanded scale.

The alternative set of attitudes we examine in this chapter involves preferences for market competition and differentials and agreement with the functionalist argument that incentives and differential rewards are needed and desirable. The overall distribution of the questions in this realm was displayed in Figure 3.4. It turns out that the variety of questions we asked reflecting functionalist arguments about the desirability of differential rewards as incentives did not have strong enough statistical associations to generate a reliable composite scale. So in this conceptual domain we again rely on a single question in which respondents were asked how much they agreed or disagreed with the statement "Only when income differences are large enough will individuals have the incentive to work hard" (bar 6 in Figure 3.4). We refer to this item as our measure of the view that "rewards [are] necessary."[17]

Finally, the other measure of preferences for market competition and differential rewards comprises responses to five questions in which respondents were asked to state varying degrees of agreement or disagreement with the following statements: "The good thing about market competition is that it inspires people to work hard and be creative"; "When every person can freely pursue his own benefit, society as a whole will also benefit"; "A free market is crucial to the economic development of our country"; "As long as there is equality of opportunity, even if there are differences between rich and poor it is just"; and "Even if there are differences between the rich and poor, people have the right to keep the wealth they have earned." These items were combined into a composite scale that we term favors "market competition."[18]

These four measures form the basis for the statistical analyses presented in the next section, with prefer equality and government leveling intended to reflect a desire for less inequality, and rewards necessary and market competition intended to reflect an appreciation of unequal rewards and thus presumably also greater satisfaction with the shape of current inequalities.

As in Chapter 6, our initial simple-minded expectation about what these four measures represent was confounded by the actual response patterns of Chinese citizens. We anticipated that responses to prefer equality and government leveling would be positively correlated and that responses to rewards necessary and market competition would also be positively correlated, but that the first two measures would be negatively correlated with the last two measures. The reality turns out to be much more complex than this simple expectation, as Table 7.1 reveals. To be sure, responses to prefer equality are negatively correlated with market competition, while responses to rewards necessary and market competition are positively correlated. However, the remainder of the coefficients in the table are contrary to our initial expectations. It is particularly striking that the correlations of the government leveling scale with the other measures are all the opposite of our original expectations. Government leveling is correlated negatively with the prefer equality measure, and positively with both the rewards necessary and market competition measures, the latter being the strongest association by far in the table.

These associations indicate that it would be misleading to consider that our four measures successfully tap contrasting preferences for equality and inequality. The government leveling scale does not imply a preference for equal distribution, much less for the government to control all resources as it did under socialism. Instead the constituent items reflect a desire for the government to promote affirmative action measures that can be seen as aimed at leveling the playing field by promoting greater equality of opportunity (not equality of results). That approach is compatible with enthusiastic support

TABLE 7.1
Correlations among equality and inequality measures

	Prefer equality	Government leveling	Rewards necessary	Market competition
Prefer equality	1.00			
Government leveling	−.10***	1.00		
Rewards necessary	.12***	.07***	1.00	
Market competition	−.12***	.41***	.16***	1.00

***$p \leq .001$

for market competition. Both principles are part of the dominant ideology that prevails in advanced capitalist welfare states today: Markets should be relied on as the dominant distributive mechanism, but government policy and welfare benefits should be used to limit inequalities by leveling-up measures in order to make market competition more fair than in a laissez-faire capitalist regime. Nonetheless, the items in the government leveling scale reflect more dissatisfaction with the status quo than the items in the market competition scale, since to date the Chinese government has done relatively little affirmative action of the sort mentioned in the government leveling questions.[19] These complexities should be borne in mind as we proceed to examine which groups of Chinese citizens have approving and disapproving attitudes toward the four measures we are considering in this chapter.[20]

THE SOCIAL CONTOURS OF PREFERENCES
FOR EQUALITY AND INEQUALITY

Which groups display the most agreement with our two measures about preferences for equality and government leveling, and which are most inclined to favor incentives to motivate hard work and to approve of market competition? In the pages that follow we examine the results of our statistical analyses of these issues. The social background and geographical location factors that we use here are the same as in Chapter 6, with one exception. Because we consider the unfair inequality scale described and analyzed in Chapter 6 a particularly central measure of distributive injustice attitudes, in this chapter and the two that follow we use that scale as an additional subjective attitude predictor that may affect other inequality attitudes. In terms of our initial expectations in this chapter, this means asking the following question: Do Chinese citizens who have a particularly strong sense that current differences between who is rich and who is poor are due to societal unfairness express stronger support than others for egalitarian distribution and for government leveling, and do they also express less support than others for the value of incentives to motivate hard work and the benefits of market competition and differentials? To examine these possibilities, we present regression analyses in a two-step sequence, showing the coefficients of each inequality attitude measure first with our standard set of background predictors and then with these same predictors plus one additional subjective predictor, the unfair inequality scale. (In the tables, the regression analyses are labeled "model 1" and "model 2" to correspond to these two steps, with a parallel approach followed in the next two chapters.)

What can we say about which social and geographical background characteristics are associated with support for equal distribution and government leveling? The correlation and regression analyses of these first two measures of preferences for different aspects of equality are presented in Table 7.2. The first feature of the table to note reinforces our earlier conclusion that these two pro-equality measures are not, in fact, simply slightly differing measures of the same egalitarian attitude syndrome. For the most part the coefficients for prefer equality and government leveling are the opposite of one another, indicating that the kind of person likely to prefer egalitarian distribution is, in fact, likely to disapprove of government leveling, and vice versa.

Examining the first three columns in Table 7.2, which concern the preference for equal distribution, several generalizations emerge. First, in terms of the occupation and residence groupings, farmers are most supportive of equal distribution, rural others somewhat supportive, and urban residents less so. In terms of other traits affecting the tendency to prefer equality, people who had bad personal or family inequality-related experiences in the last three years are significantly more likely to agree, while the well-educated, those with state-enterprise employment histories, and those who live far from any city are more likely than others to oppose egalitarian distribution.[21] As we saw in Chapter 6, there appears to be some curvilinear relationship between the prefer equality attitude and respondent age, with the middle-aged most likely to express agreement, but this effect is not large enough to be statistically significant. The addition of the unfair inequality scale as a predictor (in model 2) does not have any significant impact, and we are able to explain a modest 8 percent of the variation in the prefer equality attitude. In addition to the negative effect of increased years of education, most other indicators of high social status (for example, professional and managerial occupations, household income, CCP membership, improved living standards, and high social status relative to peers) also have significant negative correlations with prefer equality. However, when other traits are controlled for in our regression analyses, these effects tend to cancel each other out, and only the years of education coefficient remains statistically significant. Farmers, rural others, and those who have had bad family experiences in the current market environment are most likely to favor

TABLE 7.2
Correlations and regressions of attitudes favoring equality

	Prefer equality			Government leveling		
	R	Model 1 Beta	Model 2 Beta	R	Model 1 Beta	Model 2 Beta
Objective: Occupation and residence						
Farmer	.12***	.10*	.10*	−.14***	−.09*	−.08*
Rural nonfarm	−.01	.03	.03	−.05**	−.09***	−.08***
Migrant	.02	.05	.05	.02	.00	.01
Rural others	.05**	.05*	.05*	−.14***	−.11***	−.11***
Urban others	−.03	.02	.02	.08***	.03	.03
Urban unemployed	−.02	−.01	−.01	.09***	.04	.05*
Unskilled and semiskilled workers	−.06***	omitted	omitted	.05**	omitted	omitted
Skilled workers	−.04*	.03	.02	.08***	.02	.02
Self-employed	−.02	.00	.00	.03	.01	.01
Routine nonmanual	−.09***	−.03	−.03	.08***	.04	.04
Professionals	−.06***	.01	.01	.06***	.00	.00
Managers and cadres	−.09***	−.01	−.01	.04*	−.01	−.01
Objective: Demographic and socioeconomic						
Female	.05**	.02	.02	−.08***	−.04*	−.04*
Age	.05**	.17	.18	−.01	.06	.01
Age-squared/100	.04*	−.18	−.19	−.01	−.05	−.01
Years of education	−.20***	−.15***	−.16***	.21***	.16***	.15***
Married	.01	−.01	−.01	.01	.02	.03
Han ethnicity	−.02	.00	.00	.14***	.08***	.08***
Log of household income	−.15***	−.04	−.04	.14***	.04	.04
CCP member	−.08***	−.02	−.02	.09***	.04*	.04*
SOE employed	−.13***	−.05**	−.06**	.12***	.00	−.00
Access to unofficial information	−.09***	.03	.03	.09***	−.03	−.04
Objective: Geographic						
East region	.05**	omitted	omitted	.02	omitted	omitted
Central region	−.09***	−.13ns	−.14ns	.11***	.10ns	.09ns
West region	.06**	.00	.01	−.18***	−.06	−.06
Distance to city	.04*	−.11***	−.11***	−.20***	.00^^^	.02^^^
Province marketization	.02	−.05	−.05	.08***	.06ns	.06ns
Subjective						
Five-year standard of living trend	−.05**	−.02	−.02	−.02	.03	.04*
Relative social status	−.06***	.01	.02	−.05**	−.09***	−.08***
Bad experiences scale	.12***	.07**	.06**	.02	.07***	.06**
Unfair inequality scale	−.01		.03	.22***		.16***
R-squared		.08	.08		.13	.15

ns Coefficient no longer significant after correction for case clustering.

^^^ Coefficient significant beyond $p = .001$ level after correction for case clustering.

r = Bivariate correlation coefficients; beta are standardized regression coefficients from ordinary least squares regressions.

*.01 < p ≤ .05   **.001 < p ≤ .01   ***p ≤ .001

egalitarian distribution, and the well educated, those affiliated with SOEs, and those living far from any city (once occupational groups are controlled for statistically) are less likely to do so.

Turning now to the predictors for preferences for government leveling, rural occupational groups are in general less likely to express this sentiment (despite the expressed preference by farmers and rural others for egalitarian distribution), and urban groups in general, particularly the urban unemployed, are more likely to do so. (Migrants resemble other urban residents rather than other rural-origin groups on this score.) Other objective predictors related to advantaged social status are generally associated with support for government leveling, with the net influence of years of education, Han ethnicity, and CCP membership remaining statistically significant in the regression models. In general these patterns again contradict the notion that disadvantaged groups will be most likely to favor government efforts to limit and regulate inequalities.[22] When we examine the subjective predictors in the bottom section of Table 7.2, we see a different story. Although those who report improvement in their family living standards over the last five years unexpectedly express approval for government leveling, the conventional wisdom is supported for the remaining subjective predictors. People who feel they have low social status compared to their peers, who have had bad inequality-related experiences, and who feel that current patterns of inequality are shaped by unfair factors are significantly more likely than others to favor government leveling.

How can we make sense of these apparently contradictory patterns in which objective status advantages and subjective status disadvantages are both associated with support for government leveling? First, as observed earlier, the government leveling scale does not express a preference for strict equality, but more of an affirmative action orientation designed to promote equality of opportunity but not equality of results. Those who have been doing well and enjoy high social status are not particularly threatened by a government leveling approach, and the well educated, in particular, are likely to be supporters of affirmative action in any society, not just in China.

The questions used to construct this scale all involve entrusting the government with taking steps to produce a fairer distribution of rewards and opportunities. In China citizens whose lives and careers are most closely connected to the state and its policies, and who have benefited by that connection, are likely to voice approval. In the words of Davis (1993), these groups have a history of being "supplicants to a socialist state." In contrast, those who have had a more distant relationship with the state or feel they have not been benefiting or have even been harmed by the state and its policies tend to oppose government leveling, even if they would prefer to live in a more equal society. The clearest example of this syndrome is visible in the pattern of associations in Table 7.2 for farmers, who prefer equality but nonetheless tend to oppose government leveling.

Table 7.3, which parallels Table 7.2, presents the statistical analyses of the two remaining inequality attitude measures in this chapter: rewards necessary and market competition. Here our statistical models explain only a paltry 3 percent of the variance in the view that inequalities are necessary to provide incentives for hard work (see the final row in Table 7.3). The strong and/or statistically significant coefficients for rewards necessary also do not fall into a pattern that is readily interpretable. We had initially expected that people with high social status who have benefited from the reforms would agree with this functionalist statement, but only in the positive coefficients for relative social status and perhaps Han ethnicity are there signs of this pattern. In fact, there are a similar number of indicators of disadvantaged social status being associated with agreement that rewards are necessary—for example, with the middle-aged and those who score high on the unfair inequality scale tending to agree that rewards are necessary. It is hard to see a clear pattern in these results.

In examining the results in Figure 3.4 in Chapter 3 we noted that respondents presented with a variety of statements reflecting arguments about the positive functions of inequality for individual incentives and societal development were generally as likely to disagree or give neutral or can't decide responses as to agree. We noted that these patterns indicate that the government has had limited success in convincing Chinese citizens that current inequalities are justified by the positive functions they perform in society. Given these patterns, it is not that surprising that there seems to be substantial noise and randomness in responses to the rewards necessary question in Table 7.3, and as a result for responses to this question not to have a clear anchoring in particular social groups or geographic locales.

Critics in the United States and elsewhere point out fairly obvious logical problems with functionalist arguments in general. The claim that material rewards and incentives play a positive role in motivating individuals to gain skills, take on responsibilities, and work diligently may seem persuasive and even obvious. However, how can one tell whether a particular income gap or other inequality is attributable to functional necessity, or is instead the product of other forces, such as the selfish manipulations of the rich and powerful? Justifying the need for some inequalities on functionalist grounds cannot, or at least should not, lead one to conclude that the full spectrum of actual inequalities in any society is the product of functional necessity.[23] It would seem that our Chinese respondents are aware of the tension between alternative explanations of the inequalities within which they live. In response to our rewards necessary question, 50.4 percent of the citizens we interviewed agreed or strongly agreed that income differences

TABLE 7.3
Correlations and regressions of attitudes favoring inequality

	Rewards necessary			Market competition		
	R	Model 1 Beta	Model 2 Beta	R	Model 1 Beta	Model 2 Beta
Objective: Occupation and residence						
Farmer	−.01	.05	.06	−.14***	.03	.03
Rural nonfarm	−.01	.00	.00	−.03	−.03	−.03
Migrant	.00	.02	.02	.04*	.07**	.07**
Rural others	−.01	.01	.01	−.07***	.00	.00
Urban others	−.02	.01	.01	.03	.04	.05
Urban unemployed	.05**	.05	.05	.04*	.07**	.07**
Unskilled and semiskilled workers	−.01	omitted	omitted	.01	omitted	omitted
Skilled workers	.02	.02	.01	.07***	.04	.04
Self-employed	.03	.01	.02	.06***	.03	.03
Routine nonmanual	−.04*	−.05*	−.06*	.09***	.05**	.05*
Professionals	−.00	−.00	−.00	.07***	.03	.03
Managers and cadres	.02	−.01	−.01	.08***	.01	.01
Objective: Demographic and socioeconomic						
Female	−.02	−.02	−.02	−.10***	−.07***	−.07***
Age	−.01	.38**	.38**	−.09***	.09	.05
Age-squared/100	−.02	−.38**	−.39**	−.09***	−.13	−.09
Years of education	.04*	.03	.02	.24***	.11***	.10***
Married	.04	.02	.02	−.02	.00	.01
Han ethnicity	.04*	.06**	.06**	.11***	.11***	.11***
log of household income	.02	−.01	−.02	.18***	.04	.03
CCP member	−.00	−.01	−.01	.07***	.01	.02
SOE employed	−.05**	−.06*	−.06*	.09***	.02	.03
Access to unofficial information	.06***	.06*	.06*	.21***	.12***	.12***
Objective: Geographic						
East region	−.02	omitted	omitted	−.03	omitted	omitted
Central region	.06***	.11ns	.11ns	.12***	.17ns	.17ns
West region	−.05**	.10ns	.10ns	−.12***	.01	.02
Distance to city	−.06***	−.06ns	−.05	−.14***	.06^^	.07^^
Province marketization	.02	.08ns	.08ns	.02	.06ns	.07ns
Subjective						
Five-year standard of living trend	.03	.02	.02	.09***	.07***	.08***
Relative social status	.06***	.04	.05*	.11***	.01	.01
Bad experiences scale	−.03	−.03	−.03	−.07***	.02	.01
Unfair inequality scale	.06***		.06**	.12***		.07***
R-squared		.03	.03		.12	.13

ns Coefficient no longer significant after correction for case clustering.

^^ Significant beyond $p = .01$ level after correction for case clustering.

r = Bivariate correlation coefficients; beta are standardized regression coefficients from ordinary least squares regression.

*.01 < p ≤ .05   **.001 < p ≤ .01   ***p ≤ .001

are necessary to motivate individuals to work hard (Figure 3.4, bar 6), but at an almost identical 50.9 percent agreed or strongly agreed with a statement elsewhere in our questionnaire that "the reason why social inequalities continue to persist is because they benefit the rich and powerful" (Figure 3.1c, bar 2).

Turning to the final scale in Table 7.3, market competition, the associations are similar to those observed with the government leveling scale in Table 7.2. Because we discovered in Table 7.1 that these two attitude scales are positively rather than negatively correlated, this similarity is not all that surprising. Nonetheless, this finding does contradict our initial expectation that respondents who favored government leveling would disagree with statements about the virtues of market competition and that champions of market competition would oppose government efforts to promote equality.

In terms of specifics, the first column under market competition shows a pattern similar to that reported in Table 7.2 for government leveling, with rural occupational groups generally opposing market competition and urban occupational groups expressing agreement. The one difference is that migrants join other urban groups in advocating market competition, while they neither favor nor oppose government leveling. Once we control for other background traits in the two regression models, however, the other three groups with rural registration do not differ significantly from the comparison group of urban unskilled and semiskilled workers. However, migrants, the urban unemployed, and routine nonmanual workers are all significantly more likely than the comparison group to favor market competition. This is a curious finding, given that these groups are somewhat marginal within the status hierarchy of cities and might be expected to feel that they have not derived fair benefit from new opportunities. Nonetheless, these are the groups that speak most approvingly of market competition.[24] Perhaps these groups share a conviction that they would be able to do even better than at present if current institutionalized preferences enjoyed by other groups were weakened via more fully developed market competition.

In terms of demographic and socioeconomic characteristics , before we control for other traits there is a tendency for the advantaged (those with more education, higher incomes, party membership, and so on) to voice approval of market competition, while women tend to disapprove. Once we control for other background factors, the disapproving view of women is still visible, as is the net approving effect of being highly educated and belonging to the Han ethnic group. However, the other coefficients are no longer statistically significant. Curiously, those with more sources of information beyond the official media, a trait we thought might foster independent and relatively critical attitudes, is actually associated with a net approving attitude toward market competition.

The pattern of associations between the geographic location measures and market competition once again defies easy interpretation. Looking only at the correlation coefficients, it appears that residents of central provinces favor market competition, while residents in western provinces and respondents far from any city are opposed. However, once we control for other background predictors and correct for the clustering problem in our geographic variables (as discussed in Chapters 5 and 6), the effect of region becomes insignificant, while the effect of distance to the city is reversed. All else being equal, the net impact of living far away from any city is to favor market competition. At best we see hints here, as with some of the coefficients in the first two sections in Table 7.3, that approval of market competition is most likely among Chinese who are somewhat marginal.

Finally, the first three subjective measures show associations with market competition that fit the conventional wisdom, with both people whose standard of living has improved and people who see themselves as doing better than their peers voicing approval, while those who have had bad inequality-related experiences in recent years tend to disapprove. However, when we control for other background factors in the regression models, only the association with an improvement in the family's living standard remains statistically significant. In contrast, the positive association between the unfair inequality scale and market competition contradicts our initial expectation. We had assumed that people who see unequal opportunities, dishonesty, and special connections as major factors explaining why some people are rich and others are poor would be less likely than others to put their faith in market competition, but that is not the case. Such individuals express a preference for more extensive and fair market competition, rather than for increased limits on such competition through government regulation.

CONCLUSIONS

This chapter examines which social groups in China and which locales express the most support for substantially greater equality, and which groups and locales instead support the sorts of highly differentiated rewards and incentives that China's reform era leadership has been promoting. (The latter question will return in another guise in Chapter 8, where we examine the social contours of approval and disapproval of specific kinds of institutionalized preferences and discrimination, for example, toward the rich and toward disadvantaged migrants.) However, our quest in the current chapter has been, in effect, thrown off the rails by the complexities of our survey results. What have we learned?

First, the findings reinforce conclusions suggested in Chapter 3: There is not that much support, and no clear social constituency, for either highly egalitarian or very inegalitarian principles of distribution. Most Chinese do not support strict equality as the dominant distributive principle. Insofar as they would prefer China to be somewhat more equal than it is today, their clear preference is to achieve this by leveling-up measures that reduce the size and extent of deprivation of the poor, rather than by limits on the incomes of the rich or redistribution from the rich to the poor. It is also true that most Chinese do not favor a dominant or exclusive emphasis on unequal incentives and rewards as a motivating principle. Insofar as they approve of market competition and unequal results, their clear preference is for such competition to take place on a level playing field with something approaching equality of opportunity. So there is little sign of nostalgia for the leveled-down egalitarianism of the Cultural Revolution, but there is also little attraction to the unbridled competition and resulting inequalities that might be expected in early capitalism.

What does find substantial support among Chinese citizens is a formula involving distribution principles that balance equality and inequality. That formula should appear familiar to citizens in Western capitalist societies; it bears a strong resemblance to the combination of market capitalism and the welfare state that has long been the dominant public ideology in Western Europe and North America. Market competition, rather than government provision and regulation, should be the dominant mechanism of distribution. But that competition should give every Chinese citizen a roughly equal chance to be successful through dint of talent, training, and hard work. It would be desirable for the government to help make the competitive opportunities more equal than they are at present, particularly by affirmative action to make China's poor citizens more economically secure and thus more capable of competing for new opportunities. Given the popularity of what might be called these liberal capitalist (rather than laissez-faire capitalist or socialist) orientations in China today, the measures taken by China's post-2002 leaders to redress severe disadvantages (such as abolishing the rural tax on grain and waiving rural school fees) are no doubt welcomed.

Given the dominance of middle-ground views on the equality and inequality question, we have discovered that many attitudes that we had assumed would be in conflict are, in fact, quite congenial with one another. Chinese who feel that the free market is crucial, that all Chinese should be free to pursue their own personal benefits, and that individuals have the right to keep what they have earned (all aspects of market competition) also support the notion that the government should promote a somewhat reduced level of overall inequality by providing extra help to the poor and disadvantaged (government leveling). Those who feel that there is too much unfairness in the current patterns of who is rich and who is poor tend to favor both government leveling and market competition, evidently because they feel the combination would produce a fairer pattern of distribution of incomes than exists at present. Another way to state the latter relationship is to observe that Chinese who think current inequalities are unfair do not favor government interventions to limit the role of markets and the inequalities they produce, but instead wish to level the playing field on which market competition operates in the hope that improved market competition will produce fairer patterns of inequality. Equal opportunity and equitable inequalities are preferred, and Chinese citizens join their counterparts in Western societies in recognizing that neither principle is currently being fully realized.

Assuming that there is a fairly coherent syndrome of attitudes favoring a balance between equality and inequality maintained by a mixture of market competition and government efforts to aid the poor and disadvantaged, in which social groups and locations is the support for this liberal capitalist approach most likely to be expressed? Focusing on the common patterns in the associations with government leveling in Table 7.2 and with market competition in Table 7.3, several generalizations emerge. In general there is more approval of this ethic in urban groups than in rural ones, among those whose family living standards have improved, among the well educated, in the majority Han ethnic group, and among males. These patterns suggest that support for the middle ground between equal and unequal distribution is associated with having an advantaged status position.[25] However, still other figures in the table indicate associations between support for government leveling and market competition and at least relatively marginal social status. It is not the highest-status urban occupational groups that voice the most support for both government leveling and market competition, but instead the more marginal routine nonmanual workers and the unemployed (plus migrants and those living far from the city in the case of market competition). Perhaps a similar note is sounded by the fact that those who say that current inequalities are unfair (see the final subjective predictor row in each table) are also more likely than others to voice support for both government leveling and market competition. We speculate that the combination of some status advantages and some marginality indicates that support for the balancing of equality and inequality is most likely to come not from those who have had the most success, but instead from those who are doing well enough to have some faith in their ability to succeed via market competition in today's China and who wish there were more equality of opportunity and equitable rewards so that they could achieve the better status and higher living standards they feel they deserve.

The survey results reviewed in this chapter display a fair amount of disagreement and uncertainly about what sort of pattern of inequalities in China would be fairer than the current patterns. Even though many Chinese agree with the general proposition that there is too much inequality in China today nationally (see the first bar in Figure 3.1), there is not much support for a more egalitarian pattern of distribution. Rather than revealing signs of widespread nostalgia for the perceived greater equality of the socialist era and Maoist distribution rules, most Chinese instead favor liberal capitalism and vibrant market competition made fairer by government affirmative action to reduce the disadvantages the poor face in that competition.

Looking below these general patterns, there also does not appear to be a clear and solid constituency in China for a more egalitarian distribution pattern. Even farmers, the occupational group most likely to agree with the prefer equality statement, are less likely than other groups to trust the government with efforts to promote affirmative action. The attitudes of Chinese citizens on the issues considered in this chapter seem once again to point more to social stability than to instability, insofar as most citizens feel that the gap between their preferences for equal opportunity and equitable differentials and the reality of current inequalities is not too large. From the results we reviewed earlier in this study (particularly via the questions displayed in Figure 3.2 and in the unfair inequality measure discussed in Chapter 6), it appears that most respondents felt that this was the case in 2004. There is, of course, no guarantee that this general acceptance of current patterns of inequality as at least not grossly and systemically unfair will remain true in the future.

CHAPTER EIGHT

Views on Stratification and Class Conflict

In previous chapters we have seen evidence that the average Chinese citizen would prefer to live in a society that occupies a middle ground on inequality, one that resembles the welfare state or liberal capitalist ethic promoted in advanced market economies. In such an ideal society, existing inequalities would be equitable in the sense that they would reflect differential skills, contributions, and other merit factors, and the state would provide certain minimum subsistence guarantees and affirmative action policies to enable the poor and disadvantaged to have a fair chance to compete for opportunities to improve their lives—in other words, measures to promote equality of opportunities. Implicitly this sort of society would not have clear class or other cleavages or sharp conflict between strata or classes over distributive injustice. Chinese society does not match this idealized vision. According to the conventional view, social tensions and group conflict are on the rise in China due to resentments over the wealth accumulation, status transmission, and entrenched privileges fostered by market reforms.

Our goal in this chapter is to examine variations in Chinese citizens' views on such stratification trends. Within which social groups and in which locations is there the most criticism of current patterns of status transmission and the strongest sense that Chinese society is characterized by sharp social cleavages and group conflicts stemming from the very unequal lives that Chinese lead today?

China's failure to match the ideals of equity and equality of opportunity is not unusual. No actual society comes at all close to providing either equality of opportunity or rewards fully commensurate with individual merit, and it is debatable whether China is any more deficient in this regard than are other societies. This failure occurs despite the fact that the public values in most modern societies extol equality of opportunity and equitable rewards and officials all over the globe urge their citizens to work and behave in ways to help realize these goals.

The reasons no society comes close to realizing the ideals of equality of opportunity and social equity are complex, and we cannot explore them fully here. However, a central process is the universal tendency toward social stratification. The terms *inequality* and *stratification* are often used interchangeably, but they do not mean the same thing. *Inequality* refers to an objective feature of the distribution of resources and opportunities at one point in time in which some people have more than others. *Stratification* refers to a tendency for such a structure of inequality to persist over time and even over generations (see Duncan 1968; Tilly 1998). Analytically, we can conceive of a society with high inequality but weak stratification (if there is high upward and downward mobility, so that one's position at one point in time is not a good predictor of one's position at a later time, and even less so of one's children's positions). We can also imagine a society with relatively low inequality but rigid stratification (that is, a caste society in which everyone stays in the same position indefinitely, but where there are only modest differences in income and other resources between those at the top and at the bottom).

Societies can differ in how rigidly they are stratified, but no modern society has, or could have, inequality without developing stratification. Individuals and families who have high status have an understandable tendency to try to preserve and enhance their advantages over time, to use their extra resources to benefit those close to them, and to pass at least some portion of their power and privileges to their children and later generations. A wide variety of mechanisms facilitate this effort, including acquiring property and wealth, cultivating personal ties with patrons and the powerful, marrying well, using income to secure a better life and a richer cultural environment for family members, and avoiding extended and intimate contact with those of low status.[1] At the other end of the scale, the poor and otherwise disadvantaged do not possess the property, personal connections, purchasing power, and other resources that would enable them to compete for educational opportunities, jobs, or other desirable outcomes on an equal footing.

Stratification is not simply the result of the competitive but unequal striving of individuals and families; it also results from state policy and social institutions. For example, laws governing private property and inheritance tend to foster status transmission, as do regulations and customs that restrict or deny entry of people of the wrong strata or ethnic groups to particular neighborhoods, clubs, and organizations. Alternatively, some affirmative action policies and practices may facilitate the entry of the disadvantaged into higher social strata. In any case, there is a strong tendency toward stratification in every modern society—for the structure of inequalities that exists today to shape in powerful ways the structure of inequalities of tomorrow and of subsequent generations. Even if we could magically wipe out all social inequality in a society and give each citizen an equal starting point in terms of income and other resources, new structures of stratification would emerge and become entrenched within a few years and certainly over generations (see Kelley and Klein 1981; Tilly 1998). We use a variety of terms to refer to these tendencies—for example, *status transmission* and *class reproduction*. The complexity and rigidity of stratification patterns can vary from society to society, as indicated above by the hypothetical contrast between high-inequality and low-stratification societies on the one hand and low-inequality and high-stratification societies on the other hand.

Another important feature of systems of social stratification is the extent of animosity and conflict between those situated in lower and in higher strata. Again it may be useful to think conceptually in terms of extreme cases. In one society people may tend to see themselves as situated somewhere along a ladder of strata differentiated by such factors as income, occupational status, and ethnicity, but without much sense of conflict or shared grievances toward those in other strata. At the other extreme would be a society in which key groups have sharply different lives and opportunities and in which groups with lower status feel a strong sense that they are being mistreated and exploited by the unfair manipulations of a dominant group or groups (with the latter returning the feelings of animosity).[2]

More to the point in terms of the current chapter, popular views of the nature of the stratification system may differ. One individual may see China today as a society characterized by inequality, but without rigid stratification and with relatively weak social conflicts between unequal groups and strata; another individual may see China as rigidly stratified, with pervasive and sharp group conflicts over distributive injustice issues. Before we can examine which survey respondents take one or the other of these two contrasting views, it is necessary to consider the way in which China's recent history, and particularly experiences during the decades spent under centrally planned socialism, shaped both the stratification patterns that China exhibits today and popular evaluations of those patterns.

SOCIAL STRATIFICATION UNDER CHINESE SOCIALISM

When the Chinese Communist Party (CCP) gained national power in 1949, its leaders saw the transformation of the existing stratification hierarchy as one of their primary goals. Mao and his colleagues were shaped in their thinking by the Marxist faith they subscribed to, and they interpreted that stratification system primarily through the lens of social classes in the Marxist sense. In the social sciences generally, the term *social class* is conventionally used to refer to stratification based on differences in economic position and material resources (rather than, say, on differences in political power, ethnic status, or other noneconomic characteristics). What is meant by *social class*, then, is *economic class*, although the economic or material criteria for class membership and boundaries differ from one theoretical framework to another. Marxist analyses of stratification are narrower than this; Marxists focus primarily on property ownership as the defining and differentiating feature of social classes (rather than, say, income, occupational status, or standard of living).[3]

Major goals of the Chinese Communist revolution were to classify the Chinese population in terms of property ownership (or lack thereof), to redistribute some forms of property from the haves to the have-nots (accomplished with regard to agricultural land through the national land reform campaign of 1950–53), and eventually to eliminate private ownership of productive property entirely (accomplished in the socialist transformation campaigns of 1955–56).[4] Thus after 1956 Chinese society no longer had social classes in the orthodox Marxist sense (groups with differing possession of productive property), and a Marxist might have assumed that at that point Chinese society would also cease to have any basis for class conflict. Did the basic changes in the structure of Chinese society in the 1950s mean that the status transmission processes that produce stratification had also been undermined? What does being a socialist society mean in terms of stratification?

Both the realities of stratification in China during the socialist era and official debates and polemics on class issues in the Mao era are considerably more complicated than Marxist theory implies. First, the elimination of private ownership of productive property eliminated one important basis for class formation and reproduction, but others continued during the 1960s and 1970s, and centrally planned socialism created new institutional mechanisms that promoted status transmission. The result was a society that was not egalitarian in any meaningful sense, and that in some ways was rigidly stratified. How to think about and analyze the nature of stratification in those years is a puzzle that has bedeviled Chinese leaders and ideologists as well as foreign analysts.

Mao Zedong, a decidedly willful person, persisted in trying to analyze and promote an understanding of Chinese society in class terms even after 1956 and to perceive of that society as riven by sharp class conflicts, some of which he did his best to provoke. By the last decade of his life, the Cultural Revolution years of 1966–76, this focus had produced copious confusion and even violent factional battles, in part because at various times Mao emphasized three distinct versions of class analysis, each with a different meaning and different implications.

First, at times Mao and his followers emphasized what might be called "old classes," since the focus was on the property that families had owned before the revolution. During the 1950s each family went through a process that resulted in receiving a class label based on its property before 1949 (examples include landlord, rich peasant, middle peasant, poor peasant, capitalist, and worker; see Kraus 1981). The old class labels were recorded in household registration and other personnel files and were inherited (patrilineally) by subsequent generations. By the time of the Cultural Revolution, the labels had ceased to have any meaningful relationship to the family's current economic position. For example, a young person with a landlord label might be an ordinary and perhaps relatively poor commune member whose long-deceased grandfather had owned a larger than average share of village land. Nonetheless, a complex system of favoritism and discrimination based on these labels was maintained to the end of the Mao era, justified in part by the claim that those with "bad class" labels (such as landlord and capitalist) were secretly scheming to regain control of the property their families had lost in the revolution and thus had to be regularly "struggled" against (see Unger 1984; Croll 1981).

However, the primary focus of class struggles during the Cultural Revolution revolved not around these old classes, but instead around the dangers posed by what might be called "new class" tendencies. Here Mao and his radical followers were borrowing a line of thinking that can be traced to Yugoslav Marxist heretic Milovan Djilas's classic work on the new class in state socialist societies (1957), although there is no evidence that Mao had read or directly borrowed from Djilas. Djilas had noted that even though private ownership of the means of production had been eliminated in all state socialist societies, actual control over such property and, indeed, over all other important resources in state socialist societies (such as education, communications, the military, and medical care) was much more powerfully concentrated in the hands of a small number of individuals than was the case in any capitalist society.[5] Those individuals were the top leaders of the Communist Party and the highest ranks of the party-state bureaucracy who owed their positions not to entrepreneurship, acquisition, property, and wealth, but to political performance and loyalty.[6] They enjoyed a range of special privileges and institutions (such as special housing, chauffeured limousines, vacation resorts, special medical clinics, and privileged access to foreign goods) based not on their financial resources, but on their bureaucratic ranks and political positions.

Over the years Mao developed an antipathy toward the privileges and status transmission of the new elites in the socialist society he had created, and many of the developments of the Cultural Revolution were motivated by a desire to attack and prevent what Djilas would have termed new class tendencies.[7] Mao's rivals within the top leadership of the CCP were referred to as people in power taking the capitalist road ("capitalist roaders" for short), and many of the leveling-down innovations discussed in Chapter 1 (such as requiring administrators and intellectuals to leave their posts to engage in prolonged manual labor, sending educated urban youths to the countryside, and eliminating the college entrance examination system) were aimed at combating the tendencies, clearly visible in China in the 1950s and 1960s, for those in high-status positions to try to preserve their status, enjoy special privileges, and pass advantages on to their children. So whereas old class dangers stemmed from status transmission based on property ownership before the revolution, new class dangers were produced by the concentration of power inherent in contemporary socialist institutions.

To make things even more confusing, a third class analysis framework, which I call "thought classes," was popularized during the Cultural Revolution years. Anyone who was sufficiently loyal to Mao and active in promoting Cultural Revolution values might be deemed to have a proletarian class viewpoint, no matter what that person's family's class label was or the bureaucratic position the individual (or his or her parents) occupied. Anyone who deviated from the mandatory values of the period could be charged with displaying a bourgeois class standpoint, again no matter the person's class label or position. Political virtue and loyalty alone were the grounds for determining an individual's thought class position, a curiously "idealistic" rather than "materialistic" framework of class analysis to be promoted in an avowedly Marxist society. In Cultural Revolution conflicts, given these competing class frameworks, it became easy to find a class framework that would place you in a good class and your opponents in a bad class position, an ambiguity that helped exacerbate the very real conflicts that occurred at the time.[8] Table 8.1 summarizes the multiple class analysis frameworks that were in play during the Cultural Revolution era.

The obsessive analysis of Chinese society in class terms during the socialist period had a number of drawbacks. First and most obvious, it contributed

TABLE 8.1

Competing social class frameworks during the Cultural Revolution

	Old classes	New classes	Thought classes
Good classes	Pre-1949 worker, poor peasant, revolutionary soldier	Current workers, commune members, soldiers	Anyone with proletarian views
Bad classes	Pre-1949 landlord, capitalist, "bad element"	High-ranking officials, intellectuals, other elites	Anyone with bourgeois views
Mode of class struggles	Be suspicious of and struggle against those with bad class labels	Struggle against capitalist roaders; cleanse via labor	Criticize and attack bourgeois elements

to the very visible tendency to identify and exacerbate some class conflicts that, in orthodox Marxist or perhaps even in other terms, had no clear material or structural basis. The result, as Deng Xiaoping and other reformers observed subsequently, was an exaggerated and prolonged state of conflict and chaos that damaged Chinese society and the prestige of the CCP. A second drawback is that this obsession with class obscured and diverted attention from a number of other important social cleavages in China that did not readily fit in any of the competing class frameworks—for example, the rural-urban gap, ethnic group cleavages, military-civilian tensions, and regional inequality.[9] State policy under socialism exacerbated some of these other cleavages (particularly the rural-urban gap), but they were not seen in social class terms, and so these cleavages remained largely invisible. A final drawback is that by trying to analyze China's state socialist society in terms of social classes, the analogies with stratification in capitalist societies were emphasized, and the contrasts were deemphasized.

Since the socialist transformation campaigns of 1955–56 basically eliminated property-owning classes in China, one might have concluded that class analysis was no longer a useful framework for analyzing stratification in socialist China. In fact, some Chinese leaders voiced this view during the mid-1950s (see Whyte 1993). At roughly the same time, Khrushchev was turning a parallel conclusion into official state policy in the Soviet Union: The USSR could no longer be described as composed of social classes, certainly not of antagonistic social classes, and henceforth it made the most sense to think of different occupational and other groups as strata existing in relative harmony within a "state of the whole people."[10] If class analysis was no longer a productive or accurate way to view stratification in Chinese socialism, what alternative framework would work better? From 1962 onward Mao insisted on the primacy of class analysis and class struggle, and he threatened to punish any who thought otherwise, so possible answers to this question were not pursued while he remained alive.

A few ideas about a more useful approach to analyzing social stratification in state socialist societies generally, and in the Mao-era socialist system in China in particular, can be suggested (see also Wang 2008; Whyte forthcoming). First, drawing on ideas of Karl Polanyi (1944), Milovan Djilas (1957), Ivan Szelenyi (1983), Andrew Walder (1986), Yanjie Bian (1994), and others, state socialist societies differ in key respects from capitalist societies, particularly by being organized via a unitary bureaucratic hierarchy in which the primary distribution mechanism is bureaucratic allocation and redistribution, rather than by a diversity of organizational forms operating within a distribution system that is primarily organized in terms of market exchanges. In a state socialist society the name of the game for individuals is competition for bureaucratic favor, thereby to secure entry into, and progression up through the ranks of, particular organizations. Success in climbing the hierarchical rank structure brings material and other rewards, but one's rank and place in the bureaucratic hierarchy, not one's income or accumulated wealth, determine status and lifestyle. In the absence of a meaningful labor market, the income and benefits one might earn by working in a different organization or locale are not bargaining chips that can affect status and remuneration.

In this structural setting, conceptions of bureaucratic hierarchy and rank are much more useful in thinking about and analyzing stratification than are conceptions of social class. One of the notable features of state socialist societies is that the sorts of occupational groups that are most often used in non-Marxist analyses of social classes in modern capitalist societies—for example, with managers, professionals, lower white-collar workers, service workers, manual workers, and farmers occupying varying statuses in the class hierarchy—do not display much in the way of class-linked tendencies or class-related common interests. For example, under normal circumstances, socialist factory workers have their fates too closely linked to their placement within their firm's bureaucratic hierarchy and to the ranking of their firm within the larger industrial hierarchy to develop much in the way of working-class consciousness and actions to promote and defend workers' interests generally.[11] In this setting individuals may develop a powerful sense that their fate is closely linked to their work unit and all their colleagues in that unit, even though the latter differ in occupations, rank, and other ways.[12] Given the nature of Chinese society under socialism, a better analogy than social classes for understanding socialist stratification might be the internal ranking systems of an army, the Catholic Church, or the U.S. federal government (see Bauman 1972).

The absence of meaningful social classes does not mean that status transmission processes are absent in a state socialist society, or that the overall stratification structure is minimal or weak. Rather, the distinctive nature of socialist institutions and the distributive system in such societies (particularly the dominance of bureaucratic allocation over market distribution) means that stratification is primarily structured by bureaucratic regulations and by the people in political power who devise the bureaucratic structures and rules, not by financial resources, human capital, or other assets of individuals that come to the fore in a market society. In a socialist society at any point in time, the existing bureaucratic rules and procedures favor some groups and certain criteria for the best treatment and for upward mobility and thus set in place certain kinds of status transmission processes (but not others). At a later time bureaucratic authorities may change their minds and alter the rules of the stratification game, the mobility opportunities and status transmission prospects of previously favored groups will be blocked, and groups that were previously discriminated against will find themselves in favor and able to improve their lives and enhance the future opportunities of their children.[13]

The resulting overall stratification patterns may be hard to predict because the patterns are determined not simply by the fact of being a socialist society but also by the particular bureaucratic educational and career mobility rules adopted. For example, the criteria for selecting and promoting individuals into political careers and leadership changed multiple times in complex ways in China—from emphasizing rural roots and participation in the revolutionary struggle, to urban working-class credentials (in the 1950s), to specialized education and technical training (in the early 1960s), to political loyalty and the proper class background (during the Cultural Revolution), and back to higher education and specialized training (in the 1980s and beyond). In the wake of Mao's death, advanced education went from being irrelevant or actually harmful to a person's political career prospects to being essential, while family class background went from being central to irrelevant. Although the criteria changed, the nature of special treatment and privileges enjoyed by those above certain ranks and in certain key enterprises and organizations remained more constant. Before China's market reforms, many desirable services and resources were not available for purchase, but were distributed in a highly subsidized fashion through processes of bureaucratic allocation. The assortment to which a person was entitled depended on the nature and bureaucratic status of the person's work unit and his or her rank and relationships within it.

A number of other specific features of status transmission under Chinese socialism cannot be deduced in a simple manner from the fact that China is a state socialist society. For example, although China did not follow the North Korean model of having the revolutionary leader succeeded by one of his offspring, the top CCP leadership was packed with the wives of the top leaders during the Cultural Revolution. That tendency disappeared after Mao's death and the purge of the "gang of four" (the most prominent of whom was Mao's widow). In the late 1970s and early 1980s family status transmission operated closer to the bottom of the stratification order, rather than at the top. Employment in state factories could be "inherited" by a son or daughter; after the mid-1980s that practice was repudiated.[14]

Sharp changes in the regulations and institutions affecting stratification do not mean that China was not a highly stratified society in the socialist period. The stratification patterns may have operated on different principles than those in a capitalist society, but it would be hard to make the case for weak stratification in socialist China. In fact, one could characterize Chinese society during the 1960s and 1970s by a formula that sounds like an oxymoron: a classless, highly stratified society. What this formula refers to is the fact that social classes had ceased to exist in the conventional sense (classes based on economic position and resources) after the 1950s due to socialist transformation, but that other powerful stratifying tendencies, the products of socialist institutions, still structured the lives of Chinese citizens.

As noted earlier, in the view of many analysts China's most severe and durable social cleavage today is not between social classes, but between China's rural and urban citizens. The rigidity of that cleavage stems particularly from socialist policies and institutions of the 1960s and 1970s, not from China's traditional society or from the post-1978 market reforms. How the rural-urban divide became so wide and rigid is a complex story (see Cheng and Selden 1994; Chan 1994; Solinger 1999; Wang Fei-ling 2005; Whyte 2010a). The background illustrates the ability of socialist bureaucrats to shape and alter the stratification system.

During the 1950s there was a huge movement of individuals and families out of China's villages and into the cities to respond to new opportunities and to fill the rapidly expanding bureaucratic structures of the CCP leadership (see Kirkby 1985; Howe 1971), a flow that can be seen as an acceleration of the long-standing Chinese pattern of relatively free geographical and social mobility (see the discussion in Chapter 1). A large proportion of today's older urban residents are former villagers who acquired urban jobs and housing during the 1950s. After the end of that decade, and particularly after the economic depression caused by the Great Leap Forward, the leadership instituted new regulations (promulgated in 1958, but not effectively enforced until 1960) that prevented virtually all rural-to-urban migration in China.[15] For the next two decades Chinese rural residents were essentially socialist serfs bound to the soil, whose agricultural household registrations (*nongye hukou*) consigned them to an inferior caste status (see Whyte 1983; Potter 1983). Even after migration restrictions were relaxed in the 1980s, enabling rural residents to migrate into the cities and seek urban jobs and other opportunities, in almost all cases they retained their agricultural hukou and still are treated as second-class citizens, not entitled to most of the urban services and public goods that those with urban hukou are entitled to.

What had been throughout Chinese history a fairly permeable social barrier between city and countryside that remained highly porous for the first decade after the revolution became what one author calls "an invisible wall" (Chan 1994) that effectively ensured that people with rural status and their children remained members of a substantially separate and lower-status caste. Urban opportunities were available only to those born to parents with urban (nonagricultural) hukou. In the reform period the rural-urban walls have crumbled, and at any time in recent years well over 100 million migrants have been living and working in China's cities, but with treatment and opportunities that are decidedly inferior to those enjoyed by urban citizens. So one prominent legacy of Chinese socialism is a caste-like stratification barrier between China's rural and urban citizens that has no counterpart in China before 1949 or in any modern capitalist society.[16] One of our goals in this chapter is to see how the views of today's Chinese citizens about this altered but still very important aspect of Chinese stratification vary.

With the launching of China's economic reforms in 1978, the stratification situation became more complicated. For the most part the bureaucratic allocation system continued to operate, although the rules affecting status transmission changed in key ways (for example, by the institution of mandatory retirement procedures for officials—see Manion 1993; by dramatically increased emphasis on educational credentials for bureaucratic appointments and promotions; and by allowing rural residents to migrate to the city). With the further development of the reforms in the 1990s and beyond, and with the return of private enterprise, foreign firms, and property-based wealth, alternative status transmission structures and procedures resembling those in capitalist societies reappeared in China for the first time since the 1950s. A labor market began to reemerge, and some individuals who were not happy with their prospects in state jobs could "go down into the sea" (*xiahai*) by entering a private or foreign firm or even starting a private business. Others who were fired or laid off from their state jobs were forced to look elsewhere, mainly by seeking private employment. Goods and services that had been bureaucratically allocated and subsidized became available through the market, although initially at higher unsubsidized prices, particularly benefiting those with newfound wealth.

A particularly dramatic example of this transformation is provided by urban housing reforms carried out starting in the late 1990s, which essentially gave most urban residents legal title to the apartments they had been living in and renting (most often from their work units, which provided preferential financial arrangements to make possible the transition from renter to private owner). As a result of this reform, urban residents could rent out or sell their apartments if they were able to afford better housing elsewhere. Within a few years luxurious housing estates mushroomed in and around China's major cities, drawing the most successful and prosperous citizens away from work unit housing compounds. Many other goods and services underwent changes with similar consequences. For example, medical insurance coverage was sharply reduced, and it collapsed almost completely in the countryside, forcing most Chinese citizens to seek medical care on a fee-for-service basis. Existing public hospitals and new private medical clinics began to introduce more modern and expensive medical equipment and medications; some could afford them, but they were out of reach for many. Chinese universities shifted from the Soviet-style free-plus-stipend system to a more capitalist-style tuition system, again making ability to pay more of a factor in access to higher education.

Although all these changes involved the growing role of market distribution and ability to pay in determining citizen access to valued resources and opportunities, they did not come about through any sort of natural or inevitable development of markets themselves. Rather, bureaucratic decisions at the highest levels set in motion the shift from straight bureaucratic allocation of these goods and services to increasing reliance on market distribution. In other words, China's bureaucratic authorities changed the rules of the game once again, only for the most part the change involved adopting institutions and policies modeled after those in advanced capitalist societies (to replace the socialist institutions originally modeled after those in the Soviet Union). The net result is that the stratification system in China today is a complex mixture of retained and still strong bureaucratic allocation mechanisms combined with increasingly pervasive market distribution. Both bureaucratic allocation and market distribution contribute distinctive types of status transmission to the overall stratification system of contemporary China.

Today it is no longer misleading to talk of social classes in China; income, wealth, and market position now play roles similar to those played in class reproduction in capitalist societies. Wealthy families can now use their financial resources to purchase bigger, better, and more exclusive housing than other families can afford, and they can pay for better and more advanced schooling for their children, better medical treatment for family members, and in general a more privileged lifestyle. In China's large cities, the consequences of these changes are particularly visible in residential resegregation, as wealthy families move away from work unit compound apartment blocks that formerly housed employees of high and low rank into new and luxurious housing developments where their new neighbors are all similarly prosperous. Urban landscapes that used to be structured by ubiquitous work unit compounds (where rank rather than class was the dominant organizing principle) are increasingly becoming stratified and resegregated by social class.[17]

MEASURES OF STATUS TRANSMISSION
AND CLASS CONFLICT

Based on this brief historical overview, we can now describe the measures used in this chapter to examine variations in citizen attitudes toward contemporary social stratification as well as perceptions of the severity of inequality-related social conflicts. We examine processes that have their roots in socialist institutions and those that stem from China's market reforms and emerging class dynamics, using the questions whose overall survey distributions were displayed in Figures 3.5, 3.6, and 3.7 in Chapter 3. In that chapter we saw that in general large majorities of our respondents approve of the market-based phenomenon of rich families procuring better housing, schooling, and medical care for their families (Figure 3.5, bars 2 through 4). They largely disapprove of two status transmission practices with roots more in socialist bureaucratic practices: officials' use of their positions to gain better treatment for their families (Figure 3.5, final bar) and the systematic discrimination against rural migrants in the cities (Figure 3.6). These overall response patterns directly contradict the conventional view that many Chinese are unhappy about inequality and stratification trends produced by market reforms and are nostalgic for the patterns of stratification that existed in the era of centrally planned socialism.

On the question of the severity of conflicts between advantaged and disadvantaged groups in Chinese society today, our respondents had varied perceptions, but in general low levels of group conflict were more commonly identified than high levels (see Figure 3.7). Still the question remains: In which social groups in China, and in which locations, is one most likely to find anger about the contemporary tendencies for rich families to purchase better lives, for officials to obtain privileged treatment, and for migrants to be discriminated against, as well as perceptions that group conflicts over inequality issues are severe?

Through preliminary analyses we combined and reduced the measures in Figures 3.5, 3.6, and 3.7 to yield four measures to assess views on current stratification tendencies and inequality conflicts. The first two measures concern contemporary status transmission processes whose roots lie in the centrally planned socialist system before 1978 that live on in China despite market reforms. First, we wanted a measure that would summarize critical attitudes toward institutionalized discrimination against rural migrants in the cities—in other words, discrimination against Chinese citizens whose household registration (hukou) status is agricultural and not local.[18] We drew on the items displayed in Figure 3.6 and constructed our summary scale from five of those items: "It is fair that people with household registrations in the city have more opportunities than those with household registrations in the countryside"; "It is fair that rural migrants cannot easily obtain household registration in the city"; "It is fair that children of rural migrants are not permitted to attend schools in the city"; "It is fair that rural migrants are prohibited from performing certain occupations in the city"; and "It is fair that rural migrants are not allowed to obtain urban welfare benefits." Each question had the familiar five response categories ranging from strongly agree to strongly disagree. Thus the summary scale we construct from these five items is a measure of the strength of opposition to current patterns of discrimination against rural migrants in the cities, a measure we refer to here as oppose hukou bias (anti-hukou bias for short).[19]

Next we wanted a comparable measure of opposition to privilege-seeking and status transmission among Chinese officials—the current version of China's bureaucratic new class. In this case the political constraints affecting our project resulted in only a single question in our questionnaire that we can use for this purpose, in which respondents were asked to respond to the following statement: "It is fair that those who hold power enjoy a certain degree of privileged treatment," again with response categories ranging from strongly agree to strongly disagree (Figure 3.5, final bar). We use this single item as our second measure of socialist stratification, which we refer to as oppose power privilege (anti-leader privilege for short).[20] Although these two measures are rooted in China's prior socialist institutions and policies, they are both very much part of current patterns of inequality in China. Indeed, the cities were not home to substantial numbers of migrants until the reforms and associated changes "liberated" them from being bound to their rural places of origin, and the various forms of discrimination against them we inquired about are very much part of the current social reality. Similarly, people in high political positions continue to receive special treatment and privileges in a number of respects.[21]

The other two measures are intended to reflect features that are more the product of market reforms and the inequalities and class conflicts that these may have stimulated. First, we construct a summary score from the three questions about rich people using their finances to purchase better lives for themselves and their children (Figure 3.5, bars 2 through 4)—"It is fair that those who are able to pay for it to give their children better educational opportunities"; "It is fair that rich people can purchase better homes than other people"; and "It is fair that rich people can enjoy better health care than other people"—again with response categories varying from strongly agree to strongly disagree. This summary measure thus indicates opposition to the rich using their wealth to purchase better lives, and we refer to this summary measure as oppose rich transmit status (or anti-rich transmit for short).[22]

Finally, we constructed a summary measure designed to reflect respondent perceptions that current social cleavages in China are characterized by sharp conflicts. For this purpose we used the responses to the six items displayed in Figure 3.7. In each case the respondent ranked a particular social conflict along a five-point scale ranging from no conflicts to very large conflicts: "between poor people and wealthy people," "between employers and employees," "between people with agricultural hukou and nonagricultural hukou," "between migrant workers in the cities and laid-off city workers," "between Han Chinese and ethnic minorities," and "between people in coastal areas and those in inland areas." The resulting measure thus summarizes perceptions that Chinese society is riven with severe inequality-related group conflicts, and we refer to this scale as a measure of perceived inequality conflicts.[23] Hu Jintao, the post-2002 CCP leader, has been very concerned about making China a more harmonious society and thereby minimizing the tendency to perceive inequality conflicts. We have four measures of critical views about current stratification and class conflict to examine who is most likely to be angry about these particular departures from equality of opportunity and intergroup harmony: anti-hukou bias, anti-leader privilege, anti-rich transmit, and inequality conflicts.

Table 8.2 examines how the pattern of responses to these four measures of critical attitudes toward current Chinese patterns of stratification are related to one another. In the majority of cases the figures show that respondents critical of one of the dimensions of current stratification are also critical of the others. However, that pattern is broken for perceptions of inequality conflicts. Only respondents who are critical of the rich transmitting their advantages to their families and children are likely to perceive current inequality conflicts in China as severe. The respondents who are particularly angry about status transmission tendencies rooted in socialism (anti-hukou bias and anti-power privilege) are not more likely than others to see Chinese society as characterized by severe inequality conflicts. In fact, those who are angry about officials seeking and obtaining privileges are not any more or less likely than others to see severe conflicts related to inequality, while those who are most opposed to discrimination against migrants are actually significantly less likely than others to perceive severe conflicts in society ($r=-.09$). These results hint at two somewhat different orientations toward stratification in China today, with some people most concerned about unfair patterns of status transmission rooted in China's socialist past but not perceiving Chinese society generally as full of sharp group conflicts, and others most exercised about the ability of the rich to purchase better lives today and seeing this as one aspect of a society divided into sharply opposed groups.

TABLE 8.2
Correlations among stratification and conflict measures

	Anti-hukou bias	Anti-leader privilege	Anti-rich transmit	Inequality conflicts
Anti-hukou bias	1.00			
Anti-power privilege	.34***	1.00		
Anti-rich transmit	.08***	.27***	1.00	
Inequality conflicts	−.09***	−.01	.11***	1.00

***$p \leq .001$

We next examine the variations in opposition to current stratification patterns in Table 8.3 with the two summary measures of critical attitudes toward features of stratification rooted in socialist institutions: anti-hukou bias and anti-leader privilege. The predictor variables and regression models are the same as those employed in Chapter 7. Looking first at opposition to institutionalized discrimination against rural migrants, it is important to note that although the migrants themselves and perhaps farmers are significantly more likely than the comparison group (unskilled and semiskilled workers) to oppose such urban bias, there is otherwise not much variation in these attitudes across occupational and residence status groups. One advantaged urban group, professionals, is also significantly more likely than the comparison group to oppose discrimination against migrants. None of the urban occupational groups aside from the unskilled and semiskilled workers display any net tendency to be biased against migrants, as one can see from the small beta coefficients for models 1 and 2.

Why is this pattern notable? An implicit assumption of much previous discussion of China's distinctive rural-urban caste system (Solinger 1999; Wang 2005) is that most Chinese urban citizens look down on rural residents as less educated and civilized, more disorderly, and even dangerous and thus as proper objects for control and discrimination. By implication, urban authorities maintain China's distinctive rural-urban caste system at least in part to avoid antagonizing urban citizens. However, we find no evidence of any systematic support for hukou bias among urban occupational groups in general in Table 8.3. This finding builds on the patterns seen earlier in Figure 3.6, where large majorities of our national sample expressed opposition to each of the specific kinds of discrimination against rural migrants that we inquired about. Perhaps migrants and farmers, the primary victims of this discrimination, are somewhat more vocal in opposing these practices than others, but most urbanites also have critical attitudes.

The remaining patterns of association with our anti-hukou bias scale are not clear, and in some regards the results appear contradictory. The best-educated respondents are significantly more likely than others to be critical of hukou bias, but those who have more access to unofficial communications (through travel, access to news beyond the official media, use of the Internet, and so on) are less likely to be critical of discrimination against migrants.[24] Also, we find attitudes more critical of discrimination against urban migrants among those living far from any city.[25] So the main message of this analysis is that there are only modest differences in the responses of the rural-origin victims and the urban-origin beneficiaries of the discriminatory practices against migrants.

Looking at the somewhat comparable figures on critical attitudes toward privileged treatment for those in power (columns 4 through 6 in Table 8.3),

TABLE 8.3
Correlations and regressions of opposing socialist stratification

	Anti-hukou bias			Anti-leader privilege		
	R	Model 1 Beta	Model 2 Beta	R	Model 1 Beta	Model 2 Beta
Objective: Occupation and residence						
Farmer	−.01	.10*	.09	−.09***	−.01	−.01
Rural nonfarm	−.00	.01	.00	.02	.01	.01
Migrant	−.06**	.09***	.09***	−.03	−.03	−.03
Rural others	.06**	−.02	−.02	−.02	−.02	−.01
Urban others	−.02	.03	.03	.04*	−.00	−.01
Urban unemployed	.02	.04	.04	.04*	.03	.03
Unskilled and semiskilled workers	−.02	omitted	omitted	.03	omitted	omitted
Skilled workers	.01	.01	.02	.02	−.01	−.01
Self-employed	−.01	.03	.03	.01	.03	.03
Routine nonmanual	.03	.02	.02	.05**	.02	.02
Professionals	.05**	.06**	.06**	.04*	.00	.00
Managers and cadres	.00	.03	.03	.01	−.01	−.01
Objective: Demographic and socioeconomic						
Female	−.04*	−.03	−.03	−.04**	−.00	−.01
Age	−.08***	−.20	−.19	−.02	.07	.05
Age-squared/100	−.08***	.11	.10	−.02	−.07	−.05
Years of education	.07***	.14***	.14***	.11***	.13***	.13***
Married	−.02	−.01	−.01	−.04*	−.04	−.03
Han ethnicity	.02	.04*	.04*	.01	.01	.01
Log of household income	.00	−.00	−.00	.06**	.01	.01
CCP member	.04*	.04	.04	.06***	.04	.04
SOE employed	.02	.03	.03	.07***	.03	.03
Access to unofficial information	−.10***	−.18***	−.18***	−.02	−.10***	−.10***
Objective: Geographic						
East region	−.08***	omitted	omitted	−.03	omitted	omitted
Central region	.10***	.04	.04	.04*	.02	.01
West region	−.02	−.07ns	−.07ns	−.01	−.01	−.01
Distance to city	.03	.05*	.05*	−.03	−.02	−.02
Province marketization	−.08***	−.08ns	−.08ns	−.05**	−.07ns	−.07ns
Subjective						
Five-year standard of living trend	.05**	.03	.03	−.01	−.01	−.01
Relative social status	−.00	−.02	−.02	−.02	−.05*	−.05*
Bad experiences scale	−.03	−.01	−.01	−.05**	−.04*	−.04*
Unfair inequality scale	−.02		−.02	.06***		.03
R-squared		.06	.06		.03	.03

Note: Beta are standardized regression coefficients from ordinary least squares regressions.

ns Coefficient no longer significant after correction for case clustering.

*.01 < $p \leqq$ .05   **.001 < $p \leqq$ .01   ***$p \leqq$ .001

only a few associations emerge as strong or statistically significant, and we can explain very little of the variation in this measure with our range of predictors (R-squared = .03). Before controlling for other measures, it appears that urban occupational groups tend to be more critical of the privileges of the powerful than are rural groups (column 4), but when we control for other background measures (columns 5 and 6), there are no significant differences across occupational and residence status groups. None of these groups is significantly more or less likely to object to privileged treatment for the powerful. (In Figure 3.5, bar 7, there was fairly broad condemnation of this practice within the full national sample.)

The respondents who have status advantages of various types and may have more connections to the powerful than do others do not display a systematic tendency to be less critical of the privileges of the powerful, and it appears that the opposite is the case to some extent. Those who feel they have higher status relative to their immediate peers than others (on our relative social status measure) do express somewhat fewer critical attitudes, but the well educated, professionals, those with high incomes, members of the Han ethnic group, and CCP members express views more critical of the privileges of the powerful (column 4). Once we control for the other predictors (columns 5 and 6), only the years of education coefficient remains statistically significant.[26] The initial positive coefficient with CCP membership seems to indicate that these patterns are not simply a reflection of the "red versus expert" tension in any Leninist society, with those who rise due to merit and expertise resenting those who gain privileges by political criteria. Nonetheless, it is notable that the strongest coefficient in columns 5 and 6 indicates that those who have attained the highest levels of education are the respondents most likely to be critical of the privileges of power.

The remaining associations of note in the table once again defy our expectations or ready explanations. We see again the tendency for those with access to unofficial communications to be less likely to be critical than others of the privileges of the powerful, and even more surprisingly that those who have had more bad inequality-related experiences (loss of jobs, inability to pay bills, and the like) to also be less likely to be critical than others. These patterns do not provide much added understanding of who is most likely to object to the powerful receiving privileged treatment. In other words, here, as in some other inequality attitude measures employed in the current study, critical attitudes are not clearly rooted in discernable social niches, whether involving disadvantages or otherwise.

The two measures analyzed in Table 8.3 concern forms of contemporary institutionalized status transmission that are a product mainly of China's socialist period, rather than of the workings of the market reforms. We saw in Chapter 3 that there is fairly general agreement in the national sample as a whole that both discrimination against migrants and according privileges to the powerful are unjust and undesirable. This general disapproval likely contributes to the relative lack of strong associations in the columns of Table 8.3. While there is some sign that more of those who suffer from the discriminatory practices involved in the hukou system are critical than other people, in general there are few signs that the presumed beneficiaries of these practices voice support for them.[27] Rather, in general urbanites and those with several kinds of status advantages, particularly the well educated, are more likely than others to express critical attitudes. Again the simple-minded idea that you can deduce people's attitudes by a simple self-interest calculation based on their current status attributes proves a very poor guide to respondent attitudes.

Table 8.4 examines two sets of attitudes that are associated in the public mind more with market reforms and their consequences than with prior socialist institutions and practices—critical views toward the rich using their wealth to purchase better lives for their families and perceptions that Chinese society is full of sharp inequality-related conflicts. Looking first at the occupational and residence status groups and their views on the rich transmitting their status, we see little overall variation with one curious exception: The urban unemployed, whom we might expect to be particularly resentful about not having the finances to pursue better housing, schooling, and health care for their families, in fact are significantly less likely than the comparison group of unskilled and semiskilled workers to object to wealth buying better lives.[28] The occupational groups that are most likely to be well off or to have the potential to become well off—the self-employed (including entrepreneurs), professionals, and the manager and cadre category—do not show any tendency to be less critical than others of status transmission by the rich. Once again assumptions based on objective self-interest are a poor basis for understanding inequality attitudes.

Looking at other predictors associated with advantaged status at the bivariate correlation level, it appears that having a high income, being a member of the dominant Han ethic group, and perceiving that one is better off than one's local reference groups (relative social status) are each associated with fewer critical attitudes toward status transmission by the rich. However, other indicators of advantage, such as being highly educated or belonging to the Communist Party, are not associated with acceptance of status transmission by the rich, and when we control for other predictors in the regression models, the association with family income also is eliminated. One other enigmatic pattern is that residents of central provinces are significantly less likely than those in the east (other things being equal) to have critical attitudes toward the rich purchasing better lives for their families. So there is at best weak or contradictory evidence in these results for the notion

TABLE 8.4
Correlations and regressions of opposing market stratification

	Anti-rich transmit			Inequality conflicts		
	R	Model 1 Beta	Model 2 Beta	r	Model 1 Beta	Model 2 Beta
Objective: Occupation and residence						
Farmer	.03	−.03	−.03	−.03	−.06	−.04
Rural nonfarm	−.00	−.03	−.03	−.06***	−.09***	−.08**
Migrant	−.03	−.04	−.04	−.02	−.05	−.04
Rural others	−.01	−.04	−.04	−.02	−.05*	−.05*
Urban others	−.01	−.08*	−.08*	.05**	−.05	−.04
Urban unemployed	−.05**	−.08**	−.08**	−.01	−.06*	−.06*
Unskilled and semiskilled workers	.03	omitted	omitted	.06***	omitted	omitted
Skilled workers	.01	.00	.01	.02	−.03	−.03
Self-employed	.01	.01	.01	.02	−.03	−.02
Routine nonmanual	−.01	−.01	−.01	.00	−.04*	−.05*
Professionals	.00	−.01	−.01	.04*	−.01	−.01
Managers and cadres	−.01	−.02	−.02	−.01	−.06**	−.05*
Objective: Demographic and socioeconomic						
Female	.00	.02	.02	.05**	.07***	.07***
Age	.01	−.25	−.27	−.00	−.04	−.07
Age-squared/100	.02	.29*	.30*	.01	.08	.10
Years of education	−.01	.05	.05	.06***	.03	.02
Married	−.04*	−.04	−.04	−.05**	−.03	−.02
Han ethnicity	−.07***	−.07**	−.07**	−.02	−.02	−.02
Log of household income	−.04*	−.00	.00	.04*	.01	.01
CCP member	.01	.01	.01	−.03	−.03	−.03
SOE employed	.01	.01	.01	.03*	.01	.01
Access to unofficial information	−.05**	−.09***	−.09***	.13***	.14***	.14***
Objective: Geographic						
East region	.04*	omitted	omitted	.01	omitted	omitted
Central region	−.10***	−.19***	−.20***	−.03	−.05	−.05ns
West region	.09***	−.08ns	−.08ns	.04*	−.01	.00
Distance to city	.07***	−.01	−.02	−.02	−.03^^^	−.01^^^
Province marketization	−.05**	−.17ns	−.17ns	−.05**	−.10ns	−.10ns
Subjective						
Five-year standard of living trend	−.03	−.03	−.03	−.03	−.02	−.01
Relative social status	−.07***	−.07***	−.08***	−.03	−.07**	−.06**
Bad experiences scale	−.01	−.03	−.03	.01	−.00	−.01
Unfair inequality scale	−.02		−.01	.17***		.15***
R-squared		.04	.04		.04	.06

Note: Beta are standardized regression coefficients from ordinary least squares regressions.

ns Coefficient no longer significant after correction for case clustering.

^^^ Significant beyond $p = .001$ level after correction for case clustering.

*.01 < p ≦ .05   **.001 < p ≦ .01   ***p ≦ .001

that social status or geographic advantages are less likely to produce criticism of the revived ability of rich people in China today to use their resources to benefit their families and foster status transmission.

A few other patterns in these results deserve comment. We see here stronger evidence than in previous chapters that age cohorts differ, but only after controlling for other predictors. The net effect of being middle-aged is to voice acceptance of status transmission by the rich, while both younger and older respondents are more likely to be critical.[29] In addition, we see again the unexpected pattern observed in Table 8.3 that those with more access than others to unofficial sources of information are less likely to be critical of the rich transmitting their status. Finally it is worth drawing attention to one pattern we don't find: We had expected that those who scored high on the unfair inequality scale examined in Chapter 6 would be more likely than others to object to the rich transmitting their status, since they would tend to see those who are rich today as undeserving. However, the coefficients for the unfair inequality scale (last row) are close to zero. Feeling that people who are rich today did not get there by fair means does not produce a tendency to depart from the general consensus we observed in Chapter 3 that it is fair for the rich to use their resources to obtain better lives for themselves and their children.

Finally, in columns 4 through 6 of Table 8.4 we examine the background factors affecting perceptions that China is a society with many sharp inequality-related group conflicts. Most respondents disagree with the high conflict characterization of their society (Figure 3.7 in Chapter 3). Looking first at the occupational and residential status groups at the bivariate correlation level (column 4), there appears to be some tendency for urban groups to perceive many social conflicts over inequality, while rural groups tend to see few such conflicts (again contradicting press reports of the "pitchfork anger" of China's peasants). However, once we control for other predictors (in columns 5 and 6), we find a curious and unexpected result that the comparison group of unskilled and semiskilled urban workers is significantly more likely than others to perceive sharp inequality conflicts, with all the other groups, rural and urban, less likely to do so (although only about half of the associations are statistically significant). The lowly status and insecure employment situation of urban unskilled and semiskilled workers might be expected to incline them to view inequality conflicts as severe. However, other groups for whom one would make the same prediction—farmers, migrants, and the urban unemployed in particular—don't share this perception of their society as conflict-filled. Also note that those living far from any city show a net tendency to perceive less inequality-related group conflict in society.

In terms of the set of objective demographic and socioeconomic status predictors, at the bivariate level it appears that a number are associated

with viewing inequality conflicts as more or less severe, but once we control
for other predictors only two of these patterns remain notable, and neither
was expected. Women are more likely than men to see sharp inequality conflicts in society today, and those who have more access than others to unofficial sources of information are also more likely to perceive sharp group
conflicts. (On the other three measures examined in this chapter, those
with high access to unofficial information were less likely to hold critical
attitudes.) Beyond the association between distance from the city and low-
conflict perceptions, none of the other geographic predictors has a statistically significant association with inequality conflicts, once other predictors
are controlled for and we adjust for the clustering problem shared by the
geographic measures.

Finally, the subjective predictors show a tendency for those who perceive that they are better off than their local reference groups to also be less
likely than others to perceive sharp inequality conflicts. However, it is worth
stressing again that we do not see in these results a general tendency for
those in advantaged social positions to be less likely than others to perceive
sharp inequality conflicts. In fact, at the bivariate level those with high educational attainment and high incomes are more likely to perceive such conflicts, although in the regression models these associations are weakened
and are no longer statistically significant. Finally, the strongest associations
in the table are with the unfair inequality scale. Those who are more likely
than others to perceive the patterns of who is rich and who is poor as based
on unfair factors are significantly more likely than others to also perceive
Chinese society as full of sharp group conflicts, and when we add this predictor to our regression model we improve our modest explanatory power a
bit (from R-squared = .04 to .06).

CONCLUSIONS

This chapter has examined variations in attitudes toward four measures of
status transmission and the inequality conflicts that such transmission may
foster. Two of these measures (anti-hukou bias and anti-leader privilege) focus on current status transmission processes with roots in the socialist institutions that preceded the reforms, while the other two measures (anti-rich
transmit and inequality conflicts) focus on tendencies more rooted in market
reforms. Overall, we have been less successful than in the previous two chapters in detecting clear patterns of which groups and locations have critical
attitudes on any of these four measures, as demonstrated by the anemic proportions of variation that our range of predictor variables can explain (with
R-squared values for these regressions ranging from .03 to .06). Although
this modest explanatory success may seem to be a problem, it does contrib-

ute to a by now familiar theme: Our analysis does not identify a clear pattern of particular social groups or of individuals in particular locales with consistently critical attitudes about current status transmission patterns and the conflicts they may engender. Instead we have variable patterns, with migrants understandably having the strongest criticisms of hukou bias, but if anything slightly fewer critical attitudes than the comparison group on the other three measures; for Han Chinese respondents to be more accepting than minorities of the rich transmitting their status, but more critical of hukou bias; and so forth.

As noted earlier, this pattern of individuals of particular types objecting to some features of current inequalities but not to others is more a recipe for social and political stability than a recipe for looming conflict and instability. Current patterns of inequality do not appear to be producing identifiably disgruntled groups who are angry across the board. In combination with the conclusions reached in Chapter 3—that most respondents object to the continuation of hukou bias and special privileges for the powerful, while most approve of the rich transmitting their status and do not view their society as riven by inequality conflicts—we see additional evidence that there is more acceptance than rejection of the new or revived forms of inequality fostered by market reforms.

However, a few somewhat general patterns are visible in Tables 8.3 and 8.4. The best-educated respondents are significantly more likely to object to both hukou discrimination and the privileges of the powerful, although they do not differ on the other two measures considered here, suggesting that advanced schooling fosters special sensitivity to departures from merit-based inequality. Respondents who feel they have higher status than their peers are less likely to express critical views on all four of these stratification measures, and for three of them (anti-leader privilege, anti-rich transmit, and inequality conflicts), the coefficients are statistically significant. Finally, we have also called attention to the curious pattern in which individuals with more access to unofficial contacts and information are significantly less likely than others to object to our three measures of status transmission (anti-hukou bias, anti-leader privilege, and anti-rich transmit status), but are significantly more likely to see Chinese society as riven by sharp social conflicts over inequality fault lines.

Taken together these few general patterns do not yield a clear and consistent story about where the strongest criticisms of current stratification patterns are likely to be found. In particular, there are few signs of the pattern suggested by the conventional wisdom on inequality issues in China—of individuals or locations that have low status or are disadvantaged in various ways tending to have critical attitudes, and for individuals and locations with high status or that have benefited by the reforms expressing fewer critical views. Even though the associations in the tables in this chapter tend to be weaker than those in previous chapters, they point to similar conclusions—to the general absence of particular groups and locales that consistently express particularly critical attitudes, with very little indication that either current advantages or disadvantages, or being a winner or a loser as a result of market reforms, translate into less or more likelihood of having critical attitudes on inequality issues. As noted repeatedly, this pattern provides little support for the claim that China is heading toward a social volcano because of rising resentments toward current stratification patterns felt by disadvantaged and angry citizens.

CHAPTER NINE

Views About Opportunities and Social Justice

Chapters 6 through 8 examined the social roots of variations in attitudes toward a wide range of features of inequality and stratification in China. In a sense all the inequality patterns and preferences considered in those chapters are preliminaries to the analyses presented in this chapter. Perceptions of current inequalities, preferences for narrower income gaps, and views about whether current patterns of stratification are acceptable may affect Chinese citizens' "bottom-line" questions about the current social order: Is the current structure of opportunities and inequality sufficiently fair that ordinary people have a reasonable chance of improving their livelihood and social status and providing a better future for their children, or is it so unfair and arbitrary that individuals cannot hope to build better lives and obtain just treatment by working hard and playing by the rules? Is it so unjust that it systematically works to the advantage of a small number of undeserving but well-connected individuals and families while providing few rewarding opportunities for ordinary citizens? These questions about upward mobility opportunities and the prospects for distributive justice are examined in this final survey analysis chapter.

Questions about optimism and pessimism about life's opportunities are also presumed to have implications for China's future political stability. If most Chinese citizens think there are ample (even if not all that equal) opportunities for individuals to be successful, improve their standards of living, and provide better futures for their children, most likely they will feel acceptance or even gratitude toward the government and its leaders, given the continuing strong role of the government in guiding the economy. However, if they perceive the current social order as thoroughly unfair and corrupt and as providing very little possibility for themselves or other ordinary citizens to get ahead, this perception is likely to fuel feelings of resentment and anger toward the authorities. Such hostile feelings may well accumulate and feed a willingness to join protest movements and other activities that threaten China's political stability. So feelings of pessimism about opportunities and fatalism about distributive injustice can be matters of considerable consequence.

Evidence summarized in Chapters 3 and 4 indicates that the average Chinese citizen is relatively optimistic about chances for ordinary people to get ahead and, at least compared to other societies, is less pessimistic about opportunities for obtaining social justice (Figure 3.8; Table 4.6). The task in the current chapter is to determine in which social groups and in which locales more-critical views on these issues are concentrated.

CHINA'S RECENT HISTORY AND VIEWS ON OPPORTUNITIES AND SOCIAL JUSTICE

When the Chinese Communist Party (CCP) came to power in 1949, its leaders pledged to create a new socialist society that would be much more just than either the imperial or republican social orders that preceded it. Greater fairness and increased opportunities would come about through two primary transformations. First, the transition to a socialist system would eliminate foreign and private ownership of productive property and the resulting exploitation of industrial labor and tenant farmers by the rich and by foreign capitalists, and wage and other benefit systems designed to fairly reward contributions to society would be implemented. The result would be a more just society in which poverty and lack of property were not serious barriers to education, employment, and other opportunities. Second, by producing rapid economic development, the structure of opportunities could be transformed, and large numbers of people would be able to shift from farming to urban jobs, from unskilled work to skilled work, from workers to technicians and engineers, and so forth.[1]

In many ways this strategy of pursuing a more just society through the dual mechanisms of creating socialism and promoting economic development was successful during the period from 1949 to 1957. Although many Chinese who had lived privileged lives before 1949 suffered precipitous losses of status, property, and even their lives, many more Chinese from humble circumstances were able to secure education, move to the city, obtain secure wage-earning jobs, and in general improve substantially their standards of living and their prospects for the future. There were no democratic elections or even opinion polls during those years, but most accounts describe the new government led by Mao Zedong as enjoying considerable popular support in the 1950s, in large measure because of the improvements in many people's lives and the optimism that these improvements inspired about more of the same (Whyte 1991).

These developments are illustrative of two analytically distinct ways in which opportunities for upward mobility of the disadvantaged can be increased in any society. Sociologists distinguish between circulation mobility and structural mobility. *Circulation mobility* refers to a situation in which the total number of opportunities available at high and low levels in society does not change, but the chances for individuals to rise from low to high status are increased (as are the chances for high-status individuals to fall, hence producing increased circulation). Generally speaking, it is hard to produce major increases in opportunities for the disadvantaged through circulation mobility alone, but the post-1949 processes of attacking, confiscating the property of, and even exiling or killing local elites and promoting individuals of humble origins into vacated high-status positions did have considerable impact.[2]

In *structural mobility* there is a relative increase over time in the number of desirable positions and opportunities, so that individuals of humble origins have more opportunities to rise to higher status without having to displace large numbers of prior occupants of high-status positions. Economic development is the primary engine producing structural mobility in most societies. Development leads inevitably to a relative decline in farming and low-skilled manual labor positions and a relative increase in mental labor and managerial positions, which have higher pay and prestige. Both circulation and structural mobility were at work in China during the 1950s, but there is little doubt that structural mobility produced by economic expansion and by the mushrooming of the bureaucratic positions needed for the new centrally planned socialist system was the primary source of major increases in upward mobility experienced during the 1949–57 period.

The subsequent two decades of Chinese socialism, from 1958 to 1978, did not sustain this early promise, as detailed in Chapter 1. Mao Zedong certainly intended for the new initiatives launched in those years, particularly the Great Leap Forward of 1958–60 and the Cultural Revolution launched in 1966, to make China an even more fair society by promoting better opportunities for ordinary workers and farmers to be recognized and rewarded. The attack on the privileges and elite tendencies of capitalist roaders in the latter campaign was designed to clear the path toward more opportunities for ordinary workers and farmers, and the resulting egalitarian rhetoric had considerable appeal to progressives and leftists around the world. However, the reality of China's opportunity structure after 1958 did not match the rhetoric.

The spectacular failure of the Great Leap Forward produced mass famine in the Chinese countryside, with at least 30 million deaths above the expected number (Yang 1996; Thaxton 2008). Even in the cities, the collapse of the Leap led to an economic depression and employment retrenchment that to some extent lasted beyond Mao's death in 1976. Living conditions remained grim even after the "three bitter years" (1959–61). Urban wages remained largely frozen, China struggled to provide its citizens with the amount of food and other goods that had been available in the 1950s, and in some realms (such as urban housing space and per capita availability of tofu), things actually were worse in 1978 than in 1957. Strict rationing may have helped to spread available food and consumer goods fairly equally within urban areas, but Chinese urbanites remember the 1960s and 1970s as times of persistent shortages and hunger. Furthermore, after 1960 China's rural citizens were prohibited from competing for the constrained urban employment and other opportunities that did exist.

China's economy registered modest economic growth from 1962 to 1978, but more in the form of increases in bridges, cement production, railway capacity, and military capabilities than in the diets and access to consumer goods of ordinary citizens. Just producing enough increase in agricultural production to keep up with China's rising population remained a struggle. Furthermore, such economic development as did occur did not produce major shifts in the patterns of employment that would have enabled many individuals to move into higher-status and better-paid jobs. In fact, for large numbers of young urban residents, the opposite was the case. After 1968, more than 17 million urban educated youths were mobilized to leave the cities and settle in the countryside to engage in farming, a campaign made necessary by the lack of sufficient expansion in the urban economy to generate more than a tiny number of new jobs. Although the CCP did its best to justify this campaign in ideological terms and portray participation as glorious, it was still a bitter pill for most of the rusticated youths to swallow (see Bernstein 1977).

The weakness of economic growth after 1957, and the resulting anemic creation of high-status and desirable jobs, made the competition for opportunities that did exist even more sharp. Popular anxieties over available opportunities fed into Cultural Revolution struggles. The more proletarian ethos mandated during that period included a prohibition on overt expressions of personal desire for material rewards and career advancement, sentiments that could get a person branded as hopelessly bourgeois and in need of criticism, reeducation, or worse. The CCP propaganda machinery worked hard to convince the population that only if individuals suppressed personal material and career desires and devoted themselves fully to the benefit of society would China be able to develop and eventually provide prosperous lives for all.[3] But proclaiming these slogans did not change popular mentalities. Most Chinese citizens struggled to preserve some security in their lives in the midst of the chaos of the period without any great hope of achieving better conditions. However, the political battles of the period did provide one arena in which to compete for upward mobility, as the targets of Cultural Revolution struggles were deposed, replaced in many instances by those who had led the attacks against them.

Perhaps the clearest example of the failure of Cultural Revolution reforms to produce increased opportunities for China's disadvantaged citizens involves university enrollment procedures. During the Cultural Revolution China's campuses were wracked by factional struggles, and no new college students were enrolled between 1966 and 1970. The pre-Cultural Revolution method of selecting college students primarily based on their scores on national entrance examinations was attacked as helping to enable young people from high-status families to gain college entrance, because they had the family resources and cultural capital to prepare for and score well on the exams. The national entrance exam was therefore eliminated, as was direct progression from upper middle school graduation to college. Instead young people were expected to work or serve in the army for at least two years after completing upper middle school before they could be considered for college entrance. Then through a process of coworker consideration within work units and local leader approval, presumably based more on factors such as work performance and political attitudes than on academic potential, individuals were nominated to match the number of college enrollment slots allocated to a particular commune, factory, or military unit. Hence the new college enrollment system of 1970–77 is referred to as the era of "worker, peasant, soldier" college students (Pepper 1996; Han 2000; Andreas 2004).

Although these university enrollment reforms were designed to foster increased opportunities for disadvantaged Chinese youths to obtain college educations, they failed to do so. There is evidence that, rather than increase enrollment of "ordinary" young workers, peasants, or soldiers, well-connected families were enabled to use their influence over local authorities to secure nominations of their sons and daughters for scarce college spaces (Pepper 1996). The main reason the reform failed, however, was a sharp decline in university enrollments compared to the years before the Cultural Revolution. In 1965, 674,000 students were enrolled in Chinese universities (a substantial drop from the peak of 962,000 in 1960). In 1974 only 430,000 university students were enrolled, and the figure had still not returned to pre-Cultural Revolution levels by 1976, when 565,000 were enrolled.[4] So not only were no new students enrolled from 1966 to 1970, but even after 1970 China was enrolling fewer students than before. The structural mobility profile of university places had gone into reverse. Although no systematic data on the backgrounds of China's college students in the 1960s and 1970s are available, it is hard to believe that anything other than a decline occurred (relative to the number of eligible youths) in college opportunities for youths from ordinary worker and farming families.

Thus the optimism produced by increased upward mobility opportunities during the 1950s was not sustained during the remainder of Mao's rule.

Instead constrained circumstances for most Chinese meant at best maintaining rough stability in their living standards, and at worst experiencing actual declines, with reduced opportunities for most kinds of upward mobility—from farming to nonagricultural work, from middle school to college, and so forth. During the final years of Mao's life, the regime's propaganda apparatus made a sustained effort to convince the Chinese population that things were getting better and that Cultural Revolution struggles had created a more just society, but given the straitened circumstances in which the population lived, one can imagine that this was a very hard sell.

The situation has changed dramatically since China's market reforms were launched in 1978. Once again both circulation mobility and structural mobility mechanisms are at work, particularly the latter. In terms of circulation mobility, purges of beneficiaries of the Cultural Revolution and new mandatory retirement policies (Manion 1993), combined with heightened emphasis on educational credentials and job performance, produced a new shuffling upward and downward of China's status hierarchy. A much more powerful mechanism was economic development that, in combination with such other changes as administrative decisions allowing rural citizens to migrate in search of jobs in the cities and the massive expansion of college enrollments, have produced huge increases in opportunities for upward mobility in the three decades since the reforms were launched.[5]

The revived potential for status transmission by rich families discussed in Chapter 8 clouds the picture somewhat, as does the switch to charging college tuition and a range of other changes making access to resources and opportunities dependent on ability to pay. In addition, the state's determined reforms of the inefficient state-owned enterprise sector starting in the mid-1990s produced unemployment and loss of benefits for many who had enjoyed favored treatment in that sector under Mao, even though the private and foreign-owned sectors of the economy grew at a rapid rate, providing some opportunities for those who had lost state jobs. On balance, the way in which China's impressive economic growth has generated new job opportunities, increases in family incomes, improved availability of food and consumer goods, and dramatic reductions in the proportion of families living in poverty seems likely to more than counterbalance popular concern about the way rising inequality and emergent class stratification may be restricting the opportunities for disadvantaged Chinese to improve their lives. One of the clearest indications of popular optimism comes from a question we asked about how the respondent's family's living standard compared with that in 1999. Fully 63.9 percent said their families were doing better or much better in 2004.

In reflecting on the transition from the Mao era to the reform era, one is struck by the contrasts between rhetoric and reality about the creation of opportunities for economic improvement and upward social mobility. In the Mao era, generally speaking, there was greater rhetorical emphasis on eliminating injustices and promoting equality than after 1978, but following initial success in promoting mobility opportunities, the failed policies and excessive zeal in attacking advantages and elites produced a grim reality in which many Chinese had to focus their energies on avoiding downward mobility rather than on strategizing about how to get ahead. In the reform era, at least until recently, there has been much less focus in official rhetoric about social equality issues, and China's leaders have repeatedly encouraged some Chinese to get rich before others. Stratification based on social class factors like income and personal wealth and reflected in sharply diverging lifestyles of the rich and the poor has returned to Chinese social life with a vengeance. Yet beneath this declining emphasis on equality in official pronouncements, the repudiation of the Cultural Revolution excesses and extraordinary economic growth have together produced dramatic increases in upward structural mobility opportunities. Those increases have stimulated something else to return with a vengeance—Chinese families strategizing about how to get ahead under the conditions of market competition.

What matters for China's political stability are not objective trends in jobs, university enrollments, and other indicators, but popular perceptions and sentiments regarding upward mobility opportunities. The evidence reviewed in Chapters 3 and 4 indicates that a majority of our survey respondents were optimistic about current opportunities in 2004. For example, 63.1 percent said they expected their families to be doing better or much better economically in five years, and 61.1 percent expressed agreement with the statement that hard work is always rewarded (Figure 3.8, bars 1 and 5). These expressions of optimism about opportunities are generally stronger, sometimes substantially so, than those of survey respondents in other countries, particularly in Eastern Europe during the 1990s (Table 4.6). On the other hand, fairly sizable proportions of our survey respondents expressed concerns about obtaining social justice, including 50.1 percent who agreed with the statement that government officials don't care what ordinary people think (Figure 3.8, bars 6 through 8). However, fewer Chinese than citizens in other societies expressed such concerns; the proportion of Americans who agreed that government officials don't care about the views of ordinary people was 64 percent, of Russians 69.7 percent, and of Japanese 74.7 percent (Table 4.6). In sum, the majority of Chinese express relatively optimistic views about future mobility opportunities and even about the possibilities of obtaining social justice, particularly when their responses are viewed in comparative perspective.

However, there was considerable variation in responses to questions about mobility opportunities and the prospects for obtaining social justice, with substantial minorities expressing more-critical views. Our task for the remainder of this chapter is to determine which social groups and people in which localities expressed the most pessimism about mobility opportunities and the most negative or fatalistic views about the prospects for ordinary Chinese to obtain social justice.

MEASURES OF PESSIMISM ABOUT MOBILITY
OPPORTUNITIES AND SOCIAL INJUSTICE

To analyze the social roots of pessimism about opportunities for economic improvement and social mobility and feelings of distributive injustice, we make use of selected items whose overall distributions were reported in Figure 3.8. From those responses we have constructed three measures: a measure of pessimism about individual mobility opportunities, a measure of pessimism about opportunities in Chinese society generally, and a measure of fatalistic feelings about social injustice.

The measure of pessimism about individual opportunities is constructed from two similar questions included in our survey: "Five years from now, do you estimate that your family economic situation, compared with what it is now, will be much better, a little better, no change, a little worse, or much worse?" and "Based on the current situation in the country, the opportunities for someone like you to raise their living standard are still great. Regarding this statement, do you strongly agree, agree, feel neutral, disagree, or strongly disagree?" We used the same technique as in earlier chapters to create a combined scale based on responses to these questions, with high scores indicating pessimism about opportunities for individual and family economic improvement.[6] We refer to this measure as lack of individual opportunity.

The second scale is constructed from responses to three statements about opportunities to get ahead in Chinese society generally: "Currently, the opportunities to be successful are the same for all people"; "In our country, hard work is always rewarded"; and "Whether a person gets rich or suffers poverty is his or her own responsibility." The familiar five categories ranging from strongly agree to strongly disagree were used to record responses, and the scale was based on a combination of responses to all three statements, so that a high score means disagreement with statements about favorable opportunities to get ahead in China today based on individual effort.[7] We refer to the resulting summary scale as lack of societal opportunity.

The final measure is intended to reflect feelings of pessimism or fatalism in regard to injustice issues. It is based on the following three statements, which again use the familiar five-category response scale from strongly agree to strongly disagree: "Since we are unable to change the status quo, discussing social justice is meaningless"; "Looking at things as they are now, it is very difficult to distinguish what is just and what is unjust"; and "Government officials don't care about what common people like me think." These items were reversed, so that high scores indicate strong agreement with each of the pessimistic views about social justice, and we refer to the resulting scale as feelings of injustice.[8]

Table 9.1 examines the intercorrelations among the three scales. We would expect to find significant positive correlations, and that is the case for two of the three associations. Individuals who are pessimistic about their chances for raising their standard of living also tend to be pessimistic about opportunities in Chinese society generally and to have strong feelings of injustice. However, the correlation between views on lack of societal opportunity and feelings of injustice is essentially zero.

In our examination of the social and geographical predictors of variations in these three measures of attitudes about opportunities and social justice, the same predictor variables and regression models are employed as in previous chapters. The results are displayed in Table 9.2. Several patterns are particularly notable. First, once again rural respondents, farmers in particular, are more likely to have positive views than most observers have assumed. On lack of societal opportunity and feelings of injustice, rural respondents are generally less angry and more optimistic than the comparison group, with farmers even more so than other rural groups. Even on the lack of individual opportunity scale, the views of rural respondents are no more likely to be critical than the views of the comparison group of unskilled and semiskilled urban workers.

A second striking pattern indicates that the most reliable guide for determining how likely an individual is to be optimistic about getting ahead in the future is how well the person says he or she is doing today as compared with the past. Responses to the question comparing the respondent's present situation to his or her situation five years earlier are very strongly correlated with faith in the existence of individual opportunities; together with the other subjective indicators in the final section of Table 9.2, they enable

TABLE 9.1
Correlations among opportunity and injustice measures

	Lack of individual opportunity	Lack of societal opportunity	Feelings of injustice
Lack of individual opportunity	1.00		
Lack of societal opportunity	.19***	1.00	
Feelings of injustice	.17***	–.01	1.00

*** $p \leq .001$

TABLE 9.2

Correlations and regressions of lack of opportunity and feelings of injustice

	Lack of individual opportunity			Lack of societal opportunity			Feelings of injustice		
	R	Model 1 Beta	Model 2 Beta	R	Model 1 Beta	Model 2 Beta	R	Model 1 Beta	Model 2 Beta
Objective: Occupation and residence									
Farmer	.03	-.02	-.01	-.17***	-.25***	-.25***	-.10***	-.22***	-.21***
Rural nonfarm	-.09***	-.02	-.02	-.02	-.10***	-.10***	-.03	-.06*	-.06*
Migrant	-.03	.01	.01	-.03	-.10***	-.10***	.05**	-.03	-.03
Rural others	-.00	-.02	-.02	-.05**	-.13***	-.14***	-.02	-.07**	-.06**
Urban others	.09***	.02	.02	.10***	-.07*	-.07*	.05**	-.03	-.03
Urban unemployed	.10***	.02	.02	.08***	-.03	-.03	.08***	-.03	-.02
Unskilled and semiskilled workers	.01	omitted	omitted	.12***	omitted	omitted	.06***	omitted	omitted
Skilled workers	.02	.02	.02	.03	-.04	-.05*	.04*	-.01	-.02
Self-employed	-.04**	-.01	-.01	.06***	-.00	-.00	.01	-.04	-.03
Routine nonmanual	-.05**	-.03	-.03	.07***	.00	-.00	-.01	-.04	-.04*
Professionals	-.08***	-.05**	-.05**	.04*	-.04	-.04	-.01	-.05*	-.05*
Managers and cadres	-.10***	-.06**	-.05**	-.01	-.04*	-.04	-.04*	-.06**	-.05**
Objective: Demographic and socioeconomic									
Female	.03	.02	.02	-.00	.02	.02	-.02	-.03	-.03
Age	.24***	.25*	.20	-.01	-.20	-.22	.06***	.47***	.41***
Age-squared/100	.23***	-.06	-.02	-.01	.22	.24	.05**	-.42***	-.37***
Years of education	-.15***	.05*	.04	.16***	.11***	.10***	-.01	.04	.02
Married	.06***	-.00	.00	-.08***	-.05*	-.04*	.04*	.02	.03
Han ethnicity	-.02	.01	.01	-.02	-.03	-.03	.03	.02	.02
Log of household income	-.19***	-.05*	-.05*	.08***	.04	.04	-.07***	-.10***	-.11***

	(1)	(2)	(3)	(4)	(5)	(6)	(7)	(8)	(9)
CCP member	-.02	-.01	-.00	.03	-.01	-.00	-.06**	-.07***	-.06**
SOE employed	.09***	.11***	.10***	.14***	.06**	.05**	.02	-.04	-.04
Access to unofficial information	-.19***	-.07***	-.08***	.01	-.09***	-.10***	-.05*	-.05*	-.05*
Objective: Geographic									
East region	-.09***	omitted	omitted	.01	omitted	omitted	-.07***	omitted	omitted
Central region	.05**	.06ns	-.02	-.02	-.06ns	-.07ns	.11***	.18*	.18*
West region	.06***	.12ns	.13ns	.01	-.01	-.01	-.05*	.18*	.19*
Distance to city	-.01	-.04	-.03	-.09***	-.00	.00	-.16***	-.17***	-.15***
Province marketization	-.00	.04	.04	-.04*	-.07ns	-.07ns	.04*	.14ns	.14ns
Subjective									
Five-year standard of living trend	-.44***	-.31***	-.31***	-.13***	-.07***	-.07***	-.13***	-.05**	-.04
Relative social status	-.34***	-.14***	-.14***	-.11***	-.12***	-.13***	-.09***	.01	.02
Bad experiences scale	.21***	.06**	.04***	.01	.01	.01	.12***	.10***	.08***
Unfair inequality scale	.13***		.10***	.11***		.06***	.25***	.10***	.20***
R-squared	.29	.29	.30	.09	.09	.10	.11	.11	.15

ns Coefficient no longer significant after correction for case clustering.

r=Bivariate correlation coefficients; beta are standardized regression coefficients from ordinary least squares regressions.

*.01 < p ≤ .05   **.001 < p ≤ .01   ***p ≤ .001

us to be much more successful in explaining variations in the lack of individual opportunity scale than in the models in any other table in this study (R-squared = .29–.30).

Before we control for other factors, it appears that people in low-status urban occupational categories share feelings of lack of individual opportunity, and that more high-status urbanites (and rural nonfarm workers) are optimistic. Once we control for other factors in our regression models, the only occupational categories with net differences of views from the comparison category of urban unskilled and semiskilled workers are the two highest-status urban categories, professionals and managers, both of which express more optimistic views about individual opportunities.

For the most part the correlations in the remaining three sections of Table 9.2 fit conventional expectations for the lack of individual opportunity measure, with more pessimism expressed by respondents who are older, less educated, married, have lower incomes, are or were employed in state-owned enterprises, have experienced declines in family living standards, perceive themselves as doing less well than others, have had multiple inequality-related bad experiences, and perceive the differences between who is rich and who is poor largely in terms of unfair structural factors.[9] These patterns are still visible when we control for other predictors in our regression equations, except for one unexpected reversal: With other background factors controlled for statistically, the years of education predictor reverses sign, indicating a net tendency of the highly educated to be slightly more pessimistic about individual opportunities for economic improvement. Since the best-educated respondents are even more likely to score high on the lack of societal opportunity scale (columns 4 through 6), we suspect that this finding is a reflection of the syndrome (familiar in other societies) of the best-educated being more critical of the social order than people with less education.

For the most part the lack of individual opportunity scale varies in expected ways, with higher percentages of the people we would expect to have worse prospects in the future expressing criticism, but with two primary exceptions: The best-educated also tend toward more pessimism on this measure even though they should be well-situated to take advantage of future opportunities,[10] and China's rural citizens, who would be expected to show pessimism, don't.

In examining the factors explaining variations in the lack of societal opportunity scale (columns 4 through 6), perhaps most dramatic are the low scores recorded by rural respondents. Before controlling for other factors, it appears that there is a fairly general pattern for rural respondents to be more optimistic and for urban respondents to be more pessimistic. However, once we control for other predictors, it is the comparison group of unskilled and semiskilled urban workers that stands out for high scores signaling pessimism, with urban skilled workers and urban others joining the rural groups in having significantly lower scores. All four rural categories show a net tendency to score lower than any urban group, with farmers most likely to have positive views. Despite their manifestly low social and economic status, China's farmers are more likely than any other occupational group to agree that "hard work is always rewarded" and that "becoming rich or staying poor is an individual's own responsibility." As we stressed repeatedly in this study, there is little sign in these figures of the "pitchfork anger of peasants" that recent press accounts see arising from China's growing inequality gaps.

In terms of objective demographic and socioeconomic predictors, we have already noted that those with the most schooling tend to score high on lack of societal opportunity, as do those who are not married, who are or were employed in state-owned enterprises, and who lack access to alternative and unofficial sources of information. There is also a sign of a tendency for more of the youngest and oldest respondents to score high on lack of societal opportunity than of middle-aged people, although the differences are not quite large enough to be statistically significant. None of the regression coefficients for the geographic predictors are statistically significant. Aside from the coefficients for education, it is hard to know what to make of this miscellany of associations.

We find expected patterns in the panel of subjective predictors, with respondents who say they are doing better than in the past and better compared to their neighbors scoring low on lack of societal opportunity, and those who rank high on the unfair inequality scale scoring high. Only the essentially zero coefficients for the bad experiences scale do not fit the expected pattern of association with high scores on lack of societal opportunity. So the most general patterns that emerge for the lack of societal opportunity scale are that urban occupational groups (particularly unskilled and semiskilled workers), the best educated, people who feel they have been doing poorly compared with the past or with their neighbors, and those who perceive the current patterns of who is rich and who is poor as unfair tend to score high on this scale, while China's farmers are particularly notable for their low scores and positive views about societal opportunities.

In columns 7 through 9 of Table 9.2 we examine the associations of our predictors with the feelings of injustice scale. As observed earlier, we see a variation on a familiar theme in the occupation and registration status categories. The most striking pattern, and the one that departs the most from the conventional view, is that farmers are the least likely of all the groups to have strong feelings of injustice. Before controlling for other factors, low-status urban groups in general, but also migrants, harbor the strongest feelings of injustice. When controlling for other predictors, the pattern changes slightly, and the groups can be roughly ranked as follows:

Strong Feeling of Injustice

⇑

Unskilled and semiskilled workers

⇑

Other low-status urban groups, rural migrants

⇑

Other rural groups, high-status urban groups

⇑

Farmers

⇑

Weak Feelings of Injustice

It is striking that farmers stand out as the category least likely to express negative sentiments about the current social order, in this case as reflected by their scores on the feelings of injustice scale.

In terms of demographic and socioeconomic predictors of scores on feelings of injustice, we see a tendency for those with high incomes, who are members of the Chinese Communist Party, who are or were employed by state-owned enterprises, and who have high levels of access to unofficial communications to have low feelings of injustice.[11] Among these findings, the net association with employment in SOEs is unexpected, although perhaps the structured lives of such employees tend to inhibit expressing feelings of injustice. However, the most dramatic pattern in the second section of the table is the curvilinear association between age and feelings of injustice. The significant positive association with age, and the significant negative association with age-squared, indicate that middle-aged respondents are more likely than younger or older ones to express strong feelings of injustice. We have seen this pattern before (for example, in the associations with the unfair inequality scale in Table 6.2), but the coefficients are stronger here. These associations of age cohorts with feelings of injustice might be interpreted as reflecting the lost generation status of those who are middle-aged, whose lives and opportunities were most disrupted by the Cultural Revolution. However, we haven't found the middle-aged to be critical across the board in Chapters 6 through 9, and we saw a weak tendency for fewer of the middle-aged than either younger or older respondents to be critical in responses to the lack of societal opportunity scale.

The regression coefficients in the geographic predictor panel indicate that respondents in both central and western provinces display a net tendency to have stronger feelings of injustice than do respondents in the eastern provinces.[12] As we have observed before, interpretation of this pattern is complicated by the somewhat inconsistent patterns displayed for the other two geographic predictors: More respondents from highly marketized provinces also express strong feelings of injustice (although not enough for the difference to be statistically significant), and significantly more respondents who live far from any city express weak feelings of injustice. Therefore these complex patterns can't be interpreted simply as a tendency for those in less favored locales to have stronger feelings of injustice.

Finally, before we control for other factors, the pattern of associations of the subjective predictors with feelings of injustice fits conventional expectations, with those who feel they are doing well compared with the past and compared with peers expressing fewer feelings of injustice, and those who have had bad inequality-related experiences and who score high on unfair inequality expressing more. Once we control for other predictors, the first two associations are weakened substantially, and the associations between feelings of injustice and both bad experiences and unfair inequality mainly stand out.[13]

In sum, critical attitudes on feelings of injustice are expressed mostly by the middle-aged and by those in low-status urban occupations, who reside in or near urban areas away from China's coast, who have low incomes, who have had bad inequality-related experiences, and who view the current pattern of who is rich and who is poor as unfair. It is once again striking that China's farmers are less likely than any other group to express feelings of injustice.

CONCLUSIONS

In this chapter we have reviewed China's experience in creating (or failing to create) opportunities for Chinese citizens to improve their standards of living and social status. Chinese socialism made a strong start in this realm during the 1950s, but then failed to live up to early expectations, producing strong popular anxieties about simply maintaining living standards during the 1960s and 1970s, without much hope for upward social mobility. Given China's strong historical tradition of honoring self-improvement and family advancement to wealth and power, the unrewarding social order that existed for most of the 1958–78 period likely provided a wellspring of frustrated aspirations that contributed to the sense of crisis after Mao's death that convinced Deng Xiaoping and other reformers that drastic changes were needed.[14]

The changes produced by the reforms have been dramatic. Most Chinese have improved their standards of living, diet, and material possessions substantially, and some have become fabulously wealthy. Although China's economic growth has continued to race ahead (at least until recently), the implications for mobility opportunities have to some extent changed over time. As noted earlier, the early years of the reforms have been characterized as a period of reform without losers because popular living standards had been so depressed and personal incomes, access to consumer goods, and most other indicators improved so rapidly. Since the mid-1990s darker clouds have appeared. Average personal incomes have continued to rise, and urban residents have been given ownership rights to their housing, but the state's determination to reform the inefficient state-owned enterprise system and to smash the iron rice bowl of guaranteed jobs and benefits enjoyed by those employed in that sector has produced downward mobility into unemployment and poverty to go along with increased upward mobility opportunities. The phrase "reform without losers" no longer fits the situation in China after the mid-1990s.

Despite these more mixed recent trends, we saw in Chapters 3 and 4 that in many respects our Chinese survey respondents remain optimistic that they and other Chinese will be able to improve their standards of living in years ahead through old-fashioned hard work and individual and family effort. Their views on general questions about social justice are more mixed, but compared to citizens in other societies Chinese citizens still seem unusually optimistic. Despite China's inability to sustain reform without losers, the fairly positive views about opportunities for upward mobility and about social justice likely contribute an important source of stability to the current system. We didn't see any evidence in Chapters 3 and 4 of widespread feelings that opportunities for upward mobility are lacking.

Variations in the attitudes of our respondents toward upward mobility and social justice present a mixed and not altogether consistent picture, but one that does not suggest a threat to China's political stability. It is true that, as in earlier chapters, more of the best-educated Chinese have critical attitudes toward some of the measures examined here than do other people, so some concern about the views of China's best and brightest citizens is warranted. In general critical attitudes are expressed by low-status and disadvantaged urban groups, but positive views are expressed by both high-status urban groups and by rural residents. It is again striking that, on two of our three measures, farmers stand out as the group least likely to express critical and fatalistic views. People living in the central and western provinces (for feelings of injustice), those who report they are not doing as well in the past or as their peers, those who view the current patterns of who is rich and who is poor as unfair, those who lack access to unofficial sources of information, and perhaps those who are middle-aged (for feelings of injustice) or are older in general (for lack of individual opportunity) are more likely to express critical attitudes on opportunity and social justice issues than are others (although not all of the associations are statistically significant). However, these disparate patterns still do not demonstrate that particular groups and locales depart from the general consensus by being angry and pessimistic about these issues. The patterns that do emerge in many ways contradict the conventional wisdom—for example, with anger more likely in low-status urban groups in interior cities rather than in the countryside.

In the concluding chapter of this study we put the findings of this chapter together with those of the three that preceded it. Our goal is not only to present a broader summary of the survey results, but also to move toward a more coherent explanation of the complex and often unexpected findings reported in these pages.

Conclusion: Beyond the Myth of the Social Volcano

In the last thirty years China has undergone momentous changes. It is not misleading to characterize these changes as the People's Republic of China's second social revolution, equal in scope and impact on the lives of its citizens to the socialist transformation that occurred during the 1950s. In many respects the economic reforms that provided the motor for these changes have been successful, producing impressive and sustained economic growth rates and major improvements on virtually all measures of development. However, the study reported in these pages was stimulated by one major social trend that many see as more worrisome—dramatic increases in social inequality. As discussed throughout this book, in the last decade or so it has become conventional to assert that ordinary Chinese citizens are increasingly angry about rising inequality and that their anger might eventually erupt in a social volcano of widespread protests against the distributive injustices unleashed by market reforms and hectic economic growth. This study, based on the first systematic nationwide sample survey of popular Chinese attitudes toward inequality trends and distributive injustice issues, was designed to critically examine the conventional wisdom. In this closing chapter we briefly summarize our results and discuss how to explain the predominantly positive and optimistic view of Chinese citizens about current inequalities, and we will also ponder the implications of our findings for China's future social and political stability.

As will be obvious to the reader by now, our survey data indicate that the conventional wisdom is misleading or simply wrong in most respects. In briefly reviewing our findings here, it is useful to answer the major research questions that guided the study.

1. In general how angry or accepting are ordinary Chinese about current patterns of inequality in their society?

There is no simple answer to this question. We posed many different questions about inequality and distributive injustice issues, and the answers from survey respondents varied for each question, and from one question to another (as discussed in Chapter 3). On balance, though, it is striking that most survey respondents voiced more acceptance than anger about current inequalities. To be sure, most respondents felt that the gap in incomes nationwide was too large, and they objected to some other aspects of current inequalities, such as the practice of laying off state factory workers in order to cut costs and the systematic discrimination faced by urban migrants. However, the prevailing view is that, despite some unjust features and practices, overall patterns of inequality in China today are fair enough to enable ordinary citizens to get ahead and prosper based on hard work, talent, and training. Our data show little support for the notion that Chinese citizens reject as unfair the new market principles and practices within which they have to operate, or that they harbor nostalgia for the distribution principles and practices of the previous socialist system.[1] Still less do we find signs of the widespread feelings of outrage that one of the opening epigraphs, from *New York Times* reporter Joseph Kahn (2006), claimed is provoked by current wealth gaps. Some Chinese are angry and upset about particular features of current inequalities, but generally these are minority sentiments, not the prevailing popular view.

2. Which features of current inequality patterns are Chinese citizens most angry about, and which do they view in a positive light?

As summarized in previous chapters, most Chinese citizens have accepted a set of distribution principles that have more in common with a liberal capitalist welfare state than with either an egalitarian socialist system or unbridled capitalism. Most approve of rich people being able to use their wealth to provide better lives for their families, and they don't favor systematic redistribution from the rich to the poor or limits on the maximum income people can earn. In part these attitudes are grounded in the perception that the most important factors distinguishing the rich from the poor in China today are talent, training, and hard work, rather than dishonesty, unfairness in the distribution of opportunities, or other non-merit factors. So Joseph Kahn's assertion (2006) that "many people believe that wealth flows from access to power more than it does from talent and risk-taking" is contradicted by our survey evidence. If wealth in China today is generally earned by merit and is therefore deserved, it probably shouldn't be limited or redistributed away to others. However, most survey respondents do favor other types of measures to reduce inequality through government interventions to combat the inegalitarian consequences of market competition—for example, giving extra help to the disadvantaged so that they can compete and guaranteeing jobs and minimum income levels to the poor. In other words, Chinese today are egalitarians to the same extent as citizens of most modern societies, favoring certain affirmative action efforts to ameliorate persistent poverty and disadvantage. They favor equality pursued by leveling up even as they disapprove of equality pursued by leveling down. As noted in Chapter 1, this is very different from the egalitarianism of the late Mao era, in which all advantages and displays of differentiation from ordinary workers and peasants were discouraged.

The general popular approval of meritocratic competition in the market and of affirmative action to help the poor also means that when Chinese citizens see features of current inequality patterns that deviate from these principles, they view them as unjust and get angry. There are two particular examples of this tendency in our data, both of which involve the persistence in the reform era of practices with roots in the socialist era. Most respondents object to special privileges for people in political power and to the systematic discrimination experienced by urban migrants. In other words, it is striking that the strongest objections are raised about socialist-era practices, not about new inequalities spawned by market reforms. Most Chinese citizens have accepted and seem to be comfortable operating within the market system that the reforms have created. We might even speculate that the severe form of socialism imposed by Mao and his radical colleagues during the Cultural Revolution era (with all material incentives essentially abolished) produced negative reactions that have made the popular acceptance of the differentials and inequalities of today's China more palatable. However, this acceptance comes with an important qualification. Chinese citizens accept current inequalities because they believe that for the most part they fairly reflect the differential efforts and merits of individuals and families who are competing in the marketplace created by the post-1978 reforms. If their perceptions change and if large numbers begin to feel that the rules of the inequality game are stacked against them, with benefits mostly monopolized by the rich and powerful, popular outrage and resentment will likely break to the surface. However, there were no signs of this happening when the survey was administered in 2004.

We are suggesting that the trends in China fit a pattern of tolerance for inequalities in the course of economic development that Albert Hirschman described as the "tunnel effect" (Hirschman and Rothschild 1973). The analogy is with lanes of drivers stuck in a tunnel. If one lane starts to move after an irritatingly long time, drivers in the other lanes will feel relieved, not angry. They will interpret the good fortune of drivers in the freed lane as something they will soon share. However, if after another irritatingly long period only that single lane is moving, drivers in the other lanes may become apoplectic. The critical issue for China is whether the current situation in which citizens see rising inequality as representing new opportunities rather than injustice will be sustained.

3. Compared to citizens in other societies, are Chinese more or less angry about current inequalities in general, and about particular features of current inequality patterns?

Chapter 4 compared Chinese responses to questions about inequality and distributive injustice issues to survey data from other post-socialist transition societies in Eastern Europe as well as from selected advanced capitalist countries. This is obviously not as systematic a comparison with other societies as would be desirable, and we are also hampered by the fact that some of our comparison surveys were conducted in the 1990s. Despite these limitations, it is nonetheless striking that the comparisons reinforce conclusions about Chinese citizens' general acceptance of current patterns of inequality. Even the pattern of more than 70 percent of those surveyed perceiving income gaps in China as too large turns out to be a moderate amount of disapproval in comparative terms; more than 90 percent of respondents in some East European countries say that income gaps in their countries are too large. On very few questions are Chinese more critical than citizens in the other countries used in our comparison, and on many questions Chinese views are more positive or approving (see the summary in Table 4.7).

In some cases Chinese views are more positive than views in most East European countries, although not very different from the sentiments of citizens in advanced capitalist societies. In other cases Chinese citizens are even more positive than are citizens in the advanced capitalist societies included in the comparison—the United States, the United Kingdom, West Germany, and Japan. For example, Chinese are substantially more optimistic about the chances for ordinary citizens to improve their livelihoods, about the likelihood of the proportion of rich people increasing, and about the proposition that hard work is always rewarded, and they are also much more likely to feel that talent and hard work are primary explanations of why some people are rich and others are poor. In other words, there is little evidence that most Chinese harbor misgivings and anger about the market society in which they have to operate, and in some respects they are even more bullish about their market-based economy than are citizens of the most advanced capitalist societies. Given the radical socialist ideology that Mao tried to instill in the population, these accepting attitudes represent an extraordinary change.

Our survey findings conflict with the conventional wisdom about rising anger over inequality issues in China, but they coincide with the results of other recent research on Chinese public opinion. A 2007 Pew Foundation comparative survey of a substantially larger sample of forty-seven countries found that Chinese survey respondents are perhaps the world's greatest optimists (Pew Global Attitudes Project 2007). About 62 percent of Chinese said that they were better off than five years earlier (the comparable figure from our 2004 survey is 63.9 percent), and a stunning 86 percent said that they believed the next generation would be even better off than they were (we did not ask this question). This figure is higher than in any of the other countries surveyed by the Pew researchers, using a sample that included all regions of the world and both developing and developed societies. The Pew Foundation survey findings have been met with some disbelief as well as with questions about whether the fact that China is still ruled by the Communist Party inevitably produced a positive bias. Later in this chapter we again discuss the issue of the validity of our survey findings and our reasons for discounting the possibility (in the Pew survey and in ours) that such positive views can be dismissed as the product of political pressures or biases.

4. Within China in which social groups and in which local areas is there the most anger about inequality and distributive injustice issues?

Answering this question is complex, in part because there are many different attitudes and attitude scales involved, rather than a single or simple summary measure of anger about inequality and distributive injustice. In Chapters 6 through 9 we examined a wide range of indicators in an effort to determine the social contours of discontent about current inequalities in China. In all we examined and analyzed variations within our sample on twelve different measures of critical attitudes about current inequalities: excess inequality, harmful inequality, and unfair inequality in Chapter 6; prefer equality and prefer government leveling in Chapter 7; anti-hukou bias, anti-leader privilege, anti-rich transmit status, and inequality conflicts in Chapter 8; and lack of individual opportunity, lack of societal opportunity, and feelings of injustice in Chapter 9.[2] A summary of findings regarding the social contours of variation in these twelve measures is presented in Table C.1. In the cells of that table, a plus sign indicates a significant positive regression coefficient between the inequality scale in question and that respondent background characteristic—in other words, a net tendency for the background trait in question to be associated with more-critical attitudes on that inequality measure. Likewise, a minus sign indicates a significant and negative regression coefficient between that inequality measure and the social background trait in question—a net tendency for the background trait to be associated with less-critical attitudes toward that aspect of inequality. Blank cells indicate that the regression coefficients in question were not statistically significant.

Because the patterns shown in Table C.1 are simply a summary of the results reported earlier in Chapters 6 through 9, we highlight only a few overall patterns here. First, there are considerable differences in the patterns

TABLE C.I
Summary of critical attitudes about inequality

	Chapter 6			Chapter 7	
	Excessive inequality	*Harmful inequality*	*Unfair inequality*	*Prefer equality*	*Government leveling*
Objective: Occupation and residential					
Farmer	−	−	−	+	−
Rural nonfarm	−	−			−
Migrant	+				
Rural others	−	−		+	−
Urban others					
Urban unemployed					+
Unskilled and semi-skilled worker	+	+	+	−	+
Skilled worker					
Self-employed					
Routine nonmanual					
Professional					
Manager and cadre					
Objective: Demographic and socioeconomic					
Female					−
Age					
Age-squared/100					
Years of education	+	+	+	−	+
Married					
Han ethnicity	+				+
Log household income					
CCP member		−			+
SOE employed	+			−	
Access to unofficial information	−				
Objective: Geographic					
East region					
Central region					
West region					
Distance to city	+	−		−	+
Province marketization					
Subjective					
Five-year standard of living trend		−	−		+
Relative social status	−		−		−
Bad experience scale	+	+	+	+	+
Unfair inequality scale	n.a.	n.a.	n.a.		+
R-squared	.10	.11	.08	.08	.15

Note: Cell entries are based on regression coefficient significance levels and inferred from the other coefficients in the case of omitted comparison groups. Blank cells mean that none of the models had significant regression coefficients.

− = Significantly less likely to express the critical attitude regarding inequality patterns.

+ = Significantly more likely to express the critical attitude regarding inequality patterns.

n.a. = Not applicable.

	Chapter 8			Chapter 9		
Anti-hukou bias	Anti-leader privilege	Anti-rich transmit status	Inequality conflicts	Lack of individual opportunity	Lack of societal opportunity	Feelings of injustice
+					−	−
			−		−	−
+					−	
			−		−	−
		−			−	
		−	−			
−		+	+	+	+	+
					−	
			−			−
+				−		−
			−	−		−
			+			
		−		+		+
		+				−
+	+			+	+	
					−	
+		−				
				−		−
						−
				+	+	−
−	−	−	+	−	−	−
		+				−
		−				+
						+
+						−
			−			
				−	−	−
	−	−	−	−	−	−
	−			+		+
			+	+	+	+
.06	.03	.04	.06	.30	.10	.15

of predictors of critical attitudes toward inequality across the twelve scales. This inconsistent pattern means that in general respondents do not have uniform attitudes toward different aspects of inequality. Instead, a particular background trait may be associated with critical attitudes on inequality measure X and with accepting attitudes on inequality measure Y. So any attempt to assess how angry particular kinds of Chinese citizens are about current inequality patterns needs to be precise about the aspect of inequality involved. As noted earlier, the fact that feelings of anger regarding current inequality are not concentrated in a particular social group or locale is another strong indicator that the social volcano scenario is a myth.

Despite considerable variations in the social contours of inequality attitudes across the twelve measures used in this study, some relatively consistent patterns emerge. For the most part these patterns contradict the conventional wisdom, as noted in earlier chapters. It is common to assume that respondents in groups and locations that have low status or have lost out in competition for the benefits of China's reforms are angry, while those with high status and those who have benefited disproportionately from the reforms are satisfied with current inequality patterns. We find, in contrast, that current objective status is a very poor guide to inequality attitudes.

China today, as in the Mao era, is notable for the wide status and income gaps between city and countryside (Wang 2005; Khan and Riskin 2005; Gustafsson, Li, and Sicular 2008). However, in examining the top section in Table C.1 we see that where there are differences, generally rural groups (except migrants) are significantly less likely than the comparison group of urban unskilled and semiskilled workers to have critical attitudes toward many of the aspects of inequality we examined in this study.[3] In general more urban occupational groups express critical attitudes than do rural groups on most of our inequality measures, and in some instances more of the urban unskilled and semiskilled workers are critical than are some other urban occupational groups. Even within urban areas it is not the lowest-status group (the urban unemployed) who are most likely to express critical attitudes, and on most inequality measures the highest-status urban occupational groups (professionals, managers, and administrative cadres) are not significantly less likely to be critical than the comparison group of unskilled and semiskilled workers.[4] In short, anger about current inequalities cannot be predicted from objective occupational categories. However, in many but not all instances, rural citizens are less likely to be critical about current inequalities than their urban counterparts, despite the many disadvantages they continue to suffer.

In the second section of the table, which concerns other objective demographic and socioeconomic characteristics of survey respondents, we see a pattern of the most highly educated respondents holding significantly more critical opinions than others about many, although not all, aspects of current inequalities. As noted earlier, although this pattern also contradicts the conventional expectation that high status is associated with fewer critical attitudes, it does resonate with a substantial amount of research in Western societies, where prior studies suggest that the highly educated around the world tend to be especially sensitive to and concerned about inequality issues.

The other fairly consistent pattern in this section has been noted repeatedly as more of a surprise. There is a general tendency for fewer respondents who have access to a wide variety of sources of information that make them less dependent than others on the official media to be critical about many (but again not all) aspects of current inequalities. As discussed earlier in this book, we designed the set of questions concerning access to unofficial information with the expectation that individuals who score high on these measures will have more critical attitudes than will others. This assumption was based on the fact that China's political system is still highly authoritarian, with the Chinese Communist Party (CCP) exercising fairly tight control over the media and using that control to regularly and forcefully communicate the message that the current social order is fair and is worthy of popular support. Given this context, many observers have assumed that access to information from outside of China, access to the Internet, and other practices that reduce dependency on the official media foster more-critical views about the state of Chinese society. However, in our survey data we find the opposite pattern, with people with access to unofficial sources of information being less critical of current patterns of inequality. Why this should be the case is something of a puzzle, although some recent analyses of China suggest that savvy young people who are well-connected to the Internet and other alternative sources of information in general tend to be fierce nationalists rather than critics of the status quo (for example, Osnos 2008).[5]

It is also worth noting patterns we don't see in this second section of Table C.1. In much previous research on social mobility and access to valuable resources in China (such as housing), family income and Communist Party membership tend to be important predictors, leading to a view that possession of some material and political advantages tends to promote success in gaining other advantages, as is the case in other societies. However, we find that family income and membership in the Chinese Communist Party are relatively unimportant predictors of attitudes toward our various inequality attitudes. Party members and people with high incomes don't show much sign of being more accepting than others of current inequality patterns. Once again this pattern contradicts the conventional view that having an advantaged status in China fosters acceptance of the status quo.

Combining the patterns in the first two sections of Table C.1, we see some evidence that differential responses to current inequalities are linked to status positions in the previous socialist system. Urbanites in general, the well-educated, and in some instances members of the Han ethnic group and those with links to state-owned enterprises tend to have critical attitudes toward some aspects of current inequalities and would like the government to do more to limit inequalities. In contrast, rural people in general (with the partial exception of migrants) and farmers in particular, even though they are at the bottom of the status hierarchy, are less likely to be critical of current inequalities and are also less likely to favor state intervention to promote greater equality. As suggested in earlier chapters, this pattern may be interpreted as showing that those who were favored in the socialist system—"supplicants to the socialist state" (Davis 1993)—are likely to regret the loss of their favored positions that occurred with market reforms and to want the state to make greater efforts to limit current inequalities. Those at the bottom of society, China's farmers, who were systematically disadvantaged under the socialist order, see more potential for gain based on market competition and have little inclination to trust the government to manage the stratification order today.

The patterns for the various geographic predictors displayed in the third section of Table C.1 appear somewhat contradictory and difficult to interpret. Most of the regression coefficients for geographic measures are not statistically significant, and there are about as many negative as positive associations among coefficients that are significant. Whatever we make of these patterns, they once again contradict the conventional view that critical attitudes toward current inequalities are consistently found among those in the most disadvantaged locations.

The conventional view finds support only in the final section of Table C.1, which summarizes the associations of inequality attitudes with several subjective indicators. Here we find some tendency for fewer of those who report that their standards of living have improved compared to five years earlier and of those who have high social status relative to their local reference groups to be critical than are other people, and for more of those who have had bad inequality-related personal or family experiences during the last three years or who feel that the differences between who is rich and who is poor are attributable primarily to unfairness to express critical attitudes, although not all the associations are consistent and statistically significant. In a sense, respondents who feel they are winners in the highly competitive and unequal society that China has become tend to view current inequalities more positively than do those who feel they are losers, but such feelings vary within any social group or geographical locale and cannot be predicted or assumed based on the objective social status characteristics of respondents, such as their incomes or their membership in the CCP.

To sum up, our survey data indicate that despite considerable variation, there are some modestly consistent patterns in the social contours of feelings about inequality and distributive injustice issues. For example, there is a tendency to find accepting views about current inequalities among Chinese living in rural areas (farmers in particular), among those with high access to unofficial sources of information, and among those who subjectively report that their lives have improved and that they are now better off than the people with whom they compare themselves. There also is a general tendency for the highly educated, those in low-status urban occupations, and those who have had bad recent personal or family experiences related to inequality to be more angry about these issues. These patterns are modest at best (as shown by the modest sizes of most statistical coefficients and of the summary R-squared statistics at the bottom of Table C.1), and they don't provide a clear or consistent picture of where anger about current inequalities is concentrated. The dominant tendency is for Chinese citizens to broadly accept current inequalities, with anger fairly broadly dispersed across the social landscape rather than heavily concentrated in particular groups or geographic locations.

VALIDITY OF THE FINDINGS

What if our survey data are wrong, and not the conventional wisdom? Two tendencies can undermine the validity of our findings: survey bias and false consciousness. *Survey bias* refers to a possibility that in the still tightly controlled political system of China, respondents may be afraid to reveal critical attitudes and will instead answer questions with more positive views than they really feel. *False consciousness* refers to the possibility that, given the CCP's near monopoly control over the mass media and other means of communication, the authorities may succeed in getting respondents to have positive feelings about current inequalities (and to convey such feelings in answers to survey questions), even though in terms of their actual situations they might be expected to have critical attitudes.[6] Both mechanisms make it possible that the responses in surveys such as ours may be tilted in a positive direction, although strictly speaking only survey bias challenges the validity of the data. If false consciousness is operating, our survey may accurately report what respondents are feeling, but those feelings may be tilted positively by the influences of the political system on the lives of the respondents.

Questions of bias are an issue in surveys in any society, although perhaps more so in China, given the nature of the political system there. In any society it is difficult to assess whether or how seriously biases may be affecting survey data. We don't think these are serious threats to the accuracy of the data and conclusions from the 2004 China inequality and distributive justice survey. To reiterate themes discussed in Chapter 2, the methods we employed and the pattern of survey results provide reassurance.

First, our methods employed best practices designed to obtain accurate and unbiased responses to survey questions. The questions were carefully designed to avoid indicating which responses were expected or desired, and respondents were reassured in advance about the academic purposes of the survey, the voluntary nature of interview participation, the confidentiality of their answers, and the lack of any connection with a Chinese government agency. Also, respondents were interviewed by locally recruited and trained interviewers (mainly students from local colleges in each region) without any indication that foreigners were involved.

Surveys are now increasingly familiar in Chinese society, and it seems unlikely that respondents would have been afraid to state their honest opinions. One of the notable changes in China over the last thirty years has been the transformation of the political atmosphere and the loosening of political controls, even though the Chinese Communist Party remains in charge. In the late Mao era political controls were so tight, and fear about getting in trouble for a chance remark so strong, that it would have been impossible to conduct a survey such as ours. The situation has changed so much that Chinese citizens generally feel safe expressing a variety of critical attitudes privately and even in conversations with strangers, even though they know it is still dangerous to voice highly critical opinions publicly. In this context, the standard survey methods we employed seemed sufficient to reassure respondents that they didn't need to tilt their answers in a pro-government direction.[7]

The patterns in the survey data provide a second level of reassurance. Even though the majority of Chinese citizens gave fairly positive and optimistic answers to many questions, they were quite critical in response to certain specific questions —for example, by saying there is too much inequality in China today, that inequality poses a threat to stability, that those in power should not be given special privileges, that it is unjust to dismiss workers in order to reform factories, and that systematic discrimination against urban migrants is unfair. Furthermore, 27 percent of Chinese respondents said that they or members of their families had experienced unjust treatment by local officials within the past three years.[8] Although we lack comparative data that would enable us to put this figure in context, such a substantial number belies the idea that respondents were constrained by Chinese politics to give Pollyanna responses. Overall, survey responses ranged from highly accepting to quite critical, rather than being consistently favorable to the views and policies of the Chinese government.

Patterns such as the greater acceptance of current inequalities by farmers and the greater anger of the well-educated might be considered an indication of the operation of false consciousness. However, we are reassured because fewer respondents with the most access to unofficial sources of information, who presumably should be most immune to false consciousness promoted by government propaganda, in fact tended to have critical attitudes toward current inequalities than did other respondents. The data do not show a consistent pattern suggesting that acceptance of current inequalities can be explained by ignorance about how bad and unfair those inequalities are.

A final consideration that leads us to trust our data lies in the extent to which our understanding of trends in Chinese society over time is consistent with the survey results. That is the topic of the following section of this chapter.

INTERPRETATIONS

Why are the Chinese citizens we surveyed much more accepting of than angry about most aspects of current inequality patterns? In particular, why are members of some of the most disadvantaged groups, particularly farmers, more accepting of and less angry about distributive injustice issues than their more advantaged counterparts? Why is the conventional wisdom on these issues so wrong? Changes in China in the last several decades help explain the general acceptance and optimism of ordinary citizens about current inequalities.

The conventional view is based on a set of generalizations and causal assumptions in which late-Mao-era social patterns are believed to have been relatively egalitarian and to have provided substantial security of employment, incomes, and public goods for Chinese citizens, despite the lack of opportunity for migration, job changes, upward social mobility, and other individually initiated actions. The reform-era changes, in particular the switch from socialist allocation to market competition, are seen as increasing the opportunities for individually initiated changes and upward social mobility, but as undermining the equality and security of Chinese citizens. The conventional wisdom assumes that some individuals feel grateful for the material improvements in their lives, while others are angry about the loss of the equality and security that socialism used to provide.

It is our contention that this conventional story is highly oversimplified and distorted. Socialism did provide a fair amount of equality and security within favored urban work organizations. However, even in cities there were multiple grounds for dissatisfaction with material life under socialism—with sharp differences in the material conditions of people employed in different work units and in different cities, with largely fixed incomes and increasing consumer scarcities, and with bureaucratic allocation that provided the highly ranked and powerful with special goods and services that were out of reach for ordinary urbanites. Chinese socialism in the 1960s and 1970s produced a social order that was highly inequitable, in that individuals who acquired more training, worked harder, produced more output, and made innovations were not rewarded for their contributions, even while those most deft at demonstrating political loyalty might earn promotions (Shirk 1984).

Rural residents faced an even more unrewarding social system in the communes, experiencing quasi-feudal bondage to their villages and mandatory grain cultivation without the kinds of income and other security enjoyed by members of the urban workforce. Commune members for the most part could compete with their neighbors only to earn more work points and thus a larger relative share of the local income pot (which was not supported by the state, and might well be dwindling, producing egalitarian impoverishment), and they were not able to do any of the other things villagers had done over the centuries to survive and improve their lot, such as engaging in handicraft production and commerce or seeking their fortunes elsewhere. At the extreme, in the Great Leap Forward that occurred forty-five years before our survey, millions of Chinese rural residents shared the egalitarian fate of dying in a mass famine (see Yang 1996; Thaxton 2008). As in the cities, there was a fair amount of economic equality within any one production team, but there were large income differences across villages and regions that the state did nothing to counteract, and the enforced equality within localities was as inequitable as it was for urban citizens. The extreme rigidities of the socialism that existed in China in the wake of the Cultural Revolution, and the emphasis on equality pursued by Mao and his radical colleagues through unpopular leveling-down policies, produced strong grounds for feelings of distributive injustice before the launching of market reforms in 1978. This is not a story of today's inequality and distributive injustice replacing socialist equality and distributive justice.

Viewed in this light, it is not just the extraordinary rate of economic growth, the rise in average living standards, and the increased chances for upward mobility unleashed by the reforms that produce positive feelings among Chinese citizens; to a considerable extent, many (but obviously not all) aspects of the increased inequalities in China today also foster popular approval.[9] Deng Xiaoping and his reformist colleagues argued that the kind of socialism Mao promoted was unjust because it didn't properly reward differential talents and contributions, and that a social order based on market competition would produce fairer results. Our survey indicates that most Chinese agree with Deng's view. Chinese who were stuck for years in the various bureaucratic niches of Mao-era socialism now have new options and possibilities. Even though leaving their niches to engage in market competition and mobility introduces new risks and dangers, in many cases exit provides the potential for major improvements in incomes and consumption patterns.

Given China's extraordinary economic growth, many more Chinese have experienced material gains than have suffered losses. One indicator is provided by the five-year standard-of-living trend question used as a subjective predictor in Chapters 6 through 9. In response to a question asking them to compare their family's living standard in 2004 with that of five years earlier, 63.9 percent of respondents said it was somewhat or much better, 29.3 percent said it was about the same, and only 7.5 percent said that it was somewhat or much worse. Although China's rising tide is not lifting all boats, it is lifting enough of them, and rapidly enough, to inspire confidence even among those who are not doing so well.

It seems likely that today's patterns of inequality remind many Chinese, particularly those in the older generation, of patterns from before 1949. If that is the case, current inequalities may be interpreted by some respondents as a return to a normal historical situation of high inequality tempered by high social and geographic mobility, after the socialist interlude of abnormal restrictions on both inequality and mobility.[10] A social order with huge gaps between rich and poor, few caste-like barriers to upward mobility, a stress on education as the route to advancement, and a strong expectation that the government will monitor and maintain the fairness of economic competition is a legacy that goes back many centuries. Chinese citizens exist in a more competitive market environment today, but they can make more decisions for themselves and their families with some hope of succeeding, and they are no longer so dependent on the bureaucratic gatekeepers of the prior socialist order. So it is not just China's booming growth that fosters positive attitudes, but also the possibilities that current inequalities provide and how they contrast with the rigidities that characterized Chinese socialism. We started this project by assuming that our focus should be on determining how Chinese citizens weigh the balance between the positive factor of general income gains against the negative factor of increased inequality. However, based on our survey results, it now seems more appropriate to consider Chinese citizens viewing both increased incomes and wider (but more equitable) inequalities as positive trends.

How can we explain not just the general acceptance of current patterns of inequality, but also the contours of variations in inequality attitudes across the Chinese social landscape? In responding to this question, we focus on the puzzle of the positive attitudes of China's rural residents, and of farmers in particular, compared to the attitudes of urbanites. Why is it that, despite remaining pretty much at the bottom of China's social hierarchy, farmers are more likely than others to see current inequalities as fair? Where is the "pitchfork anger of peasants" mentioned in recent press reports (Time Asia 2006)?

The importance of subjective factors in shaping inequality attitudes, as discussed in regard to the patterns in Table C.1, may help to explain this counterintuitive finding. Reform-era changes have opened new possibilities for economic improvement that were denied villagers during the collective era. Farmers are no longer locked into a form of socialist serfdom as members of communes. Given the rigidity of controls over their lives in the collective era, in a sense China's farmers had nowhere to go but up, and they have been liberated by market reforms. They can now contemplate possibilities beyond staying put and growing grain—for example, cultivating specialized crops, obtaining work in a rural factory or construction team, making and trading household handicrafts, engaging in rural and rural-to-urban commerce, migrating to the city in search of work, and starting a private business. Even though variable access to and success at pursuing these opportunities has led to increased inequality, when farmers form their attitudes about the fairness of the current social order, they are most likely to be influenced by the inequalities in their local communities rather than by the opulent lives of new millionaires who live in distant cities. As shown in Figure 3.1a, most respondents see the inequalities in their local communities as appropriate rather than excessive. In this regard, the subjective influence of comparisons with the past and with local reference groups may explain why farmers have more positive attitudes than we might expect. Perhaps recent reductions in rural taxes and fees also contribute to improved feelings about the current system. We inquired about the tax and fee burden elsewhere in our questionnaire, and more than 70 percent of rural respondents reported that the amount they had to pay had decreased over the three years prior to our survey. A final influence on the inequality attitudes of the rural population is our earlier observation that they were more victims of the socialist state than successful supplicants to it, and that experience seems to have left a legacy of preferences for competition in revived markets without strong desires for the government to intervene and engage in redistributive policies.

We don't mean to imply that China's farmers have no grounds for anger about their situation, only that such anger is not based primarily on perceptions that current inequalities are excessive and unfair. Most rural protest incidents in recent years have involved procedural injustices rather than distributive injustice—for example, the unfair burden of rural taxes and fees until recently, inability to block nearby enterprises from emitting contaminating pollution, or the confiscation of village land for development without proper consultation or compensation (see Bernstein and Lu 2003; O'Brien and Li 2006). Nor are we saying that China's rural residents are generally happy about their lives or that reports of peasant anger are inaccurate. Our survey focus is inequality and distributive injustice, and we are simply concluding that, insofar as rural residents in China today are angry, widening inequalities since 1978 are not a prime factor provoking such feelings. Such inequalities may be viewed as symbolic more of enhanced opportunities than of social injustice.

It is also not entirely surprising that more urbanites tend to have critical views about current inequalities than do villagers, despite their many advantages and the more rapid improvement of their living standards. Unlike peasants, they are unlikely to feel they have nowhere to go but up. The opportunities to become very rich are greater in the cities, but city residents also face the prospects of losing jobs, benefits, and incomes. While facing the perils associated with market reforms and the smashing of the iron rice bowl of state employment security, urbanites also have more examples close at hand of new millionaires and their lavish and segregated lifestyles. Confronted with contrasts between their own difficult struggles and the fabulous success of others, the fact that they are doing much better than most farmers will not provide much comfort. The same subjective comparisons with the past and with others in the local community that incline farmers to be accepting of current inequalities make a higher percentage of urban residents angry.

CONCLUSIONS

Based on both the quality of our survey data and the detailed discussion of the Chinese context, we feel confident in rejecting the conventional wisdom. Most Chinese citizens have accepted and are busily organizing their lives under the new market principles and heightened inequalities unleashed by China's reforms since 1978. Although attitudes vary and all Chinese like some features of the current structures of inequality more than others, we find little evidence of the claimed high and rising levels of popular anger about inequality issues, and we see few signs that China is heading toward a social volcano due to widespread discontent over inequality and distributive injustice issues. If anything, Chinese attitudes about current inequalities probably are more conducive to political stability than to instability.

This conclusion brings us to the fifth research question posed in the Introduction: Does the pattern of Chinese citizen responses to our questions about inequality and distributive injustice issues indicate that popular opinion in these realms is a potential source of future political instability? For the time of the survey (in 2004, to be precise), the answer is a resounding no.

In some ways this conclusion is remarkable and even ironic. China is still ruled by the Chinese Communist Party that came to power in 1949. Under Mao the CCP proclaimed that socialism was the route to both economic development and a more just society. After Mao's death in 1976, Deng Xiaoping and other CCP leaders did not relinquish the historical stage in order to allow advocates of markets and democracy to dismantle the increasingly moribund socialist system, as happened in the former Soviet Union and in Eastern Europe. Instead CCP leaders persisted in power but reversed gears economically, launching the dismantling of the socialist system they themselves had helped to build earlier and gradually but systematically replacing it with the institutions of a market system—in other words, with capitalism. So lifelong communists presided over a state-directed effort to create the kind of capitalist system they had fought to eliminate earlier, with the hope that the economic benefits would enable them to preserve political stability and hold onto power indefinitely. From the evidence of our survey, this paradoxical reversal and strategic gamble were still working in 2004, twenty-six years after market reforms were launched.

Given the relatively weak sentiments of distributive injustice in our national survey and the fact that the groups that are objectively the most disadvantaged are not the angriest, can China's leaders now take comfort in our findings and relax, knowing that they don't have to worry that political stability will be threatened if they do not take vigorous steps to make their society less unequal and more just? In our view such a complacent attitude would be misguided. Our study has focused only on distributive injustice issues, and we have just noted that there are many other kinds of injustice that can generate strong popular discontent. For example, individuals who contracted AIDS from tainted blood transfusions, who had a baby sickened by adulterated milk products, or who lost a child when a shoddily constructed school collapsed in an earthquake may legitimately be furious, even if these are not primarily distributive justice issues. By the same token, convincing Chinese citizens that the current social order is fair may depend more on such measures as improving the legal system and giving ordinary citizens opportunities to influence the people and policies that govern their lives than it does on government redistributions from the rich to the poor or reduction of the national Gini coefficient.

Even in the distributive realm, the popular perception that China's leaders are concerned about excessive and unfair inequalities probably helps dampen feelings of distributive injustice among the population, and these feelings could flare up if Chinese citizens saw their leaders becoming complacent about the problems of disadvantaged citizens. Furthermore, maintaining popular optimism about chances for people to improve their standards of living is probably possible only when a large proportion of citizens feel they are doing better than they were earlier, and that this is the case also for many if not most of the people they know. Such feelings clearly characterized our survey respondents in 2004, but a major economic downturn in China could undermine such confidence.

As we noted earlier, the explanation of how distributive justice attitudes are formed that is suggested by our results also leads us to suspect that these attitudes may be somewhat volatile, subject to change in response to altered personal and family experiences and circumstances. If we are correct that current inequalities are accepted in part because they seem more fair than the inequitable patterns of Mao-era socialism, the value of that subjective comparison will diminish as the socialist era recedes even further into the past and comparisons with how citizens were doing a decade or two earlier become a more meaningful reference point. In such comparisons, will present inequalities look so acceptable? In short, there is nothing in our survey results that says that the dominant popular view in 2004 about current inequalities—of acceptance tinged by criticism—is guaranteed and permanent, or that China's political stability could not be threatened by a broader sharing of feelings of injustice, distributive and otherwise, in the future.

As this book is being completed in the summer of 2009, China has been in the throes of a sharp economic downturn as a result of the global financial crisis. Economic growth rates have dropped substantially from the 10 percent-plus levels of recent years, Chinese exports are down sharply (by 26 percent in February 2009 compared to a year earlier, according to press reports), and more than 20 million workers have already lost their jobs. There were signs of recovery in the Chinese economy later in the year, but with substantial debate among observers regarding the extent of any rebound in popular employment and income levels. Even if we can be confident that no social volcano was looming in 2004, we cannot be quite so certain that the level of acceptance of inequalities and optimism about future opportunities that we observed then is the dominant mood today. Are Chinese citizens now more angry about distributive injustice issues than they were in 2004? Are groups that have been affected by mass layoffs and declining living standards willing to blame outside forces, and the U.S. financial system in particular, or will they turn their anger against the market-based economy that now governs their lives, and against the political elites that they count on to manage that economy? Our 2004 survey provides strong evidence that we cannot simply observe objective trends in employment and income distribution in China and draw conclusions about how popular attitudes have changed. It will be necessary to carry out new survey work on popular attitudes toward inequality issues now and in the future to determine whether the social volcano scenario can still be confidently discounted.[11]

One final cautionary lesson can be drawn from our survey results. Our data suggest that some of the measures the Chinese government is taking to counteract feelings of distributive injustice may not be aimed at the most appropriate groups and locales. We do not advocate abandoning reforms designed to improve the lives of China's farmers, but those concerned with

China's future social and political stability would be well advised to reject the assumption that objective status can be automatically equated with attitudes toward current inequalities. Assuming that feelings of injustice are an important source of potential instability, assessments of China's prospects for political stability or instability could be more confidently made by directly asking citizens probing questions, on a regular basis, about how just or unjust they feel the social order is than by computing and monitoring Gini inequality coefficients. The survey data analyzed in this study are a modest first step in that direction.

REFERENCE MATTER

Introduction

1. The failed Great Leap Forward launched by Mao Zedong in 1958 led to the deaths of 30 million or more Chinese beyond the number expected under normal mortality, a disaster attributable not to weather or other natural disasters but to misguided state policy; see Yang 1996.

2. The 2002 Gini of .45 is based on the research reported in Gustafsson, Li, and Sicular 2008. The United Nations Human Development Report for 2007–2008 (available online at hdr.undp.org/en/statistics/) gives a Gini of .469 for China, compared to .408 for the United States (the most unequal developed society), .249 for Japan, .368 for India, and .334 for Bangladesh. The same source gives Brazil's Gini index as .57 and South Africa's as .578.

3. A variety of other phrases and euphemisms are used in China instead, such as "socialist market economy." At times during the 1980s some Chinese leaders contended that China's economic problems were attributable to the fact that Mao Zedong (China's leader from the establishment of the People's Republic of China in 1949 until his death in 1976) had tried to create centrally planned socialism prematurely, before the prior stage of capitalism had been developed to the levels that Marxist theory said were necessary to support a socialist transition. Based on this reasoning, China's leaders' task should be to step back and allow the return to private property and business in order to promote market-style development but maintain the eventual goal of changing China to a centrally planned socialist system. However, such arguments have disappeared from official discourse in China in recent years. For good overviews of the economic changes in China before and after 1978, see Naughton 2007; Brandt and Rawski 2008.

4. Official statistics reported by China's Ministry of Public Security claim that the number of "mass protest incidents" nationally increased from 8,700 in 1993 to 87,000 in 2005 (Tanner 2006; Chung, Lai, and Xia 2006). After 2005 the Chinese media stopped reporting these annual counts of mass protest incidents, a development that has led to speculation that the total today is probably much higher.

5. Measurement of national income inequality is a tricky business, and there is some variation in the Gini coefficient estimates reported in different studies. Most Western estimates for recent years are, as noted earlier, more in the .45 to .47 range, rather than .53, a figure that would mean that China is approaching the levels of inequality of places like Brazil and South Africa. Gustafsson, Li, and Sicular (2008, p. 20) note that their national Gini estimate based on their 2002 survey was

essentially unchanged from the level computed from the comparable survey in 1995—about .45.

6. He Qinglian, an economics-trained journalist, antagonized Chinese authorities by muckraking articles and her book *China's Pitfall* (1997), in which she argued that the benefits of Chinese reforms were being monopolized by the well-connected. She is now living in exile in the United States. In her writings from exile she continues to publish similar views: "China's new economic elite . . . and the heads of the party-state now control 85 percent of all the wealth in China and constitute the super-rich. . . . Chinese society currently resembles a volcano on the verge of a major eruption" (He 2003, pp. 69, 71).

7. Jiang Zemin was China's top leader from 1989 until his retirement as CCP leader in 2002. In the late 1990s he initiated the Develop the West campaign designed to counteract the overwhelming concentration of foreign investment and other development activity in China's coastal regions, arguably the first of several government initiatives designed to bring about more equitable growth.

Chapter 1

1. In this book *socialism* means monopoly state or public control over the means of production and a national economy coordinated by central planning rather than by markets. Given this definition, which is based on the Marxist formulation used by the Soviet Union and later state socialist systems, many other countries that in the second half of the twentieth century were often called socialist—for example, India, Tanzania, Guyana, Sweden, and even Great Britain—do not qualify as socialist. Obviously if a more expansive definition of *socialism* is adopted, the proportion of the world's population living under socialism would have been even larger, perhaps over 50 percent. It should also be noted that in terms of the same Marxist framework, none of the centrally planned socialist countries claimed to be communist. In economic terms *communism* was defined as a future, more abundant stage after socialism in which distribution would be according to need, without the necessity of a wage system, material incentives, or perhaps even money. So communism in economic terms was a future goal that was never realized. When we refer to these systems (and to China still today) as communist, what we mean is that their political systems involved monopoly rule by communist parties, not that their economies were organized according to communist principles.

2. The nature of the Chinese dismantling of socialism differs from most other centrally planned socialist systems (except Vietnam) in that the Communist Party has remained in command and has in fact led and guided the process of market reforms. In Eastern Europe and the former Soviet Union, Communist Party rule collapsed more or less simultaneously with the start of market reforms. Given this key difference and the desire of China's leaders to foster continuity and popular legitimacy, they have not stated that they are dismantling socialism and building (or restoring) capitalism. Mao Zedong famously and repeatedly fulminated against the possibility of capitalist restoration in China, and his successors do not want to acknowledge that they have made his worst fears come true. Instead they have used a variety of formulations to claim that they are presiding over the creation of a form of market socialism or following a Chinese path to socialism. However, given the fact that by the 1990s market distribution had replaced central planning as the primary economic distribution mechanism and that public ownership of the means

of production was no longer dominant, China is no longer a socialist economy according to the traditional Marxist definition of *socialism* we are using in this study. So we will from time to time refer to China's current economy as capitalist, even if the country's leaders do not dare to use this term.

3. In the same period, even economies that were not really very socialist in terms of the Marxist definition, such as India and Great Britain, took dramatic steps to reduce the role of state ownership and controls in the economy and to increase the reliance on markets and private enterprise.

4. Laos began its own market-oriented reform program in 1986 at roughly the same time as Vietnam did, but it has been less thorough and less successful so far.

5. In this respect, Vietnam's experience with market reforms has been similar to China's, and in important respects Vietnam's reform program has been modeled on China's earlier efforts.

6. See the discussion of the paradoxes of China's economic reform path in Whyte 2009.

7. The qualifier "at least" is inserted because some would regard other turning points in China's history over the last century—for example, the downfall of the Qing dynasty in 1911, the consolidation of Nationalist rule in 1927, the coming to power of the CCP in 1949, or the Cultural Revolution launched in 1966—as on a par with the post-1955 and post-1978 social revolutions discussed here. By contrast, the most dramatic turning points in American history—the Revolution launched in 1776, the Civil War, the Great Depression, and the civil rights revolution, not to mention the feminist, sexual, and digital revolutions—involved much more partial and selective changes compared with life before these turning points.

8. The class label categories used by the CCP (landlord, rich peasant, etc.) were not part of the traditional lexicon of villagers, who tended to see their social worlds organized much more in terms of kinship groups than in stratification categories, and in fact the terminology used was derived from earlier Japanese terminology (see Kuhn 1984). So in a sense there was no clearly defined landlord social category in China until the CCP came to power and imposed this terminology nationally. (Giving each rural family official social class labels was an important and necessary preliminary stage before redistribution of land in the national land reform campaign in 1950–53, and the work teams sent into villages to manage this process were provided with regulations, pamphlets, and model examples to guide them in determining what qualified a family as a landlord, a rich peasant, an upper-middle peasant, or another newly imposed category.)

9. In other words, a major expansion of the state sector of the economy did occur during these years, but more as a result of new enterprises and projects, key portions of which were built with Soviet assistance, rather than through the state nationalizing the remaining privately owned and operated firms.

10. By a slightly different periodization, China's economic growth rate between 1952 and 1957 was about 6 percent per year, according to Western economists (about 9 percent in China's official figures), quite a respectable rate (see Yeh 1973).

11. Technically, there was a third type of enterprise that emerged from the socialist transformation: the joint state-private firm. This term was used for the private firms that were handed over to the state in 1955 in view of the fact that the former owners were given salaried jobs and received interest payments for the next decade on the assessed value of the firm assets they were giving up. However, in

reality these functioned the same as state enterprises, so they are not considered separately here.

12. Initially the capitalists who agreed to turn over their firms in the 1955 socialist transformation received interest payments on the value of the property they had turned over. However, these payments were based on often artificially low state assessments from which fines assessed in earlier campaigns were deducted, and in the Cultural Revolution these interest payments were discontinued. The more prosperous farmers were supposed to receive payments for the extra land, draft animals, and tools that they turned over to the APCs when they joined, but they had even less time to enjoy these property-based additions to income. By 1956 the lower-stage APCs, which included these property shares, were amalgamated into higher-stage APCs, and as a result all farmers were compensated from that point on only in work points based on their labor.

13. It would be too much of a diversion to explain here why the Leap was launched and the major changes and disruptions it produced, but see MacFarquhar 1983; Teiwes and Sun 1999.

14. The post-1962 communes had three administrative levels—commune, production brigade, and production team—and in most locales the brigade corresponded to a former APC and to a natural village. Daily farming was organized and compensated at the lowest level, in the production team (see Bennett 1978; Whyte 1986).

15. Brides could move at marriage into the villages where their grooms lived; rural youths who passed the college entrance examinations or were inducted into the military could leave, although not necessarily permanently; and villagers whose land was taken over by expanding state factories might be given jobs and urban household registrations. Virtually everyone else was consigned for life to the villages of their birth.

16. During the early 1950s, as noted earlier, China looked to the Soviet Union as a model and used Soviet institutions and policies as inspiration for Chinese socialism. However, by the late 1950s Mao had become disenchanted with the Soviet Union and angry at Soviet leader Nikita Khrushchev, and by 1960 the Sino-Soviet dispute had erupted into the open, with each country and its leaders denouncing the other.

17. An earlier draft of this chapter used the phrase "negative action" instead of "leveling down" to emphasize the obverse of affirmative action, but the author decided that "negative action" would be unintelligible to readers, as the policies probably were, at least initially, to Chinese citizens.

18. In the Sino-Soviet polemics of the 1960s, Soviet propagandists denounced Mao's version of socialism as designed to produce "barracks communism," a term originally used by Karl Marx to criticize nineteenth-century rival socialist theorists' ideas involving uniform poverty enforced bureaucratically.

19. Generally, urban parents were allowed to retain one of their grown children in the city in order to care for them in their old age, but the rest were expected to join the exodus to the countryside. (Most urban families had three or more children at the time.) Initially urban youths were told that they were being sent to the countryside for life, but this rule was so unpopular that by the early 1970s the authorities modified it into a promised rotation system, under which youths would be eligible for return to their cities of origin after a period of agricultural life and labor (often three years). See Bernstein 1977.

20. The truncation of educational and other opportunities affected all urban youths during this period, even those not sent to the countryside for an extended period. There is debate about whether those sent to the countryside did that much worse later in life than others in the lost generation; see Zhou and Hou 1999; Xie, Yang, and Greenman 2008.

21. In rural areas a substantial amount of the inequality among neighboring families was due to life-cycle differences related to the ratio of laborers (and thus earners) to dependents (see the discussion in Selden 1988). Poor families with many small children or aging relatives to feed and care for, but few laborers, could receive advance grain distributions from their production teams even though they wouldn't be able to pay for them fully with their work point earnings at the post-harvest accounting. These "overconsuming households" (*chaozhi hu*) accumulated debts to the team that they could hope to pay off once one or more children grew up and started earning work points.

22. The claim here is not that socialism had the same inequalities as capitalism, but that socialist societies have their own types of inequalities that, while different from those in capitalist societies, can nonetheless make them highly inegalitarian.

23. Most conventional reports of these transitions suggest that Deng and other reform-era leaders did not initially contemplate dismantling the socialist system, but instead mainly wanted to recover from the economic and political disorder and alienation produced by the Cultural Revolution. As one set of reforms led to new problems and pressures, other reforms were introduced, and eventually the leaders arrived at a much more thorough repudiation of the socialist system than initially contemplated—a change process symbolized by Deng Xiaoping's phrase quoted earlier, "crossing the river by stepping from stone to stone." This characterization of the process may be partially true, but judged from the vantage point of where China is in 2009, it looks much more like China recognized that following an only slightly modified version of the Soviet model was no longer a viable proposition, and that instead China had to move steadily toward an adaptation of the East Asian development model pioneered originally by Japan and successfully copied in Taiwan, South Korea, and elsewhere (see the discussion in Whyte 2007).

24. The 1977 national entrance exam was the first such exam given since 1965. Millions of youths whose lives and schooling had been disrupted after 1965 by the Cultural Revolution and by being sent, in many cases, to the countryside were also able to sit for the revived college entrance exams initially, resulting in extraordinary numbers of test-takers and intense competition for the still limited number of university enrollment places.

25. Susan Shirk (1984) has described this as a switch from "virtuocracy" to meritocracy.

26. The open-door policy refers to a whole package of dramatic policy reversals launched in 1978 designed to transform China from one of the most isolated and self-sufficient economies in the world to full immersion in the global economy, including welcoming foreign investment and foreign ownership, encouraging exports and imports, and seeking participation in regulating the international economic order. For an overview, see Harding 1987.

27. Initially, strict limits were imposed on how many employees could be working in such private firms (no more than seven at first), but those limits rapidly fell by the wayside.

28. I can recall being in Chengdu, Sichuan, in the summers of 1986 and 1987 and seeing the roads leading in from rural areas clogged each morning with thousands of rural traders using every possible kind of vehicle and conveyance to bring in vegetables, animals, and household manufactures—the largest of which were perhaps the pool tables balanced precariously on rickety farm carts and destined to feed the craze for pool in newly blossoming pool halls all over that city.

29. Estimates of the size of the floating population vary and depend to some extent on whether moves within the locality and from one rural area to another are included (hired rural laborers from interior provinces are now common in prosperous coastal villages), or only long-distance rural-to-urban moves. Some current estimates are in the 130–140 million range and even higher.

30. Media accounts during the 1980s featured the proliferation of "ten-thousand yuan households" that specialized in raising fish, mushrooms, rabbits, and multiple other items.

31. As noted earlier, official income statistics, particularly for this early period, are open to question. Urban residents benefited from a large number of subsidies and subsidized services to which rural people had no access, making the "real" urban-rural income gap much larger. Even without considering such subsidies, China's urban-rural income gap in all recent periods is unusually large in comparative terms (see Khan and Riskin 2005; Li and Luo 2010).

32. Since about 2003 a national effort has been launched to create a new but minimal village health insurance pooling system in rural China. However, such a system still did not exist at the time we conducted our 2004 survey.

33. Zhu Rongji had been mayor of Shanghai from 1989 to 1991, where he led the initial stages of the effort to develop Pudong. He was transferred to Beijing by CCP leader Jiang Zemin in 1991 to become vice premier, and in 1993 he entered the CCP Politburo Standing Committee while also serving as governor of the Bank of China, where he battled inflation and developed plans for the reform of SOEs, plans he pushed through when he served as premier from 1998 to 2003.

34. In virtually all rural areas housing remained privately financed, constructed, and owned throughout, so there was no comparable housing privatization campaign in the countryside.

35. Most companies listed on the Chinese stock markets do not regularly pay dividends, so the primary way that purchasing stocks can augment income is through the time-honored practice of buying low and selling high (a risky strategy, of course, as the Chinese stock market decline that began in 2007 demonstrated).

36. Between 1991 and 2004 urban household income grew by an impressive 7.7 percent a year; rural growth, while respectable, was substantially lower—4.9 percent a year (Naughton 2007, pp. 210–11). Although most individuals born in rural areas cannot readily obtain urban household registrations, an exception has generally been made for successful businessmen. If they make substantial business and/or housing investments in a city, they can receive a special "blue seal" version of the local urban household registration status (the normal registration bears a red seal).

37. However, there is one countertrend of importance. Urban poverty was not much evident in the socialist period; smashing of the iron rice bowl, unemployment, and loss of benefits in the 1990s produced an increase in urban poverty in recent years among registered urbanites (not counting poverty among the migrants); see Khan and Riskin 2001, chap. 4.

38. As noted in the epigraph at the beginning of this study, the first time Deng Xiaoping used this phrase, in a speech on January 12, 1983, the wording was "Some people in rural areas and cities should be allowed to get rich before others." As the phrase became a mantra for market reforms, it was generally shortened to something like "It is good for some people to get rich first." (My thanks to Maocan Guo for tracking down the origins of the phrase.)

Chapter 2

1. At that time I had left the University of Michigan and was teaching at George Washington University. Leslie Kish was a nationally renowned specialist on sampling methods who taught the secrets of that arcane technique for many years at the University of Michigan, where he was a professor of sociology and a senior researcher in the Institute for Social Research. He was also a key advisor to an earlier China survey project I directed.

2. Shen Mingming had received his PhD in political science at the University of Michigan in 1994, and I knew him during his student days and served on his dissertation committee. At Michigan he received his initial training in survey research methods through the Detroit Area Study and studied sampling methods with Leslie Kish.

3. The Beijing Area Study operates more like another well-known U.S. survey, the General Social Survey (GSS), than like the Detroit Area Survey (DAS). The DAS surveys are on completely different topics each year and thus involve entirely new questionnaires, whereas the GSS has certain standard modules of questions that are asked each year, with other new modules on different topics each time. A survey module is a set of questions on a particular topic or issue that may take up perhaps one-fifth to one-third of the space and time in a questionnaire.

4. Therefore, the final project research team included Albert Park, Pierre Landry, Wang Feng, Jieming Chen, Chunping Han, and myself on the U.S. side, and Shen Mingming, Yang Ming, and the staff of the Research Center for Contemporary China at Peking University on the Chinese side.

5. Pretesting of questionnaires is a standard stage in preparing to conduct a survey such as ours. Interviewees who are similar to the kinds of people who will serve as respondents in the actual survey are contacted and interviewed using the draft questionnaire. These interviews help train the interviewers, but more importantly they help to detect problems with question wording and the ability of respondents to understand and respond in a meaningful way. When problems arise, particular survey questions can be altered or even eliminated from the questionnaire entirely.

6. Specifically, there were four sampling points in the northeast region, four in north China, nine in east China, five in south China, eight in central China, three in the northwest, and seven in the southwest.

7. When a selected household had more than one eligible respondent (individuals between the ages of eighteen and seventy), we followed conventional procedures and selected one eligible person randomly using the Kish grid of random selection choices printed on the interview cover sheet.

8. Of the urban cases included in the final sample, 642 were in the base sample and 1,137 in the urban supplementary sample. Because of the over-sampling of urban areas, when an effort is made to show the distribution of attitudes for the whole adult population (primarily in Chapters 3 and 4), sampling weights are used

to correct for this over-sampling, thus yielding figures representative of all Chinese adults.

9. Since we are sampling locales with probability proportional to size, provinces that are relatively thinly populated, such as Tibet and Qinghai, have a relatively low chance of being in the national sample. That logic does not apply to populous Sichuan, but any sample such as ours that is stratified by region but not by province will exclude some provinces. Such omissions do not invalidate the representative nature of the national sample as long as the omitted provinces had a chance of being included in the sample that is proportional to their population size. (Our survey, in fact, covers a wider range of provinces than most existing China national surveys, such as the China Health and Nutrition surveys or the China Household Income Project surveys.)

10. Use of the term *standard* indicates that these procedures are all adaptations to Chinese conditions of the procedures followed in surveys in any society, not ones specifically required because our survey took place in China.

11. We again followed conventional procedures by using only alphanumeric codes on the completed questionnaires to identify the respondents, with information about the identity of respondents matched with their code numbers recorded on documents kept in a separate file, again under lock and key.

12. The issue of the use of deception is a key and contentious issue in discussions of procedures for protecting human subjects in research. Generally we did not employ, nor did we need to employ, any deceptive procedures, although perhaps the omission of information about foreign participation in designing and analyzing the survey comes close. The Chinese university and bureaucratic authorities who approved of our project obviously knew that this was an international collaboration.

13. Alison Denton Jones, a doctoral student in sociology at Harvard, performed this back-translation task.

Chapter 3

A preliminary version of this analysis was published in Whyte 2010b.

1. Throughout this chapter, the percentages presented are weighted figures designed to correct for urban over-sampling in order to yield estimates that are representative of China's adult population as a whole. How patterns of response to many of these questions vary by social group and geographical location is considered in Part II. In our Beijing pilot survey in 2000, condemnation of national income differences as excessive was more nearly universal than in our national survey in 2004, with 95.4 percent saying that national income differences were too large or somewhat too large.

2. Poor people were defined in the question as "those who cannot support basic living conditions like food, clothing, and housing," while rich people were defined as "those who can pretty much buy anything for themselves."

3. Here our question relates to a debate that cannot be openly expressed in China under current conditions: Have the economic reforms since 1978 changed China into a capitalist society, or should the system still be considered (market) socialism? The authorities in China want to foster the impression that they are developing a form of market socialism, not restoring capitalism. The responses to this question suggest that the majority of Chinese citizens are willing to give the authorities the benefit of the doubt on this score.

4. There is a missing logical link in this statement, since presumably current inequalities would not undermine social stability unless those who are poor and disadvantaged feel that their treatment is unjust and are inclined to join protests and other potentially disruptive activities. However, our respondents do not have to feel that current inequalities are inherently unjust in order to recognize that others may view them as such, and on that basis our respondents may have concluded that current inequalities are excessive and undesirable on the grounds of social instability more than of social injustice.

5. In each list there is one trait (bad luck, good luck) that cannot be easily characterized as conveying either individual merit or external influences. It turns out our interviewees treated the luck questions as reflecting more external attribution than individual merit. It might also be noted that two traits in the list of attributions for wealth (dishonesty and having connections) might be seen as reflecting "negative merit" of individuals rather than simply unfairness of the external environment.

6. In rank order, the reasons given for poverty were lack of ability, low education, lack of effort, poor character, unequal opportunity, bad luck, discrimination, and unfairness of the economic system. The attributions of wealth in rank order were ability and talent, hard work, high education, connections, better opportunities, good luck, unfairness of the economic system, and dishonesty. The two lists of traits are not exact parallels, so we don't know how respondents would have ranked an absence of personal connections as an explanation for current poverty.

7. A somewhat similar view is conveyed by the pattern of responses to a question in which respondents were asked to give their views on the statement "Whether a person gets rich or suffers poverty is his/her own responsibility." Responses varied, but 46.3 percent expressed varying degrees of agreement with this statement, while only 28.9 percent expressed disagreement.

8. We asked another set of questions related to the question of the fairness and unfairness of current inequalities. Respondents were asked to say how much influence each of thirteen traits should have on a person's salary, and then how much influence they thought each of those same thirteen traits actually have in determining salary. The traits were educational level, adverse working conditions, individual effort, size of family, job responsibilities, seniority, being male, contributions to the work unit, ties with superiors, having personal connections (*renshi ren, you luzi*), having urban household registration, age, and having specialized technical skill. The traits that respondents thought should have most influence on a person's salary were, in order, technical skills, educational level, individual effort, having personal connections, contributions to the work unit, and job responsibilities. They ranked the top traits in terms of their actual influence on a person's salary as having personal connections, technical qualifications, educational level, ties with superiors, individual effort, contributions to work unit, and job responsibilities. The main difference perceived between what should determine individual salaries and what actually does do so is that having personal connections and ties with superiors were seen as more influential than respondents felt they should be. All the other traits, which involve individual merit factors, had very similar rankings in the "should" and "actual" responses. In other words, respondents felt that for the most part the traits that should form the basis for individual salaries actually do so, the major exceptions being that

connections with superiors and ability to use personal relationships play a larger role than they should (but with the latter viewed more favorably than the former).

9. Our questionnaire included a series of questions asking respondents to compare their current standards of living with a range of reference groups, including relatives, former classmates, coworkers, and neighbors as well as more distant comparison groups—in the local city or county, in the province, and in the entire nation. Generally about 60 percent responded that they had about the same living standard as their immediate reference groups, while about 25 percent said they were below that level and about 15 percent above. Not surprisingly, in the more distant comparisons 50 to 60 percent said they were worse off, only about 35 percent said they were at about the same level, and less than 10 percent reported being better off.

10. These responses are congruent with the fact that, when asked about what traits should influence how much salary an employee is paid, family size was ranked last out of thirteen listed traits (see note 8).

11. As discussed in Chapter 1, the egalitarianism of the Mao era (particularly during the Cultural Revolution) consisted primarily of measures to limit the incomes, bonuses, and other advantages of intellectuals, officials, and other advantaged groups, rather than to provide income and job guarantees for the poor; see Whyte 1981.

12. The notion of the positive function of differential rewards is not distinctive to market-based or capitalist societies. In most socialist societies as well, the characterization of socialist distribution as involving rewards "to each according to his contributions" was used to justify a wide range of material incentives and hierarchically graded benefits and privileges from the time of Lenin onward. Polish sociologists in the 1980s argued that socialist societies were more meritocratic than capitalist societies because salaries and other rewards could be more tightly calibrated to individual training, responsibility, and contributions without the complicating factors of private property ownership and inherited wealth (see Weselowski and Krauze 1981). However, after the collapse of socialism in Eastern Europe, Weselowski acknowledged that actual socialist societies such as Poland were more meritocratic in theory than in reality; see Weselowski and Wnuk-Lipinski 1992. It was precisely this functionalist thinking that led Mao to condemn the Soviet Union and its East European satellite regimes as revisionist and to attempt to sharply limit the use of material incentives throughout Chinese society in the period from 1966 to 1976. Given this legacy, Deng and his reformist colleagues had to overcome the condemnation of material incentives in order to justify their official approval of incentives and income differentials (see Whyte 1981). In the process of market reforms, of course, they went beyond the "rewards proportional to contribution" formula of socialist societies; increasingly, China's income differentials are the product of competition in revived markets and even the power of privately owned property, not simply the result of differentiated wage and benefit scales supervised by the bureaucrats of a socialist planned economy. Ivan Szelenyi contended that in the context of a centrally planned socialist society, allowing secondary distribution via markets could actually reduce the considerable inequalities generated by bureaucratic allocation (see Szelenyi 1978, 1983), but once markets replace bureaucratic allocation as the basic distributive mechanism, as they have in China since the 1980s, they seem to lose this counterbalancing and equalizing role. Some would even

argue that China today displays the worst of both capitalism and socialism by enabling both the rich and the powerful to convert their advantages and resources into privileged lives for their families. See further discussion of these issues in Chapter 7.

13. In the socialist era, of course, those with high incomes could not readily translate this advantage into better housing, education, or medical care for their families, while those with high rank and important political positions received systematic advantages for themselves and their families in these and other realms. Evidently the legacy of the special privileges of the political elite under socialism is still a sore point with many Chinese.

14. A substantial literature documents the institutionalized discrimination experienced by China's rural hukou holders both in the Mao era and in the reform era. See, for example, Chan 1994; Solinger 1999; Zhang 2001; Wang 2005; Whyte 2010a.

15. See Wang Feng (2010), an analysis based on the same survey data. Generally the responses of rural residents and urban residents to these questions are similar, with migrants slightly more critical. More detailed examination of social background variations in attitudes toward discrimination based on hukou status is presented in Chapter 8.

16. In his statements on these issues, "On the Ten Major Relationships" (April 25, 1956) and "On the Correct Handling of Contradictions Among the People" (February 27, 1957), Mao stressed that Chinese society was characterized by a large number of mostly nonantagonistic contradictions among groups and sectors of society and that it was the task of the leadership to manage these to prevent them from becoming antagonistic (Mao 1977b). Unfortunately for Chinese society, in later years Mao forgot his own wisdom and instead focused obsessively on detecting class conflicts and waging campaigns against the antagonistic classes thus identified, real or imagined.

17. Response categories were reversed, with neutral and don't know responses placed in an intermediate category, resulting in a five-point scale from 1=no conflicts to 5=very large conflicts.

18. These were new questions designed for the 2004 survey, so there are no comparable figures from other societies.

19. For example, most Han Chinese have little opportunity for close contact with ethnic minority communities and may as a consequence see little grounds for conflict, but the Han petty merchants who were attacked and burned out of their shops in Lhasa in March 2008 by rioting Tibetans, or the Han residents affected by the Uighur rioting in Xinjiang in summer 2009, would presumably have a different view.

20. In recent years a new system of minimum income subsidies (*dibao*) has been introduced in Chinese cities. However, this system does not provide guaranteed jobs, and it is not clear whether the incomes provided are sufficient to reliably meet basic subsistence needs of recipient families. In any case the majority of the population—migrants and those living in the countryside—are not covered by the system, although some localities have launched experimental rural dibao programs in recent years.

21. Despite this general consensus that hukou-based discrimination is unjust, it is questionable whether such sentiments can serve as the basis for protest activity and political instability. Why hukou-based discrimination has been so durable

despite increasing public recognition of its unjust nature is one of the puzzles explored in Whyte 2010a.

Chapter 4

1. Where two rounds of surveys were carried out in an Eastern European country, we report only the 1996 results in this chapter. For countries in which a third round of ISJP surveys was conducted in 2005 or 2006 we show the results for that survey, except in cases where particular questions were not included in those surveys, in which case we show the results for 1996. To limit the size of the tables, we omit the results of the 1991 surveys in Estonia, Slovenia, and Holland.

2. Figures for Hungary in Tables 4.1a and 4.1b are from the 1996 round of ISJP surveys, as these questions were not included in the 2005 Hungary ISJP survey. In the comparisons in the present chapter, we are ignoring the year of the survey. In the conclusion to this chapter, we examine whether the different timing of the surveys in China and in other countries, rather than real differences in attitudes across countries, could explain the results.

3. The relatively low emphasis on reliance on guanxi expressed by Chinese respondents is a surprise, since reliance on personal connections is a much more highly elaborated and ancient cultural theme in that society than elsewhere (see Gold, Guthrie, and Wank 2002). In Russia the rigidities of state socialism in the Soviet period led to extensive use of personal connections and payoffs (*blat*) to get needed supplies and resources (see Berliner 1957). Some of the metaphors used by Soviets and Chinese are similar—using irregular or even illicit means to get things accomplished is *zou houmen* (going by the back door) in China and *na levo* (going to the left) in Russia.

4. Although China's market reforms were launched earlier than those in Eastern Europe, the fact that they took a step-by-step form rather than the big-bang comprehensive privatization form followed in Eastern Europe means that the full inegalitarian consequences of those reforms were not felt initially. For example, the rural-urban income gap narrowed until the mid-1980s and widened only subsequently, and substantial urban unemployment occurred only after the mid-1990s. See further discussion of this issue of survey timing in the conclusion to the present chapter.

5. The unfair inequality and merit-based inequality summary scales, discussed in Chapter 6, are constructed from the Chinese responses to subsets of these items (displayed in Figures 3.2a and 3.2b). Specifically, the unfair inequality score used in Figure 4.1 is the mean of the responses to questions about attributing poverty to discrimination, unequal opportunity, and an unfair economic structure and attributing wealth to dishonesty, connections, unequal opportunity, and an unfair economic structure (with each attribution varying along a five-point scale from "not important at all" to "very important," as discussed in Chapter 3).

6. It might be objected that China is the odd man out in these comparisons because its population is still largely rural, while the ISJP comparison countries are more developed and thus predominantly urban. Evidence presented in Chapters 6 through 9 indicates that rural residents and farmers in particular tend to have more-accepting and less-critical attitudes on many inequality attitude measures than do other respondents, contrary to the conventional wisdom. However, when we calculate the figures for Figures 4.1 and 4.2 based on Chinese urban respondents only, the results are not substantially different. To be specific, the mean on the unfair

inequality measures for urban respondents is 3.3, just slightly higher than the mean of 3.14 for all Chinese respondents, and still well below the means of all of the other countries except for Japan, which also has a score of 3.14. On the mean score for emphasis on talent and effort shown in Figure 4.2, Chinese urban respondents have a score of 3.74, compared to 3.68 for all Chinese respondents, with both figures well above the comparable mean for all of the other ISJP countries.

7. For example, in Eastern Europe, as in the Soviet Union, material incentives were stressed as motivational devices, but they were denounced in China after the launching of the Cultural Revolution in 1966. Similarly, the use of clothing styles to convey relative status and even gender was taboo in China in the late Mao era, and regular campaigns were launched to send the educated and elites to serve at manual labor posts in industry and agriculture, leveling-down programs that Mao's critics in the Soviet camp viewed as bizarre.

8. The reader should keep in mind that in this sorting process, the principle followed is whether or how much the pattern of Chinese responses differs from the pattern in other countries, not whether there was a higher level of agreement of Chinese respondents with the question posed. So, for example, placing "wealth due to dishonesty" in category 5 means that markedly fewer Chinese agreed with this statement than did people in the other countries surveyed.

9. We are conducting a new national survey in China in 2009 to enable us to examine the issue of changes in inequality attitudes over time.

10. Citizens in the Soviet Union were no doubt less aware of their relative backwardness than were their counterparts in Eastern Europe, but they were almost certainly more aware than their counterparts in Mao-era China.

11. These explanations point to the importance of taking past experiences and expectations of individuals into account in trying to understand their attitudes and behavior, rather than relying only on information about their current social status. See the discussion in Pierson 2004.

12. The Russian case is more complicated, with many observers feeling that there was more freedom of the press and more voicing of critical opinion when the ISJP survey was conducted in 1996 than exists today.

13. He Qinglian, an economic journalist, wrote a highly critical account of China's reforms (*China's Pitfall*), originally published in Hong Kong in 1997. A considerably sanitized version was published in China in 1998, selling a reported 200,000 copies but generating much controversy and official anger. The book was banned. He Qinglian was subjected to severe criticisms and limitations on her ability to publish new work, and she was forced into exile in 2001. She now lives in the United States.

Chapter 5

1. One way of proceeding would have been entirely empirical, rather than conceptual. That method would have involved throwing all of our seventy-plus inequality attitude questions into a giant statistical churning process called factor analysis, and allowing the computer to decide how many dimensions these questions represent and which specific questions should be combined into scales to measure each dimension. However, that type of approach is too susceptible to the GIGO syndrome (garbage in, garbage out). Since the questions included in our survey were designed with at least an implicit conceptual scheme regarding inequality attitudes in mind, our approach is to decide first on the distinct conceptual domains we want

to examine, and only then to use statistical tools to determine which question or questions in the survey provide the best measures of each sub-aspect of these distinct inequality domains.

2. The analytical strategy we employ here reveals another reason not to rely on factor analysis to construct our inequality attitude scales. As customarily employed, factor analysis produces separate scales that are constrained to be statistically independent of one another, and when this is the case, whether or how much different scales are related to one another cannot be studied.

3. The exceptions are our geographic measures and information on the gender of respondents, which are not based on questionnaire responses.

4. Note that migrants are treated as a separate category, no matter what type of urban jobs they are performing or even whether they are employed at all. In the statistical analyses that follow, we use these twelve categories to create twelve "dummy variables" that are used in computing correlations and regression coefficients. Dummy variables are substitutes for categorical variables in which, for example, first farmers=1 and the rest of the sample=0; then rural nonagricultural workers=1 and the rest of the sample=0; and so forth through the list of all twelve occupational and residential status categories. This substitution is necessary with a complex categorical variable in order to make feasible statistical computations that assume measures are linear and continuous in form, rather than categorical. In regression analyses in later chapters, one of the dummy variables has to be omitted, and the coefficients displayed indicate how each other occupation category compares with the omitted category. Throughout Chapters 6 through 9 we use the unskilled and semiskilled urban worker category as the omitted reference group for the occupational and residential status measure.

5. Strictly speaking, these measures are designed to distinguish age cohorts rather than age per se. We considered using a different measurement scheme that divided all respondents into five distinct age cohorts, but that approach yielded results that, while largely similar to those obtained using age and age-squared, were more inconsistent and harder to interpret. The age-squared term is used in statistical calculations in an effort to detect curvilinear relationships between age and inequality attitudes. We suspect that the most critical attitudes may be held by respondents who are middle aged, the age cohort most affected negatively by the disruptions of the Cultural Revolution (the lost generation mentioned in Chapter 1), and if so we expect to find a positive association between age and a particular critical attitude toward inequality, but a negative association with age-squared (the division by 100 makes the resulting age-squared coefficients more comparable to those computed for age alone). In other words, positive and negative coefficients for the age and age-squared terms, respectively, suggest that the relationship between age and the attitude in question resembles a parabola or inverted U shape.

6. In any society income distributions are highly skewed, with most families clustered at the low end of the scale, but with a few high-earners far removed at the top end of the scale. In order to perform statistical analysis using income data, making a logarithmic transformation first to make the distribution less skewed is a common procedure that we follow here.

7. The access to unofficial information scale was computed from a series of seven questions, each of which asked respondents to rate their cosmopolitanism or exposure to specific outside or unofficial influences on a scale from 1=never to 4=frequently: travel domestically within China; travel outside China; exchange

information about society's current events with relatives and/or friends within China; exchange information about society's current events with relatives and/or friends outside China; learn news from international periodicals, television, or radio; learn information other than news from international books, magazines, television programs, or movies; and use the Internet. A higher score indicates more or multiple kinds of exposure to a range of sources of information beyond the official news media.

8. There are contradictory expectations about the influence of affiliation with a state-owned enterprise (SOE). During the socialist era, individuals affiliated with SOEs generally had higher incomes, social status, and fringe benefits than those affiliated with urban collective enterprises, not to mention members of rural communes (see Walder 1984; Bian 1994). In the reform era many SOEs have had financial difficulties that have produced a sense of insecurity and declining status among their employees and retirees. The discussion in the text assumes that the latter tendency dominates in shaping the attitudes of respondents with SOE ties, but strictly speaking this is an empirical question. We also included in our questionnaire one question about what family class origin label the respondent's family used to report before these labels were abolished (after 1979). In the Mao era, family class labels, which could be sorted into good, middling, and bad categories, had a major impact on how individuals were treated and on their access to many types of opportunities (see, for example, Kraus 1981; Croll 1981; Rosen 1982). However, our measure of recollected family class label did not have statistically significant associations with most inequality attitude measures, so we omit it from the models and tables presented in Chapters 6 through 9.

9. In statistical calculations we use a dummy variable version of this region categorization. In that version east takes a value of 1 if the respondent lived in an eastern province and otherwise 0. Similarly, center takes a value of 1 when the respondent lived in a central province and otherwise 0, and west takes a value of 1 when the respondent lived in a western province and otherwise 0. In regression analyses in Chapters 6 through 9, we take the east region as the omitted reference category, so the coefficients reported there indicate whether the attitudes of respondents who live in the two other regions are significantly different from the attitudes of those who live in the eastern region.

10. Prefectural cities are intermediate in the Chinese urban administrative hierarchy, ranking between county capitals and provincial capitals. Using this measure all our urban respondents in medium or larger cities receive a score of 0, with only respondents residing in smaller cities and towns or rural areas filling the other seven categories.

11. Fan and Wang use twenty-three distinct indicators, each ranging from 0 to 10, to measure various aspects of marketization of a province; the measure we use here is the mean of these twenty-three separate indicators. Their data refer to 2002, two years before our survey, the most recent figures available.

12. We face a special problem in the statistical analysis of the associations between these geographic measures and our various inequality attitude scales in Chapters 6 through 9. All of our other predictors are based on the variable characteristics of individuals, so that the respondents we interviewed in a particular sampling point will have different values on such measures. However, the geographic measures for all respondents interviewed in one sampling point will have the same value, since they all reside in the same province and live an equal

distance from the nearest prefectural or larger city. This matters because in Chapters 6 through 9 we will be employing ordinary least squares (OLS) regression to examine how background variables are related to our inequality attitude scales, and OLS regression assumes that the background predictor values for one respondent are independent of the values for other respondents in the same locale. This clustering of the values of our geographic variables leads to underestimating the standard errors of the geographic regression coefficients in our OLS models, and therefore to a tendency to exaggerate the statistical significance of the associations of geographic variables with inequality attitudes. In other words, a basic assumption of OLS regression is violated due to the structure of our survey data, with clusters of respondents nested within locales. To correct for this clustering problem, we employed multilevel analysis, an arcane technique that enables us make corrections for clustering and thus to estimate unbiased standard errors and statistical significance levels of the various geographic coefficients in the regression models shown in the tables in Chapters 6 through 9. (My thanks to one of the original reviewers of the manuscript for Stanford University Press for pointing out the clustering problem, and to Dong-Kyun Im for figuring out how to perform the multilevel analysis to produce corrected coefficients.) The multilevel results are not reported here, but all of the subsequent regression results in which that technique made a noticeable difference in the statistical results have the effect of the correction indicated next to the coefficients in question.

13. Strictly speaking, even our objective occupation, residence, demographic, and socioeconomic predictors (other than gender and the geographic measures) are subjective in the sense that they are based on self-reported background information provided in response to our survey questions, not external objective information about respondents. However, the final three subjective predictors are not only self-reported but also entail respondents' subjective assessments of their experiences and circumstances, rather than simply their statements about, say, whether they are members of the Chinese Communist Party or how old they are. For this reason we group these three predictors in a separate category in summary statistical tables in Chapters 6 through 9.

14. The relative social status measure is computed from the mean of four questions about how respondents would rank their current living standards compared to four alternative local reference groups: relatives, former classmates, coworkers, and neighbors. In each case the response categories ranged from 1=much worse to 5=much better, so the resulting mean scale also ranges from roughly 1 to 5.

15. We asked respondents about whether they or any members of their family had had the following experiences in the past three years: being seriously ill, suffering physical injury or economic loss due to artificial or natural disasters, being laid off or becoming unemployed, having difficulty paying for medical care, dropping out of school because of inability to pay the fees, having to borrow money to cover basic living expenses, and being treated unfairly by local officials. For each experience we recorded a 1 if the respondent said he or she had experienced it and 0 otherwise. The bad experiences scale is the sum of these separate scores, thus ranging from 0 to 7.

16. In Chapters 7 through 9 we add a fourth subjective measure as a predictor of inequality attitudes for reasons explained in the introduction to Chapter 7.

Chapter 6

1. An additional reason we didn't combine the three questions into a single scale is that rural respondents were not asked the question about inequality within their work units. The five response categories are reversed, so that they range from 1=too small to 5=too large, and they are treated as if they were an interval scale for the purpose of statistical analysis.

2. The two questions about whether the proportion of poor people and of rich people are expected to increase, stay the same, or decrease over the next five years (Figure 3.1b) also did not cohere well enough to form a single scale, and we decided not to use them in subsequent analyses.

3. These four items can be combined in a scale with a reliability of $\alpha=.53$. We constructed the scale by using factor analysis to find the common factor represented by all four items and then computing the values of the summary scale from the factor scores that reflect how closely each item is associated with that common factor. In this manner items that are closer to the common factor they all share contribute more to the summary scale value than items not as closely associated. The resulting values were rescaled so that they vary from 1 to 100.

4. The main change was to include low education as an additional possible cause of poverty and high education as an additional possible cause of wealth.

5. As with the harmful inequality scale, we used factor analysis to compute values of the unfair inequality summary scale from the factor scores of the constituent items, and we rescale the resulting values so that they vary from 1 to 100. These items form a very reliable scale, with $\alpha=.74$.

6. We used factor analysis to compute merit-based inequality scale values from the factor scores of the constituent items, rescaling the resulting values from 1 to 100. The constituent items form a very reliable scale, with $\alpha=.77$.

7. In the pilot survey we conducted in Beijing in 2000, we asked these same questions and constructed comparable scales. In that survey the scales measuring unfair inequality and merit-based inequality were negatively correlated, unlike in the 2004 national survey, but the correlation was not statistically significant ($r=-.033$; see Whyte and Han 2008).

8. In most instances, where we have inequality attitude measures computed as continuous measures from multiple items, we employ ordinary least squares (OLS) regression. However, in a few instances where we have used a single item with ordinal response categories as our inequality attitude measure (as in the case of the excessive inequality measure in the current chapter), we ought to employ instead ordered logistic regression. Our computation of ordered logistic regression models in such cases produced results that were basically the same as when we computed OLS regressions (details not shown here), and so for the sake of simplicity and comparability within tables, we report only the OLS regression results here.

9. In preliminary analyses of these data, we employed simpler regression models using subsets of predictor variables. Since in general the results of those simpler models were consistent with the models shown here, and because our tables are already numerous and complex enough, we show only the final models using the complete set of predictor variables in the regressions in Chapters 6 through 9. In this and later tables we display standardized regression coefficients,

which are designed to reflect the relative influence of one predictor vis-à-vis another (by the relative size of the coefficients), rather than unstandardized regression coefficients, which tell us how much change in the dependent variable (in this case, our inequality perception measures) takes place for each unit change in a predictor variable. We follow this practice because we are mainly interested in the relative influence of our predictors compared to each other over a range of inequality attitude measures, and we are not trying to explain the exact value of any dependent variable.

10. One other consideration lying behind this approach is that the correlations among our four inequality scales displayed in Table 6.1 reflect a pattern of positive association, rather than showing the expected negative association between the merit-based inequality scale and the other three measures. That pattern indicates that we cannot view the merit-based inequality scale as in effect the opposite of the other three measures (inequality is bad in contrast to inequality is good), a pattern that is now more understandable once we realize that the merit-based inequality measure is tapping a core belief that is shared by most Chinese even if they disagree on the other attitudes we inquired about. We suspect that the unexpected pattern of correlations in Table 6.1 also reflects a tendency for some respondents to feel that many different factors (merit and non-merit) explain who is rich and who is poor, while other respondents name few factors of either type they think are important. The fact that the respondent's years of schooling have a significant positive correlation with both unfair inequality and merit-based inequality is consistent with this speculation.

11. The significant positive regression coefficient (.06) for migrants and excessive inequality means that they are more likely than urban unskilled and semi-skilled workers to view national income gaps as excessive. Since the other three rural hukou categories are significantly less likely than the comparison group to see current income gaps as excessive, that makes migrants the single most critical occupational category on this issue.

12. The general tendency for Chinese farmers to have more positive attitudes regarding a whole range of inequality and distributive injustice attitudes is the focus of Chunping Han's sociology doctoral thesis (2009), where possible explanations for this general pattern are discussed at length.

13. Elsewhere in the second panel in Table 6.2, we observe that the associations with gender and marital status are weak and not statistically significant once other variables are taken into account, and that membership in the Chinese Communist Party and access to unofficial information have contradictory associations with inequality views at the bivariate level; only an expected pattern for CCP members to be less likely to perceive current inequalities as harmful and an unexpected pattern for those with access to unofficial information to be less likely than others to view current national income gaps as excessive remain statistically significant once other variables are controlled for statistically.

14. As discussed in Chapter 5 (note 12), the values of each geographic predictor are identical for all of the survey respondents interviewed in one sampling locale, and this clustering tendency leads to underestimation of the standard errors of the OLS regression coefficients. The "ns" notation in the geographic variable panel of Table 6.2 indicates coefficients that initially appeared statistically significant but turned out not to be once the correction via multilevel modeling for this clustering tendency was employed.

15. As noted in Chapter 1, most village cooperative medical insurance systems that existed during the late Mao era collapsed during the 1980s, forcing rural residents to obtain medical treatment on a fee-for-service basis.

Chapter 7

1. In the terminology of modernization theory, perhaps the dominant social science theory of economic development for interpreting contemporary social change patterns during the 1960s and 1970s, the USSR and the United States (and such other modern industrial societies as Japan) were seen as proceeding toward inevitable "convergence" because the institutional requirements of industrial society were much the same everywhere, despite differences in historical traditions, property forms, and ideology.

2. Although this formula may seem utopian and unworkable, it is worth pointing out that ordinary families in capitalist societies operate on communist distribution principles. However, distribution according to needs at an organizational level higher than the family seems difficult to institute, and no socialist society made a serious and sustained attempt. Experiments with free food in public mess halls early in China's Great Leap Forward (1958–60) proved unworkable and were terminated fairly quickly. The most sustained and successful effort to organize a local community according to communist principles is probably the Israeli kibbutz movement (see Spiro 1956), but the rest of Israeli society, comprising the vast majority of the population in that country, has always operated on decidedly capitalistic principles.

3. As discussed in Chapter 1, although the terms *equality* and *equity* are sometimes used as if they mean the same thing, they do not. *Equality* and *inequality* refer to the objective distribution of particular resources, such as income or schooling, whereas *equity* and *inequity* refer to subjective judgments about how well the actual distribution pattern corresponds to popular preferences and values. Citizens can judge a situation to be inequitable because there is too much inequality, but also sometimes because there is too much equality.

4. To be sure, individuals and families in a socialist society can possess some personal property, such as housing, consumer durables, jewelry, family heirlooms, bank savings, and so forth, and these can sometimes be used to produce modest extra income (such as by renting out a room or collecting interest in a bank account) and can be inherited by their children. In the early days of the Soviet Union there was an attempt to abolish the inheritance of family property, but this experiment was soon repudiated as unworkable and unpopular (see Moore 1950). However, the ban on private ownership of land, banks, factories, and other productive property means that property-based income plays a very minor role in shaping overall inequality in socialist societies.

5. There is an important qualifier to this generalization about public goods. Whether bureaucratic allocation helps to increase equality or exaggerates inequality depends on the rules of eligibility for such distributions. If any citizen or even the entire population regardless of citizenship is eligible (as in the National Health system of the United Kingdom), the impact will be equalizing. But if only designated groups are eligible to receive public goods and others are excluded, this kind of public goods distribution has a decidedly inegalitarian impact. In the Mao era many public goods were distributed to urban residents only, and the effect was to foster equality within cities but stark inequality across the rural-urban divide

(see the discussion in Solinger 1999; Whyte 2010a). For Chinese society as a whole, the latter tendency dominated.

6. However, there is an extensive literature demonstrating that in revolutionary and state socialist societies, children from families enjoying high status and incomes were more likely to obtain higher education than children from worker and farm families (see Connor 1979; Kelley and Klein 1981), due in part, at least, to the ability of high-status families to provide the encouragement, cultural capital, and resources that tend to produce high entrance examination scores. This pattern was a major motivation for the Cultural Revolution effort in China to eliminate college entrance examinations and develop a model of "worker, peasant, soldier" students based on work records, political enthusiasm, and local recommendations. It is debatable whether the politicized and truncated college admissions procedures of that period actually produced more-equal opportunities for access to higher education, and within a year of Mao's death the entrance examination system was restored (see Pepper 1996).

7. Progressive piece rates involve paying a given sum per item produced up to a certain level, then an increased sum per item above that level, and so forth. After Stalin's death Khrushchev not only denounced his mass crimes, but also his transformation of the USSR into a highly inegalitarian society, and he introduced a range of policies (such as minimum pay for collective farm workers) designed to foster a return to greater social equality. In this context it is ironic that Mao Zedong denounced Khrushchev for revisionist policies departing from socialism; to a considerable extent both Mao and Khrushchev were reacting against Stalin's extremely hierarchical and unequal form of socialism.

8. Societal inequality can be reduced as much or more by out-migration from depressed areas and economic sectors as by governmental redistribution from rich to poor locales, and socialist societies tend not to foster or sometimes even allow either process.

9. In agriculture there were systems of work points rather than wages, and there were similar Cultural Revolution debates about how to modify work-point systems to place less emphasis on their material incentive component—mainly by awarding fixed work points for each day worked. Although these daily work points differed by age and gender, they did not reflect the quantity and quality of the actual agricultural tasks performed (see Whyte 1969).

10. This is not to say that China was a society devoid of individual competition during the Cultural Revolution—far from it. However, the form of competition that was dominant reflected the frenetic political atmosphere. Individuals competed within an ethos that one analyst has termed "virtuocracy" (Shirk 1982, 1984), in which they tried to do a better job of displaying political loyalty and enthusiasm than their colleagues in the hope of winning praise, political honors, and even promotion. However, they were expected to avoid displaying any interest in material advancement.

11. The clearest instance of this danger was visible in the "destroy 4 olds" phase of the Cultural Revolution in late 1966, during which gangs of roving Red Guards attacked people on the street if they were wearing clothes or hairstyles that were deemed insufficiently proletarian.

12. Rural residents did not enjoy the iron rice bowl of job, income, and benefit guarantees that urban state-sector employees enjoyed under socialism. However, the collective system of the communes did provide certain minimal forms of secu-

rity relative to neighbors, such as cooperative medical insurance and an opportunity for rural families to receive advance distributions of basic grain even if they could not accumulate enough work points to pay later for the grain they had already consumed. (Some referred to this much more modest security as a "clay rice bowl.") This was security relative only to fellow villagers, and rural residents were not thereby protected from disastrous policies in the Great Leap Forward famine of 1959–61, which led to the deaths of millions.

13. As discussed earlier in this chapter, however, capitalist societies differ from orthodox Marxist regimes in allowing property ownership and inherited wealth to serve as sources of income. China now also allows private ownership in at least some realms, and on this basis a new and growing class of very rich developers and entrepreneurs has been created. In reality, China has gone further than simply repudiating the Cultural Revolution taboo on incentives and returning to orthodox socialist principles of distribution.

14. Responses were recorded in the familiar five-category scale, ranging from strongly agree to strongly disagree, with the values reversed so that 5 = strongly agree. In statistical analyses we treat this measure as a continuous variable, although we also computed the statistics appropriate for an ordinal measure to make sure the results were basically consistent both ways (results not shown here).

15. The response categories for each statement were recorded on a five-point scale ranging from strongly agree to strongly disagree, and then reversed so that 5 = strongly agree. The reliability for this scale is $\alpha = .65$. As elsewhere in our study, the scale was constructed from the factor scores reflecting the common content of these three items, and then converted to values ranging from 1 to 100.

16. In terms of face content, there is ambiguity about whether respondents interpret the third statement included in the government leveling scale as entailing shrinking the gap between high and low incomes by raising the floor or by lowering the ceiling. Given the content of the other two included statements and the lower correlation with the fourth statement regarding imposing a maximum income limit, we assume that most respondents interpreted the third statement as mainly involving raising the income floor.

17. As with the prefer equality measure, we reversed the five response categories so that 5 = strongly agree, and in statistical analyses we treat this as if it were a continuous measure, although we double-checked the results against statistics produced using the appropriate ordinal statistical procedures (results not shown here).

18. All five questions had the standard five response categories ranging from strongly agree to strongly disagree, which we reverse so that 5 = strongly agree. The composite market competition scale was constructed from the factor scores reflecting the shared content of these items and then rescaled from 1 to 100. The market competition scale has a reliability of $\alpha = .64$.

19. Market reforms since 1978 have weakened the government's commitment to providing employment to all urbanites, allowing unemployment to increase substantially. But even in the Mao era the job provision responsibilities of the government did not apply to the rural residents who made up a majority of the population. In recent years urban areas have introduced a modest minimum income welfare benefit (referred to as the *dibao* system), but as of now, this minimum income payment system has only gradually and experimentally been spread to the countryside, and with much lower payments than urbanites receive.

20. What is most surprising in Table 7.1 is the modest but statistically significant and positive correlation between prefer equality and rewards necessary. Although the two statements appear more directly contradictory than is the case with government leveling and market competition, this finding demonstrates the tendency in research on distributive justice attitudes to find respondents agreeing with different statements that appear to be (and were designed to be) direct opposites. Human beings often subscribe to multiple general principles under different circumstances, principles that cannot all be reconciled into one consistent personal ideology.

21. Note that the distance to the city correlation is positive, but that the regression coefficients for distance to city are reversed and are statistically significant. As in Chapter 6, corrections for geographic clustering have been applied in order to determine the appropriate level of statistical significance of the regression coefficients in the geographic panels of Tables 7.2 and 7.3.

22. However, in addition to the urban employed being more likely than the comparison group of unskilled and semiskilled workers to favor government leveling, we see in the third section of Table 7.2 that there is a net tendency (controlling for other predictors) for those living far from any city to also favor government leveling. (Without controlling for other predictors, the correlation for distance to city and government leveling is negative, rather than positive.)

23. See the classic debates between functionalist theorists Kingsley Davis and Wilbert Moore and their conflict theory critic, Melvin Tumin, reprinted in Bendix and Lipset 1966; see also Lenski 1966.

24. The marginal nature of migrants and the unemployed is fairly obvious, but even routine nonmanual workers are generally disadvantaged compared to professionals, managers, and entrepreneurs. The case of migrants is complex; with respect to urban residents they face clear institutionalized disadvantages in terms of jobs and income, but compared to relatives and friends back in the villages they may feel that they are beneficiaries of market competition. We will have more to say about the complicated situation of migrants later in this study.

25. In this instance these generalizations are not made in comparison with what I have been calling the conventional wisdom; the focus is now on two scales that the conventional wisdom originally expected to have statistical coefficients contrary to one another. Some additional traits can be seen as demonstrating the tie between advantaged status and a liberal capitalist ethic, but only for one of the two scales being examined—the strong associations between CCP membership and government leveling and between access to unofficial information (which implies cosmopolitan social ties and sources of information) and market competition.

Chapter 8

1. There are many other manifestations of these tendencies, such as the efforts of people who hold political offices or run organizations to try to hold onto their positions. For the latter case, we have the classic statement of the iron law of oligarchy: "who says organization, says oligarchy" (Michels 1911). Some discussions of these multiple processes speak in terms of different forms of capital that can be accumulated and used to preserve and transmit advantaged status: financial capital, human capital, political capital, social capital, cultural capital, and so on.

2. These statements are another way of making the familiar observation that groups may vary in their degree of class consciousness. Obviously these hypothetical examples are oversimplified. In any complex stratification hierarchy, it is

possible and even likely that there will be strong conflicts between some strata and groups and relatively little conflict among other unequally situated groups.

3. One major alternative to the Marxist social class framework was provided by Max Weber, who saw social classes as defined by differential market positions, with those positions affected by such characteristics as occupation, income, and education. One implication of these contrasting conceptions is that the Marxist framework readily lends itself to a binary view of opposed social classes (bourgeois property owners versus propertyless proletarians), whereas the Weberian approach lends itself to a view of multiple social classes arranged in a ladderlike hierarchy, without clear class boundaries or necessarily much class conflict. Alternative theoretical treatments of social class exist that are not materialist, such as those that classify citizens in terms of the subjective class positions they identify themselves as belonging to (working class, middle class, and so on).

4. These campaigns have been the subject of an extensive series of studies detailing how they were carried out, and it would be too much of a detour to go into those complexities here. Suffice it to say that the initial land reform campaign was marked by substantial conflict and violence (see, for example, Hinton 1966) and that the eventual socialist transformation campaigns were much less violent (see Shue 1980; Vogel 1969).

5. Even in a capitalist society, power over resources and people is derived not simply or even primarily from property ownership, but from administrative control over the complex bureaucratic structures that dominate modern social life. See the discussion in Dahrendorf 1959.

6. These people are often called the *nomenklatura*, a term borrowed from the Russian because there is no equivalent in a non-Leninist society. The term refers to the several hundred top party-state officials who are selected and approved by the highest levels of the party, are beholden to those top leaders, and occupy the key bureaucratic positions in every sector of society. For a description of the Chinese version of nomenklatura in various periods, see Burns 1987; Heilmann and Kirchberger 2000.

7. Many observers have noted that there was considerable hypocrisy in Mao's attacks on elite privilege, seeing that he (and his wife, Jiang Qing) continued to use a wide range of travel, housing, and secluded resort privileges even while they were demanding that other elites cleanse themselves through manual labor and frugal lifestyles. See, for example, Witke 1977; Salisbury 1992.

8. The variety of classes mentioned in these three discourses were not "genuine" social classes in terms of conventional social science understanding of the term because they did not stem from stratification structured primarily by economic resources and characteristics.

9. As noted in Chapter 3, in 1956 ("On the Ten Major Relationships") and 1957 ("On the Correct Handling of Contradictions Among the People") Mao (1977a) wrote analyses indicating that he was aware of and concerned about such nonclass inequalities in the society he had created, but after 1962 his edict to "never forget class struggle" essentially halted any serious attention to them.

10. The Soviet official analysis of its own society, after the rejection in 1956 of Stalin's class policy, involved a formulation that Soviet society was composed of multiple strata within two large and nonantagonistic classes (state employees and collective farmers), and one separate stratum (intellectuals), with the class distinction

based on different forms of socialist property employed in the sectors in which individuals worked (state or collective), rather than on any differences in the property possessed by the individuals or their families. Thus all Soviet citizens, from lowly collective farmers to the first secretary of the Communist Party, were henceforth considered good proletarians because they did not own productive property and they sold their labor for wages. This formulation infuriated Mao Zedong, and he denounced it as a manifestation of Khrushchev's revisionism. Here again Mao's attempt to continue to find classes and class struggle after China's socialist transformation, not Khrushchev's repudiation of such an attempt, constitutes a clear revision of orthodox Marxist doctrine. After 1978, as noted in Chapter 1, Deng Xiaoping and his colleagues adopted essentially Khrushchev's formulation in regard to classes under socialism.

11. Even when industrial conflict does occur in state socialist societies, in most instances it involves worker protests against the leaders of a particular factory, rather than in defense of worker interests more generally or against higher authorities and the state. What made the events in Poland in the 1970s particularly dramatic was that the rise of the Solidarity movement and other developments led to an unprecedented broader movement of workers beyond firm boundaries. It is ironic that the closest thing to a proletarian revolution that the world has known occurred against socialism in Poland, and not in a capitalist society as Marx had predicted. In capitalist societies, when the role of market distribution is minimized and bureaucratic allocation is emphasized, tendencies similar to the ordinary reality in state socialist societies may be observed—say, in an American company town or perhaps in large permanent-employment Japanese firms during their heyday in the 1970s and 1980s.

12. One of the early Western journalists allowed to open a bureau in China, Fox Butterfield (1982) of the *New York Times*, conveys the distinctiveness of this mentality through a question he was asked upon arriving in Beijing and trying to register in a hotel: "Ni shi nar?" (Where are you?). Butterfield's years of studying Chinese and residence in Taiwan had not prepared him to understand what the desk clerk meant: What is your work unit? On the centrality and power of *danwei* (work unit) in Chinese socialism, see Whyte and Parish 1984; Walder 1984, 1986; Henderson and Cohen 1984).

13. As with other features of socialist societies discussed elsewhere in this study, these tendencies are not totally absent from capitalist societies. National legislation and corporate policy decisions may change the rules of the game for social mobility in a capitalist society. A telling example is the way the GI Bill opened the doors to college education to millions of ex-soldiers of working-class origins after World War II. However, in a capitalist society these bureaucratic decisions are only one part of a larger set of influences on mobility opportunities and stratification, which are primarily determined by market forces. In a state socialist society they are the only game in town.

14. At the time the rules allowed a worker in a state factory who was willing to take early retirement to arrange to have a son or daughter hired by the work unit, although not necessarily in the same job. This was referred to as the *dingti* (replacement) system. It seems to have been motivated initially by a concern to favor state workers and allow them to help a child escape being sent to the countryside, and subsequently (after 1979) to enable as many as possible of the children of state workers who had been sent to the countryside to return and be placed in

urban jobs. Once the wave of youth returning from the countryside had passed, the dingti system was abolished.

15. Exceptions made escape from socialist serfdom possible, but only for the fortunate few who were able to pass college entrance examinations, who were inducted into the military and rose high enough to be demobilized into an urban job, or who lived in villages whose lands were taken over by expanding urban factories and received urban jobs and hukou as compensation. Even marriage to an urban citizen did not entitle a person to obtain an urban hukou, and urbanites who were sent to the countryside generally lost their urban hukou.

16. The old class system discussed earlier established another important caste-like barrier between favored individuals from good class families and stigmatized individuals who had bad class labels. Since these labels were inherited patrilineally, a daughter with a bad class label could partially escape systematic discrimination if she married someone with a good class label, and their children thereby avoided the stigma of a bad class label. Sons of bad class families had no such escape opportunity, and many had great difficulty getting married at all (see Croll 1981). In 1979 China's reformers repudiated the old class system and had class labels removed from personnel records, and there is little sign today that pre-1949 class background plays an important role in stratification. The system of discrimination based on household registration, in contrast, persists and still has a powerful influence on individual status and opportunities.

17. The term *resegregation* is appropriate because Chinese cities were segregated on the basis of social class before the 1950s socialist transformation that replaced market allocation of jobs and housing with bureaucratic allocation.

18. Household registration status has long had two linked dimensions— agricultural or nonagricultural, and local or nonlocal. So, for example, farmers who live in districts incorporated within the expanded city administrative boundaries that have long been typical in China would have a combination of agricultural and local household registrations. Rural migrants from elsewhere, the preponderant category of China's reform era floating population, have nonlocal and agricultural household registrations. Reform proposals that are gradually being introduced seem aimed at phasing out the agricultural and nonagricultural categories, but at retaining the local and outsider household registration distinction. The impact of this change on rural migrants is negligible, since as outsiders they are still excluded from the category of those entitled to urban citizenship rights (see the discussion in Chan and Buckingham 2008). At the time of our 2004 survey, both types of status were still in operation and recognized by our respondents.

19. As with other summary measures in our study, the summary scale was constructed from the factor scores measuring how close responses for each constituent item were to the common factor they all share, and the resulting measure was rescaled from 1 to 100. The reliability of the anti-hukou bias scale is $\alpha=.81$.

20. As elsewhere in Chapters 6 through 9 where we use single items as an outcome measure, we treat the responses as if this were a continuous variable and thus report correlations and ordinary least squares regression coefficients. We computed and compared the more appropriate statistics (such as ordered logistic regression coefficients) and verified that the results were basically the same, but we don't report those results here.

21. We did not include questions about views on past socialist distribution patterns that no longer exist, such as wages that do not reward educational attainment or rural work points that are lower for women than for men. Our goal is not to compare how respondents view current inequalities in comparison with the patterns of inequalities that existed in the late Mao era, but rather to examine how they view a variety of current status transmission patterns that have their roots in the two different eras.

22. We constructed the summary measure from the factor scores of the constituent items, rescaled to vary from 1 to 100. The reliability of the anti-rich transmit scale is $\alpha = .71$.

23. The scale was constructed from the factor scores of the constituent items, with the resulting variable rescaled to vary from 1 to 100. The reliability of the inequality conflicts scale is $\alpha = .73$.

24. As noted in earlier chapters, when we constructed the measure of access to unofficial communications, we assumed that it reflected some combination of cosmopolitanism and capacity for forming independent and potentially critical opinions (for individuals not totally dependent on the official media and the government's views about current affairs). Insofar as this is the case, we might expect to find similar patterns of association of this measure and of the years of education measure with various inequality attitude scales. However, as the results in Table 8.3 show, this has not proved to be the case, and we find some evidence that fewer of those who have access to a variety of unofficial communications actually have critical attitudes than do other respondents. Why that should be the case is not obvious, and we ponder this question further in the Conclusion.

25. Two other patterns are visible in these figures—a tendency for the middle-aged to have somewhat fewer critical attitudes toward urban bias than do either the young or the elderly (although not enough to make these coefficients statistically significant) and for Han Chinese to be more likely to be critical of hukou bias than non-Han.

26. The relatively critical attitudes at the bivariate level of some particularly disadvantaged groups, particularly the urban unemployed, also are no longer significant in the regression models.

27. To clarify, we are not in a position to test whether those who are really powerful in China have fewer critical attitudes than others toward the privileges they enjoy, since in any representative sample survey such as ours there will be too few of the very powerful (or very rich, for that matter) to examine their views in detail.

28. Those in the urban others category also are less likely to be critical of the wealthy buying better lives, but since this is a catch-all residual category, including individuals who were never employed, students, retired people, and others, it is hard to know what to make of this second exception to the no-difference pattern.

29. The coefficients in the regression models for age and age-squared are similar and strong, but the age coefficient falls just short of being statistically significant at the $p = .05$ level. This pattern is the opposite of the age patterns observed in Chapter 6, where the middle-aged were more likely to be critical of the unfairness of current patterns of inequality than were younger and older respondents, perhaps as a result of their being members of China's lost generation. From the figures in Table 8.4 for anti-rich transmit, it is clear that the middle-aged are

not more critical across the board of the various aspects of contemporary inequality examined in the current study.

Chapter 9

1. These examples concern what sociologists refer to as intra-generational mobility—changes individuals make in their lifetimes. Perhaps even more important are potential increases in intergenerational mobility—the chances to get children launched into higher-status careers than their parents currently occupy.

2. Perhaps the most dramatic instance of the impact of circulation mobility was in rural villages, where land reform and class struggle against the pre-1949 village elites, combined with the development of new local leadership structures into which the activists in these struggles were promoted, resulted in a virtual reversal of the status pyramid of Chinese villages by 1953.

3. As the popular phrase of the period put it, *posi ligong* (smash selfishness, establish the public good).

4. Chinese educational statistics from chinadataonline.org.ezp-prod1.hu1. harvard.edu.

5. The figures on college enrollment expansion are particularly dramatic. The number of students enrolled in China's universities grew from 565,000 in 1976 to 1,730,000 in 1985, 2,063,000 in 1990, and 2,906,000 in 1995, and then shot up to 5,560,900 in 2000 and 20,210,000 in 2008, the latter figure a roughly sixfold increase from a decade earlier (chinadataonline.org.ezp-prod1.hu1.harvard.edu). Visitors to China in 2009 have been told that university enrollments presently exceed 26 million.

6. As in earlier chapters, the resulting scale was constructed from the factor scores of these two items and then rescaled to vary from 1, the most optimistic, to 100, the most pessimistic. The reliability of this scale is $\alpha=.50$.

7. The scale was computed from the factor scores computed for the three items, and then rescaled from 1 to 100. The reliability of this scale is $\alpha=.57$.

8. Again we use factor scores to create this summary scale, with the results rescaled to vary from 1 to 100. The reliability of the resulting scale is $\alpha=.70$. Note that none of the three statements refer specifically to distributive injustice. However, given the context of our questionnaire with its focus on inequality and mobility issues, we presume that our respondents answered these questions with distributive injustice issues in mind.

9. From the correlation coefficients, it appears that residents of the central and western provinces are also more likely than their counterparts in the eastern provinces to agree that there is a lack of individual opportunity. However, once we control for other predictors and correct for the clustering tendency of the geographic measures, the regression coefficients for region are no longer statistically significant. The one unexpected pattern is that respondents with above-average access to unofficial information are more likely to be optimistic than to be critical, whereas we had expected them to be more pessimistic. We have seen the same pattern in earlier chapters, and it is also reflected in significantly more positive views on the other two scales shown in Table 9.2.

10. What matters in this realm as elsewhere are relative expectations, and on multiple occasions the Chinese media have discussed complaints that China's best-educated citizens, even though favored by many reform-era changes and

opportunities, nonetheless still are not treated and rewarded as well as they should be in terms of the meritocratic policies of China's current leaders.

11. It is worth calling attention to one pattern we don't observe here. Highly educated respondents are not any more (or less) likely to express strong feelings of injustice, a departure from their generally critical responses on other inequality-related measures.

12. In column 7, before controls, respondents in the western provinces showed a tendency to be less likely to express feelings of injustice.

13. It should be noted that one of the items in the bad experiences scale is whether the respondent or the respondent's family members have been mistreated by local officials in the last three years, while one of the items in the feelings of injustice scale is agreement that local officials don't care what ordinary people like the respondent think. Therefore the significant positive association between these two scales is hardly surprising.

14. Deng and other leaders could also look over their shoulders and observe the rise of the Solidarity movement and workers' protests in Poland in the late 1970s and become aware that economic stagnation and consumer frustrations could have drastic political consequences.

Conclusion

1. This is not to say that nostalgia for some aspects of life under socialism is completely absent. Many Chinese would prefer to have more economic security along with the potential to increase their living standards—in other words, to enjoy the carrots of market competition without the sticks. However, if given a choice between secure jobs with fixed low incomes and purchasing power (roughly the situation of privileged state workers in the late Mao era) or less-secure jobs with opportunities for improved earnings and living standards, our survey data indicate that a large majority would choose the latter. There is also widespread nostalgia for the perceived less-materialistic ethics that many associate with the socialist era, in contrast to the money-grubbing tendencies many see as prevailing today (as captured by the changing of one character of the phrase "xiang qian kan" from "look forward" in the Mao era to "look to the money" today). It seems similarly doubtful, though, that many would prefer to a live again in a China in which the pursuit of higher incomes and better lives is penalized and not a realistic option.

2. We also examined variations in three measures of positive attitudes about inequality: merit-based inequality in Chapter 6 and rewards necessary and favor market competition in Chapter 7. We do not focus on those three measures here.

3. However, some rural groups, farmers in particular, were significantly more likely to prefer egalitarian distribution and to be critical of discrimination against rural migrants.

4. A plus sign in the row for unskilled and semiskilled workers and blank cells for the other urban occupational categories indicate that the unskilled and semiskilled workers are more critical than some rural categories, but do not differ significantly from the other urban groups. In other words, the row of plus signs after unskilled and semiskilled workers is somewhat misleading, since in most instances it indicates a difference from the rural categories, not from the other urban categories (unless those categories have plus or minus signs). The urban unemployed are more critical than unskilled and semiskilled workers only in voicing stronger support for government efforts to level inequalities.

5. One additional pattern that doesn't show up very clearly in Table C.1 is the impact of age cohort membership on inequality attitudes. With fair frequency in earlier chapters we saw tendencies for the middle-aged to have negative views about current inequalities (with the reverse pattern for anti-rich transmit), but many of the coefficients showing this pattern were not strong enough to be statistically significant. The patterns that hold up clearly and appear in Table C.1 are for older respondents to have more pessimism about individual opportunities and middle-age respondents to have stronger feelings of injustice.

6. False consciousness has its origins mainly in Marxist theorizing about why factory workers in capitalist societies don't feel the anger at their bosses that Marx expected them to feel. Since then the concept has been applied to a variety of other circumstances in which people think or behave in ways that the analyst thinks departs from what their true interests are. In most cases the grounds for judging what an individual's "true consciousness" ought to be are debatable.

7. As indicated in Chapter 2, we also take comfort that the response rate was about 75 percent, rather than the 99 percent that is often reported for officially sponsored and promoted surveys. The lower response rate is a clear indication that potential respondents felt that they could refuse to participate in our survey, making it less likely that those who did participate felt any sense of coercion.

8. This question was one of several items used to construct the bad experiences scale that was used in the statistical models in Chapters 6 through 9.

9. These generalizations do not apply to all features of current inequalities. For example, as shown in Figure 3.6 in Chapter 3, the extensive discrimination against urban migrants that persists today is seen as unfair by most survey respondents precisely because it is based on categorical status as a bearer of an agricultural hukou, rather than on individual merit.

10. This interpretation is the opposite of the view promoted during the Mao era that Chinese society before 1949 was an evil and corrupt social order characterized by excessive and unfair inequalities that had to be restricted or eliminated. The chaos of the Cultural Revolution may have helped to destroy popular acceptance of Mao's view and to open the door to considering the pre-1949 social order as not so bad after all.

11. The author and his colleagues are conducting a follow-up national survey on popular attitudes toward inequality issues in late 2009. If we are successful, the new survey will provide the basis for making generalizations about the patterns and explanations of changes over time in attitudes on these issues.

Alesina, Albert, and Nicola Fuchs-Schündeln. 2007. "Goodbye Lenin (or Not?): The Effects of Communism on People's Preferences." *American Economic Review*, 97: 1307–28.

Andreas, Joel. 2004. "Leveling the 'Little Pagoda': The Impact of College Entrance Examinations—and their Elimination—on Rural Education in China." *Comparative Education Review*, 48: 1–47.

Bauman, Zygmunt. 1972. "Officialdom and Class: Bases of Inequality in Socialist Society." In *The Social Analysis of Class Structure*, ed. Frank Parkin. London: Tavistock.

Bendix, Reinhard, and S. M. Lipset, eds. 1966. *Class, Status, and Power: Social Stratification in Comparative Perspective*, 2nd ed. New York: Free Press.

Bennett, Gordon. 1978. *Huadong: The Story of a Chinese People's Commune.* Boulder, CO: Westview Press.

Berliner, Joseph. 1957. *Factory and Manager in the USSR*. Cambridge, MA: Harvard University Press.

Bernstein, Thomas. 1977. *Up to the Mountains and Down to the Villages: The Transfer of Youth from Urban to Rural China*. New Haven, CT: Yale University Press.

Bernstein, Thomas, and Xiaobo Lu. 2003. *Taxation Without Representation in Contemporary Rural China*. Cambridge, U.K.: Cambridge University Press.

Bian, Yanjie. 1994. *Work and Inequality in Urban China*. Albany, NY: SUNY Press.

Brady, Anne-Marie. 2008. *Marketing Dictatorship: Propaganda and Thought Work in Contemporary China*. Lanham, MD: Rowman and Littlefield.

Brandt, Loren, and Thomas Rawski, eds. 2008. *China's Great Economic Transformation*, New York: Cambridge University Press.

Burns, John. 1987. "China's *Nomenklatura* System." *Problems of Communism*, 36: 36–51.

Butterfield, Fox. 1982. *China: Alive in the Bitter Sea*. New York: Times Books.

Centeno, Miguel. 1994. "Between Rocky Democracies and Hard Markets: Dilemmas of the Double Transition." *Annual Review of Sociology*, 20: 125–47.

Chan, Kam Wing. 1994. *Cities with Invisible Walls*. New York: Oxford University Press.

Chan, Kam Wing, and Will Buckingham. 2008. "Is China Abolishing the *Hukou* System?" *China Quarterly*, 195: 582–606.

Cheng, T., and M. Selden. 1994. "The Origins and Social Consequences of China's *Hukou* System." *China Quarterly*, 139: 646–68.

Chow, Yung-teh. 1966. *Social Mobility in China*. New York: Atherton Press.

Chung, Jae Ho, Hongyi Lai, and Ming Xia. 2006. "Mounting Challenges to Governance in China: Surveying Collective Protestors, Religious Sects, and Criminal Organizations." *China Journal*, 56: 1–31.

Connor, Walter. 1979. *Socialism, Politics, and Equality: Hierarchy and Change in Eastern Europe and the USSR*. New York: Columbia University Press.

Croll, Elisabeth. 1981. *The Politics of Marriage in Contemporary China*. Cambridge, U.K.: Cambridge University Press.

Dahrendorf, Ralf. 1959. *Class and Class Conflict in Industrial Society*. Stanford, CA: Stanford University Press.

Davis, Deborah. 1993. "Urban Families: Supplicants to a Socialist State." In *Urban Families in the Post-Mao Era*, ed. D. Davis and S. Harrell. Berkeley: University of California Press.

Davis, Kingsley. 1953. "Some Principles of Stratification: A Critical Analysis: Reply." *American Sociological Review*, 18: 394–97.

Davis, Kingsley, and Wilbert Moore. 1945. "Some Principles of Stratification." *American Sociological Review*, 10: 242–49.

Davis-Friedmann, Deborah. 1985. "Intergenerational Inequalities and the Chinese Revolution." *Modern China*, 11: 176–201.

Djilas, Milovan. 1957. *The New Class: An Analysis of the Communist System*. New York: Praeger.

Duncan, O. D. 1968. "Social Stratification and Mobility: Problems of Measurement of Trends." In *Indicators of Social Change*, ed. E. Sheldon and W. Moore. New York: Russell Sage.

Economist. 2006. "How the Other 800m Live." *The Economist*, March 22: 12.

Elman, Benjamin. 2000. *A Cultural History of Civil Examinations in Late Imperial China*. Berkeley: University of California Press.

Fan Gang and Wang Xiaolu. 2004. *Zhongguo Shichanghua Zhishu—Gediqu Shichanghua Xiangdui Jincheng 2004 Niandu Baogao* (Marketization Indexes for China: Report on Relative Progress Toward Marketization in Various Localities in 2004). Beijing: Economic Science Press.

Firebaugh, Glenn. 2003. *The New Geography of Global Income Inequality*. Cambridge, MA: Harvard University Press.

Flannery, Russell. 2007. "China's 400 Richest." http://www.forbes.com, November 1.

Gold, Thomas, Doug Guthrie, and David Wank, eds. 2002. *Social Connections in China: Institutions, Culture, and the Changing Nature of Guanxi*. New York: Cambridge University Press.

Gustafsson, Björn, Li Shi, and Terry Sicular, eds. 2008. *Inequality and Public Policy in China*. Cambridge, U.K.: Cambridge University Press.

Han Chunping. 2009. *Rural-Urban Cleavages in Perceptions of Inequality in Contemporary China*. Unpublished doctoral dissertation, Department of Sociology, Harvard University.

Han Chunping and Martin K. Whyte. 2008. "The Social Contours of Distributive Injustice Feelings in Contemporary China." In *Creating Wealth and Poverty in Post-Socialist China*, ed. D. Davis and Wang Feng. Stanford, CA: Stanford University Press.

Han Dongping. 2000. *The Unknown Cultural Revolution: Educational Reforms and Their Impact on China's Rural Development*. New York: Garland Press.

Harding, Harry. 1987. *China's Second Revolution: Reform After Mao*. Washington, DC: Brookings Institution.

He Qinglian. 1997. *Zhongguo de Xianjing* (China's Pitfall). Hong Kong: Mingjing Publishers.

———. 2003. "A Volcanic Stability." *Journal of Democracy*, 14: 66–72.

Heilmann, Sebastien, and Sarah Kirchberger. 2000. *The Chinese Nomenklatura in Transition*. Trier, Germany: Trier University Center for East Asian and Pacific Studies.

Henderson, Gail, and Myron Cohen. 1984. *The Chinese Hospital: A Socialist Work Unit*. New Haven, CT: Yale University Press.

Hinton, William. 1966. *Fanshen*. New York: Vintage.

Hirschman, Albert O., and M. Rothschild. 1973. "The Changing Tolerance for Inequality in the Course of Economic Development." *World Development*. 12: 29–36.

Ho Pingti. 1962. *The Ladder of Success in Imperial China*. New York: Columbia University Press.

Hochschild, Jennifer. 1981. *What's Fair? American Ideas About Distributive Justice*. Cambridge, MA: Harvard University Press.

Howe, Christopher. 1971. *Employment and Economic Growth in Urban China*. Cambridge, U.K.: Cambridge University Press.

Kahn, Joseph. 2006. "China Makes Commitment to Social Harmony." *New York Times*, October 12.

Kelley, Jonathan, and Maria Evans. 1993. "The Legitimation of Inequality: Occupational Earnings in Nine Nations." *American Journal of Sociology*, 99: 75–125.

Kelley, Jonathan, and Herbert Klein. 1981. *Revolution and the Rebirth of Inequality*. Berkeley: University of California Press.

Kelley, Jonathan, and Krzysztof Zagorski. 2004. "Economic Change and the Legitimation of Inequality: The Transition from Socialism to the Free Market in Central-East Europe." *Research on Social Stratification and Mobility*, 22: 319–64.

Khan, Azizur, and Carl Riskin. 2001. *Inequality and Poverty in China in the Age of Globalization*. New York: Oxford University Press.

———. 2005. "China's Household Income Distribution, 1995 and 2002." *China Quarterly*, 182: 356–84.

Kirkby, Richard. 1985. *Urbanization in China*. New York: Columbia University Press.

Kluegel, James. 1988. "Economic Problems and Socioeconomic Beliefs and Attitudes." *Research on Social Stratification and Mobility*, 7: 273–302.

Kluegel, James, David Mason, and Bernd Wegener, eds. 1995. *Social Justice and Political Change*. New York: Aldine de Gruyter.

Kluegel, James, and Eliot Smith. 1986. *Beliefs About Inequality: Americans' Views of What Is and What Ought to Be*. New York: Aldine de Gruyter.

Korzec, Michel, and Martin Whyte. 1981. "Reading Notes: The Chinese Wage System." *China Quarterly*, 86: 248–73.

Kraus, Richard. 1981. *Class Conflict in Chinese Socialism*. New York: Columbia University Press.

Kreidl, Martin. 2000. "Perceptions of Poverty and Wealth in Western and Post-Communist Countries." *Social Justice Research*, 13: 151–76.

Kuhn, Philip. 1984. "Chinese Views of Social Classification." In *Class and Social Stratification in Post-Revolution China*, ed. James L. Watson. Cambridge, U.K.: Cambridge University Press.

Landry, Pierre, and Mingming Shen. 2005. "Reaching Migrants in Survey Research: The Use of the Global Positioning System to Reduce Coverage Bias in China." *Political Analysis*, 13: 1–22.

Lau, Lawrence, Yingyi Qian, and Gerard Roland. 2000. "Reform Without Losers: An Interpretation of China's Dual Track Approach to Transition." *Journal of Political Economy*, 108: 120–43.

Lenin, V. I. 1917. *State and Revolution*. Reprinted 1971, New York: International Publishers.

———. 1949. *Sochinenia* (Works), Vol. 33. Moscow: State Publishers of Political Literature.

Lenski, Gerhard. 1966. *Power and Privilege: A Theory of Social Stratification*. New York: McGraw-Hill.

Li Lianjiang. 2004. "Political Trust in Rural China." *Modern China*, 30: 228–58.

Li Shi, and Luo Chuliang. 2010. "Re-estimating the Income Gap Between Urban and Rural Households in China." In *One Country, Two Societies: Rural-Urban Inequality in Contemporary China*, ed. Martin K. Whyte. Cambridge, MA: Harvard University Press.

Ma, Josephine. 2005. "Wealth Gap Fueling Instability, Studies Warn." *South China Morning Post*, December 22.

MacFarquhar, Roderick. 1983. *The Great Leap Forward, 1958–1960*. New York: Columbia University Press.

Manion, Melanie. 1993. *Retirement of Revolutionaries in China*. Princeton, NJ: Princeton University Press.

Mao Zedong. 1967. *Selected Works of Mao Tse-tung*, Vol. 1. Beijing: Foreign Languages Press.

———. 1977a. *Selected Works of Mao Tse-tung*, Vol. 5. Beijing: Foreign Languages Press.

———. 1977b. *Selected Readings from the Works of Mao Zedong*. Beijing: Foreign Languages Press.

Marx, Karl. 1875. *Critique of the Gotha Program*. Reprinted 1954, Moscow: Foreign Languages Publishing House.

Mason, David, and James Kluegel, eds. 2000. *Marketing Democracy: Changing Opinion About Inequality and Politics in East Central Europe*. Lanham, MD: Rowman and Littlefield.

Michels, Robert. 1911. *Political Parties*. Reprinted 1999, New Brunswick, NJ: Transaction Publishers.

Moore, Barrington. 1950. *Soviet Politics: The Dilemma of Power*. Cambridge, MA: Harvard University Press.

Murphey, Rhoads. 1980. *The Fading of the Maoist Vision: City and Country in China's Development*. New York: Methuen.

Naughton, Barry. 1995. *Growing Out of the Plan: Chinese Economic Reform, 1978–1993*. Cambridge, U.K.: Cambridge University Press.

———. 2007. *The Chinese Economy: Transitions and Growth*. Cambridge, MA: MIT Press

O'Brien, Kevin, and Li Lianjiang. 2006. *Rightful Resistance in Rural China.* Cambridge, U.K.: Cambridge University Press.

Okun, Arthur. 1975. *Equality and Efficiency: The Big Tradeoff.* Washington, DC: Brookings Institution.

Olson, Mancur. 1965. *The Logic of Collective Action.* New York: Schocken Books.

Osnos, Evan. 2008. "Angry Youth: The New Generation's Neocon Nationalists." *New Yorker,* July 28.

Parish, William. 1984. "Destratification in China." In *Class and Social Stratification in Post-Revolution China,* ed. James L. Watson. Cambridge, U.K.: Cambridge University Press.

Parish, William, and Martin K. Whyte. 1978. *Village and Family in Contemporary China.* Chicago: University of Chicago Press.

Pepper, Suzanne. 1996. *Radicalism and Education Reform in 20th Century China.* Cambridge, U.K.: Cambridge University Press.

Pew Global Attitudes Project. 2007. *Global Opinion Trends 2002–2007.* Washington, DC: Pew Research Center.

Pierson, Paul. 2004. *Politics in Time: History, Institutions, and Social Analysis.* Princeton, NJ: Princeton University Press.

Polanyi, Karl. 1944. *The Great Transformation.* New York: Rinehart.

Potter, Sulamith. 1983. "The Position of Peasants in Modern China's Social Order." *Modern China,* 9: 465–99.

Ravallion, Martin, and Michael Lokshin. 2000. "Who Wants to Redistribute? The Tunnel Effect in 1990s Russia." *Journal of Public Economics,* 76: 87–104.

Rawski, Thomas. 2007. "Social Capabilities and Chinese Economic Growth." In *Social Change in Contemporary China,* ed. W. Tang and B. Holzner. Pittsburgh: University of Pittsburgh Press.

Reykowski, J. 2004. "Unexpected Traps of the Democratic Transformation." *International Journal of Sociology,* 34: 35–47.

Rosen, Stanley. 1982. *Red Guard Factionalism and the Cultural Revolution in Guangzhou (Canton).* Boulder, CO: Westview Press.

Salisbury, Harrison. 1992. *The New Emperors: China in the Era of Mao and Deng.* Boston: Little, Brown.

Selden, Mark. 1988. "Income Inequality and the State in Rural China." In *The Political Economy of Chinese Socialism,* ed. M. Selden. Armonk, NY: M. E. Sharpe.

Shambaugh, David, ed. 2000. *Is China Unstable?* Armonk, NY: M. E. Sharpe.

Shirk, Susan. 1982. *Competitive Comrades.* Berkeley: University of California Press.

———. 1984. "The Decline of Virtuocracy in China." In *Class and Social Stratification in Post-Revolution China,* ed. J. Watson. Cambridge, U.K.: Cambridge University Press.

Shue, Vivienne. 1980. *Peasant China in Transition.* Berkeley: University of California Press.

Skinner, G. William. 2005. "The Spatial Logic of Uneven Development in Contemporary China." Unpublished paper, University of California, Davis.

Solinger, Dorothy. 1999. *Contesting Citizenship in Urban China.* Berkeley: University of California Press.

Spiro, Melford. 1956. *Kibbutz: Venture in Utopia.* Cambridge, MA: Harvard University Press.

Szelenyi, Ivan. 1978. "Social Inequalities in State Socialist Redistributive Economies." *International Journal of Comparative Sociology,* 19: 63–87.

————. 1983. *Urban Inequalities Under State Socialism*. New York: Oxford University Press.

————. 1988. *Socialist Entrepreneurs: Embourgeoisement in Rural Hungary*. Madison: University of Wisconsin Press.

Tanner, Murray Scot. 2006. "We the People (of China) . . . ." *Wall Street Journal*, February 2: A10.

Teiwes, Frederick, and Warren Sun. 1999. *China's Road to Disaster: Mao, Central Leaders, and Provincial Politicians in the Unfolding of the Great Leap Forward, 1955–59*. Armonk, NY: M. E. Sharpe.

Thaxton, Ralph. 2008. *Catastrophe and Contention in Rural China: Mao's Great Leap Forward Famine and the Origins of Righteous Resistance in Da Fo Village*. New York: Cambridge University Press.

Tilly, Charles. 1998. *Durable Inequality*. Berkeley: University of California Press.

Time Asia. 2006. "Seeds of Fury." *Time Asia*, March 5.

Tomba, Luigi. 2004. "Creating an Urban Middle Class: Social Engineering in Beijing." *China Journal*, 51: 1–26.

Unger, Jonathan. 1982. *Education Under Mao: Class and Competition in Canton Schools, 1960–1980*. New York: Columbia University Press.

————. 1984. "The Class System in Rural China: A Case Study." In *Class and Social Stratification in Post-Revolution China*, ed. James L. Watson. Cambridge, U.K.: Cambridge University Press.

Vogel, Ezra. 1969. *Canton Under Communism*. Cambridge, MA: Harvard University Press.

Walder, Andrew. 1984. "The Remaking of the Chinese Working Class, 1949–1981." *Modern China*, 10: 3–48.

————. 1986. *Communist Neo-Traditionalism*. Berkeley: University of California Press.

Wang Fei-ling. 2005. *Organizing Through Division and Exclusion: China's Hukou System*. Stanford, CA: Stanford University Press.

Wang Feng. 2008. *Boundaries and Categories: Rising Inequality in Post-Socialist Urban China*. Stanford, CA: Stanford University Press.

————. 2010. "Boundaries of Inequality: Perceptions of Distributive Justice Among Urbanites, Migrants, and Peasants." In *One Country, Two Societies: Rural-Urban Inequality in China*, ed. Martin K. Whyte. Cambridge, MA: Harvard University Press.

Weselowski, W., and T. Krauze. 1981. "Socialist Society and the Meritocratic Principle of Remuneration." In *Social Inequality: Comparative and Developmental Approaches*, ed. G. Berreman. New York: Academic Press.

Weselowski, W., and E. Wnuk-Lipinski. 1992. "Transformation of Social Order and the Legitimization of Inequalities." In *The Polish Road from Socialism*, ed. W. Connor and P. Ploszaiski. Armonk, NY: M. E. Sharpe.

Whyte, Martin K. 1969. "The Tachai Brigade and Incentives for the Peasant." *Current Scene*, August 15.

————. 1974. *Small Groups and Political Rituals in China*. Berkeley: University of California Press.

————. 1981. "Destratification and Restratification in China." In *Social Inequality: Comparative and Developmental Approaches*, ed. G. Berreman. New York: Academic Press.

———. 1983. "Town and Country in Contemporary China." *Comparative Urban Research*, 10: 9–20.

———. 1985. "The Politics of Life Chances in the People's Republic of China." In *Power and Policy in the PRC*, ed. Yu-ming Shaw. Boulder, CO: Westview Press.

———. 1986. "The Commune as a Social System." In *The Chinese: Adapting the Past, Building the Future*, ed. R. Dernberger, K. DeWoskin, S. Goldstein, R. Murphey, and M. Whyte. Ann Arbor: University of Michigan Center for Chinese Studies.

———. 1990. "Changes in Mate Choice in Chengdu." In *Chinese Society on the Eve of Tiananmen*, ed. D. Davis and E. Vogel. Cambridge, MA: Harvard University Press.

———. 1991. "Urban Life in the People's Republic." In *The Cambridge History of China*, Vol. 15, ed. John K. Fairbank and Roderick MacFarquhar. Cambridge, U.K.: Cambridge University Press.

———. 1993. "Deng Xiaoping: The Social Reformer." *China Quarterly*, 135: 515–35.

———. 1996. City Versus Countryside in China's Development. *Problems of Post-Communism* 43: 9–22.

———. 2002. "Chinese Popular Views About Inequality." *Asia Program Special Report, Woodrow Wilson International Center* 104: 4–10.

———. 2006. "Popular Attitudes Toward Income Inequality in China." Weatherhead Center for International Affairs Working Paper, Harvard University.

———. 2007. "A Sociological Perspective on China's Development Record." Paper presented at "Rule and Reform of the Giants: China and India Compared," Harvard University.

———. 2009. "The Paradoxes of China's Economic Boom." *Annual Review of Sociology*, 35: 371–72.

———, ed. 2010a. *One Country, Two Societies: Rural-Urban Inequality in China*. Cambridge, MA: Harvard University Press.

———. 2010b. "Fair versus Unfair: How Do Chinese Citizens View Current Inequalities?" In *Growing Pains: Tensions and Opportunities in China's Transition*, ed. J. Oi, S. Rozelle, and X. Zhou. Washington, DC: Brookings Institution.

———. Forthcoming. "Rethinking Equality and Inequality in the PRC." In *China: Yesterday, Today, and Tomorrow*, ed. R. MacFarquhar. Cambridge, MA: Harvard University Press.

Whyte, Martin K., and Chunping Han. 2003. "Distributive Justice Issues and the Prospects for Unrest in China." Weatherhead Center for International Affairs Working Paper, Harvard University.

———. 2008. "Popular Attitudes Toward Distributive Injustice: Beijing and Warsaw Compared." *Journal of Chinese Political Science*, 13: 29–51.

Whyte, Martin K., and William Parish. 1984. *Urban Life in Contemporary China*. Chicago: University of Chicago Press.

Williamson, Oliver. 1975. *Markets and Hierarchies*. New York: Free Press.

Witke, Roxane. 1977. *Comrade Chiang Ch'ing*. Boston: Little, Brown.

World Bank. 1997. *Sharing Rising Incomes: Disparities in China*. Washington, DC: The World Bank.

Xie Yu, Yang Jiang, and Emily Greenman. 2008. "Did Send-Down Experience Benefit Youth? A Reevaluation of the Social Consequences of Forced Urban-Rural

Migration During China's Cultural Revolution." *Social Science Research*, 37:686–700.

Xinhua. 2004. "Survey of Chinese Officials' Opinions on Reform: Beijing Daily," *Xinhua News Bulletin*, November 29.

Xu Xiaohe and Martin K. Whyte. 1990. "Love Matches and Arranged Marriages: A Chinese Replication." *Journal of Marriage and the Family*, 52: 709–22.

Yang Dali. 1996. *Calamity and Reform in China*. Stanford, CA: Stanford University Press.

Yeh, K. C. 1973. "National Income." In *China: A Handbook*, ed. Yuan-li Wu. New York: Praeger.

Zhang Li. 2001. *Strangers in the City: Reconfigurations of Space, Power, and Social Networks Within China's Floating Population*. Stanford, CA: Stanford University Press.

Zhou Xueguang and Liren Hou. 1999. "Children of the Cultural Revolution: The State and the Life Course in the PRC." *American Sociological Review*, 64: 12–26.

Italicized page numbers indicate figures and tables.

National college entrance exams, 25, 167, 207n24, 222n6
National land reform. *See* Land reform campaign
New Economic Policy (NEP), 121–22
Ningxia, 102
Nomenklatura, 225n6

Occupational status, inequality measures and, 101, *109, 186,* 188, 230n4; opportunities and, *172,* 174–78; preferences and, 129, *130, 133,* 134, 137; stratification and, 154, *155,* 157, *158,* 159
"On Correcting Mistaken Ideas in the Party" (Mao), 118
Open-door policy, 26, 207n26
Opportunities, 163–79; attitudes toward, 98; comparative views of, *81,* 82–84; current Chinese views of, 61–67, *63,* 178–79; history of, in China, 164–70, 177–78; ideals vs. reality of, 139–40; job, 57, *58;* measures of, 170–71, *171;* preferences for, 136–38; respondent characteristics and, 171–79, *172–73;* rhetoric vs. reality of, 168–69. *See also* Mobility
Optimism about social mobility. *See* Mobility
Organizations, inequality within and across, 121–23
Örkeny, Antal, 88

Park, Albert, 35
Peking University, 37, 40
Perceptions. *See* Inequality, perceptions of
Pessimism about social mobility. *See* Mobility
Pew Foundation survey, 184–85
"Pitchfork anger of peasants," 4, 115, 159, 166, 175, 195
Poland, 212n12, 226n11; Warsaw survey in, 87–88
Polanyi, Karl, 145
Political power, elite status and, 55, *56,* 65, 183, 193–94, 213n13; perceptions and, 143; stratification and, 225n6, 228n27. *See also* Anti-leader privilege measure

Political stability. *See* Stability, social/political
Poor people: defined, 210n2; trends in proportion of, 44, *45*
Post-socialist transition, 11–32; importance of, 11–13; Mao era and, 13–25; post-1978 market reforms and, 25–31
Poverty: comparative views of, 72, *73;* current Chinese views of, 46–50, *48, 49,* 211–12nn5–9; defined, 210n2; government-sponsored programs and, 50–52, *51,* 213n20; market reforms and, 27, 31, 208n37
Power. *See* Political power
Preferences. *See* Inequality, preferences for
Prefer equality measure, *186–87;* preferences and, 126–31, *128, 130,* 223n14; rewards necessary measure and, 224n20
Private ownership: capitalism vs. socialism on, 119–20, 142, 221n4, 223n13; Chinese revolution and, 164; in socialists states, 143; in Soviet Union, 121–22. *See also* Property ownership
Private sector, 26, 28–30, 149, 207n27
Privileges: socialist states and, 22. *See also* Anti-leader privilege measure
Procedural injustice, 196
Productivity, Cultural Revolution and, 23
Progressive piece rates, 122, 222n7
Property income, 30, 149
Property ownership: communist theory and, 142–45. *See also* Private ownership
Provinces. *See* Geographic location
Public goods, capitalism vs. socialism on, 119–20, 221–22n5
Public opinion, 90–91

Questionnaire design, 34–38; back translation and, 41, 210n13

RCCC. *See* Research Center for Contemporary China (RCCC)
Redistribution: Chinese communist revolution and, 142; Chinese views of, 50–52, *51;* comparative views of, 76, *77,* 78
Reform without losers, 29, 99, 178